ARABESQUE AND HONEYCOMB

Madraseh Chahar Bagh at Isfahan

# ARABESQUE
# AND
# HONEYCOMB

*by*

SACHEVERELL SITWELL

RANDOM HOUSE    NEW YORK

TO BRYHER

and to

ROBERT AND MILDRED WOODS BLISS

# CONTENTS

# LIST OF ILLUSTRATIONS

## Colour

## Plates

All the illustrations in *Arabesque and Honeycomb* are from photographs specially taken for the purpose by Alexandra Metcalfe.

# PREFACE

THIS present work has been long in maturing for it may be said that from the moment I set foot in Morocco in the spring of 1927, and saw its mosques and its human beings, I was determined to go to Persia, an ambition that was only realized in the spring of 1956. But all this time the project had been in mind. The dedication to Bryher is the measure of her encouragement in despatching my wife and myself on the summer voyage from Genoa to Istanbul in order to see the Cariye Cami; and immediately on hearing of our intention to go to Persia forwarding us in the same manner, but this time by air, from Beirut to Tehran and back again. The dedication to Mr and Mrs Robert Woods Bliss is because of their help and interest in cleaning the mosaics of the Cariye Cami, and for the wonderful early works of art that they have collected and now offered to the public at Dumbarton Oaks, their former home in Washington.

I would like to express my gratitude to Sir Roger Stevens, our Ambassador in Iran, and to Lady Stevens, for their kindness, and for all he did to advise and help me. While in Tehran we stayed in the house of Tim and Avice Marten. It is difficult to know how to express our gratitude for their friendship and hospitality. Their house was our home for nearly a month, and when first one, and then the other, returned to England before us the bond of our friendship was how much we missed them. John Russell, the Counsellor of our Embassy, is an old friend whom it was a delight to meet again in Tehran. Our thanks for many kindnesses are due, also, to Charles and Maria Wiggin, our next door neighbours during those weeks in the yellow brick compound. The patient forbearance of those in the Chancellery Office on whom I showered questions, while plans were changed continually, was beyond all praise.

My thanks are due to Princess Firouz for her letter of introduction to Dr Shadman, Keeper of the Shrine at Meshed, and his wife who is her niece. And I am particularly obliged to the friendliness of Dr Alawi who wrote letters for me to deliver in Meshed. Our stay in Meshed would have been nearly impossible but for the hospitality of Tom Cassilly, the American Consul, in the beautiful old house which he had taken over. Of Dr and Mrs Shadman I have tried to write in the body of this book. It was a delight to talk to them. And to the Keeper of the Mosque I am indebted for his help, and for an exciting ascent of one of

the minarets. After a long interval it was pleasant to meet again Mme
Arfa, who in another incarnation had been the "Russian" dancer,
Hilda Bewicke in Diaghilev's company. To Mme Moghadam, librarian
of the National Museum I owe my warmest thanks for much information she has given me, and for allowing me to reproduce the portrait of
Nasr-ed-Din Shah which belongs to her and her husband.   Our travelling companions in so many places, in Isfahan, in Persepolis, and in Shiraz,
were the Arnold Whitridges whom I cannot forbear to mention. But
neither, when thinking of Persia, can I forget Archibald Chisholm in
London from whom I have sought counsel these few years past when
hoping to go to Iran and who wrote letters of introduction for us; nor
Geoffrey Keating, another friend who knows Persia well.

To the French Ambassador to the Lebanon, Louis Roché and to
Jacqueline Roché, who made such a host of friends during the years
they were in London, our thanks are due for asking us to stay with them
in the Résidence des Pins, than which there could be no more delightful
memory. It was upon the strength of her invitation to Beirut that we
were able to form our plans for continuing as far as Tehran. While in
Beirut we received many kindnesses from Desmond and Yvonne
Cochrane, and would like to thank them, and also Mme Linda Sursock.
It was a pleasure, also, to see again an old friend Eddie Gathorne-Hardy,
now a learned authority upon the Middle East. In Jerusalem, staying
at the American Colony, we met Mrs Lynd, the granddaughter
of the founders of that philanthropic institution, and through her had
the privilege of a talk with Père de Vaux, the learned and charming
Dominican monk who is an authority on the Dead Sea Scrolls. And
when thinking of Syria I must mention Mr and Mrs Marcopoli; and
tell of the delightful experience it was to meet Dr Altounyan and his
wife, and to know something of the work this poet-doctor of Cambridge has accomplished among the ill and poor of Aleppo. Mary
Roxburghe accompanied us to Jerusalem and Aleppo. Our companion
who came with us to Cairo at short notice was Frankland Dark, with
whom we looked at the Mosque of Soltan Hassan and drove out to the
Pyramids.

Our visit to Istanbul in August 1955 was the occasion of kindness
and hospitality on the part of Michael and Damaris Stewart, who
entertained us in the Embassy and took us for a cruise on the Sea of
Marmora, occasions on which it was impossible not to evoke the
friendly and benevolent shade of Sir George Clerk with whom we
stayed at Istanbul many years before. While in Istanbul on this later
occasion we met and made friends with Lesley Blanch; and through her
met Daoud, the genial and lively personality from the bazaar with

whom more than one pleasant and amusing evening was spent. Miss
Vivienne Molesworth took us to the Byzantine churches, and to the
Mosque of Sokollu Mehmet Pacha. To her sister Miss Eva Molesworth
in London I am no less indebted for the trouble taken to arrange all the
details of our two journeys. Mr Robert Hale, my publisher, gave me
every encouragement and enabled me to journey to the Middle East.
It is a personal loss to me that his death should have occurred while I
was still working on the book and before I had time to hand him in the
finished manuscript. Mrs Jean Wormald has typed out all this manuscript and taken endless trouble over foreign spelling. My inseparable
companion, as ever, has been my wife who came with me everywhere,
has helped and encouraged me with my writing, read my proofs, and
not least by her presence has enabled me to emerge from the first person
singular in my narrative and write, at times, as "we" instead of "I".

   There has been, and there surely will be, trouble about the spelling
of names. Is it, for instance, *medersa* or *madraseh*? It is difficult to be
consistent throughout. Certainly in Morocco it is *medersa*, as all know
who have set foot in Fez. But further East it is, as certainly, *madraseh*.
Perhaps a similar case is "church" in the English countryside and
"kirk" in the Scottish highlands. The Persian national feast of Nau Ruz
is a nearly impossible problem for one sees it spelt in four or five
different ways. In Turkey there is at least a new and ugly-looking
system of orthography but in other Near Eastern countries it is quite
arbitrary. On the other hand it is possible to go too far in the right
direction as in *Baedeker's Egypt* (1929 ed.), where there are too many
circumflex accents, e.g. Soltan Qalâun, or worse still, with addition
of dots, Qûṣûn es Sâqi, with a dot under the H for Soltan Ḥasan, and
so forth. As to the rights and wrongs of this complicated question I am,
myself, too ignorant to state any opinion.* It is *souk* in North Africa
and Egypt and Turkey, but *bazaar* in Persia, and the more one becomes
involved in the muddle the worse it becomes. I have to thank my
friend Wilfrid Blunt, who was in Persia at the same time that I was,
for reading my proofs and for giving me the benefit of his advice. In
the end I have tried to conform with the system of spelling of names
for which he has sought the best authority, though it is with an inward
wrench that one writes *molla* for *mullah*, *Ramazan* for *Ramadan*, and
*Soltan* for *Sultan*. Djama becomes more easily Cami in Turkey, Brusa
becomes Bursa (and loses in the process), and Pacha masquerades for
Pasha. Wilfrid Blunt, whom I thank again, is not to blame for this.

* Nasr-ed-Din Shah, or Náṣiru'd-Dín Sháh, as in E. G. Browne's *A Year amongst the
Persians*, edited by the great Orientalist Sir E. Denison Ross, Cambridge University Press,
1926? Fath Ali Shah becomes Fatḥ-'Alí Sháh.

It now looks to my ignorant eye as though the names in this book may be correct for Persia and Turkey, but wrong in all other countries of the Middle East, and in attempting to be consistent the only certainty is that I have made mistakes.

Over another matter, if there is a preponderance of colour photographs of Persia, as compared to other countries visited, it is because of the Persian architecture in colour which is unique in the world. It seemed to be an opportunity not to be missed of illustrating the domes of Meshed and Isfahan in their natural colours. Other subjects, as, for instance, Petra, are too well known pictorially, and there is little point in introducing them. But the illustrations cover most of the places mentioned excepting Cairo and Istanbul. My thanks are due to Alexandra Metcalfe who accompanied us in Persia, and from whose gallery of photographs all the plates have been chosen. It is perhaps no coincidence that such beautiful photographs of Persia should have been taken by the daughter of Lord Curzon. There are two indispensable books for which I must express my thanks to the authors. They are *Syria* by Robin Fedden, and *Byzantium and Istanbul* by Robert Liddell. Lastly, my thanks are due to the Governors of the B.B.C. and to the Editor of *The Sunday Times* for permission to make use of material which has appeared previously under their auspices.

It would be absurd for someone who has only spent a few weeks in Persia to attempt to write a book upon that country. My remarks are confined, therefore, to those places where I have been. It is true, though, that there is little left in quantity compared with what we have in Europe, the amount of mediaeval work all told in Persia being much less than one would imagine. Mosques are not thick upon the ground as churches in Somerset or East Anglia. In all the Moslem world it is only in Cairo and in Istanbul that there is a plenitude of mosques to which no city in Europe can compare in its number of churches; not Venice, nor Florence, hardly even Rome has as many of them.

With the exception of the Moslem buildings in India I think I can say I have been to every centre of the arts of Islam. Only Konya with its Seljuq mosques and *tekkiyes* has escaped me. And of course Samarcand which could on examination prove to be not more interesting or beautiful than Meshed. There is, however, to judge from old photographs and drawings a wildness of domes in Samarcand which puts it in a class apart, and makes it belong in very truth to Central Asia. It was not part of my original intention to go to Cairo but the chance came, and in view of such recent experience of Isfahan it seemed a pity not to write of it. The chapter on Istanbul, written last, though it is the account of a journey made a year earlier, is really more of a prelude than an epilogue, but I have left it where it stands to form the last chapter in the book. I am pleased to think that after seeing the mosaics of the Cariye Cami I was able to revisit Ravenna and see San Vitale again in the summer of this year.

Throughout I have tried to write of what I have seen in terms of a working knowledge of the arts of the Mediterranean, and of Italy and Spain. That is why in order to complete the picture there are some paragraphs in the Introduction upon the Andalusian style. In the course of our recent journey we went to almost every important town in the Middle East excepting Baghdad, and comment upon those cities should be more interesting having been with open eyes to Granada and to Fez. Politics are not my subject. The concern of these pages is with works of art, and human incidents by the way. It is in appreciation of the wonders of Italy and Spain that one should look at Palmyra and Jerash, see the mosques of Cairo with the same eyes that admire the blue domes of Meshed and Isfahan, compare St Mark's in imagination with the Mosque of Omar, and the churches and palaces of Venice with the domes and minarets of Istanbul. That done and accomplished, the true picture emerges of the wonders of the East and West.

SACHEVERELL SITWELL

8 *December*, 1956.

*b*

# INTRODUCTION

THERE have been two universal world civilizations, the Roman and the Islamic. Wherever the Romans went they left roads and mosaic pavements, triumphal arches, circuses, and baths. And in like manner the Moslem world has some general features, mosques and *souks* and *hammams*, to be found everywhere from Marrakesh to Samarcand. To what extent the public baths of the Moslems, and even some features of their daily dress, are in direct descent from the Romans, it is difficult to determine. But if it is true that the Moslems took over or inherited from the Romans more than we may imagine, it is, also, the case that in its origins and early history Islam was a reforming or puritan religion. They permitted no altars, no idols, and no priesthood; nevertheless, it is true that laxity and indolence are attributed by the Occident to the turban'd East.

A question that has to be decided is where does the East begin. It may start for many persons from that first moment of being in Palermo and seeing the five red domes of the ruined church of San Giovanni degli Eremiti under the pendant *daturas*. That, indeed, is a breath of the Orient, as is the wooden Saracenic ceiling of the Cappella Palatina and its frieze of stalactites; but the theme is further complicated by Greek craftsmen whom the Norman Kings of Sicily employed on the mosaics. Or the message may come first from the Arab cloisters of Amalfi and Ravello. Whenever, and wherever it reaches one, it is a taste never forgotten and that calls for more.

Having regard to the amount of journeying required, other aesthetic tastes are almost easy in comparison. For one thing nearly all the centres are so far apart. So the theme is one that has to be kept in mind, and taken up as occasion offers. But opportunities are made, they do not happen. They have to be encompassed. I have had this book in mind for half of my life, until in this last year it seemed the time had come in which to write it. Having long awaited the chance, at last I was able to go to Persia. In retrospect, all the years become one journey, as though, which is true in a sense, it has been going on this long while; the theme, as ever, being the splendours and miseries of the world and the glory of being alive.

It was in 1919 that I first went to Toledo; and one has not to be there long to apprehend that it was a bilingual city where Arabic as well as Castilian was spoken during the lifetime of El Greco. There was the Mudéjar ceiling in one of the chapels of the Cathedral; there were Moorish arches and facial traces of the Moors. Later, came the tiled courts and stairways of Seville; but most fascinating of all, perhaps, were the cloisters with Moorish ceilings in the old Royal convent of Las Huelgas, outside Burgos, for I only saw those as late as August 1951, not long after *clausura* had been lifted and visitors were allowed inside. What a strange mediaeval world where Moslem craftsmen did interior decoration in a sacred seraglio or harem of white-clad nuns!

The Mosque of Córdoba is another matter, being work of the ninth and tenth centuries, and of earlier generations of Arabs to come to Spain. It antedates the stalactite and filigree, being, nevertheless, with its acrobatic arches somewhat of a trick conception, like some sacred fun-fair or hall of distorting mirrors a thousand years old, and therefore respectable, but of obvious intent to astonish everyone who enters. Not to be classed as North African, for its builders had in mind the mosques of Egypt and of Mesopotamia. They brought with them the orange tree which had come to Arabia by way of China not long before, hence the "court of oranges" (Patio de las Naranjas) of Córdoba and of Seville. Those orange groves are so much proof of long journeying and that it was no local style.

It has been told before how the same architect Jebîr the Moor built the Tower of the Giralda at Seville, the Tower of Hassan at Rabat, and that of the Koutoubia at Marrakesh; all three of them minarets. Seville was summer capital of the caliphs, and winters were spent at Marrakesh. By now, for it is late in the twelfth century, many of the Spanish Moslems were of purely European descent. They were in no sense Africans or Moors. They were every bit as "Spanish" as the Christians were. And it is now that we get the indigenous or Andalusian style, an amalgam of elements, Arab, Berber, and Spaniard, practised on both sides of the Straits, in Morocco and in Southern Spain.

One had become familiar with *azulejos*, whether pronounced in Spanish or in Portuguese, and their Moorish equivalent which is *zellijes*, and this is important because so many Moslem buildings all over the world of Islam could be qualified as kiosques or pagodas. That is to say, they have a china surface. In Persia it produced an architecture in colour such as the world has never seen. But in the hands of the Andalusian Moors it was productive of abstract patterns. Of such are the *azulejo'd* courts of Granada, and the tiled patios of Seville. But the highest to which this art attained in Moorish hands is in the public fountains of Marrakesh, that of El Mouasine, in particular, with projecting wooden porch or hooded cornice carved in stalactite, and tiled panels of parhelions and rayed suns.

The most famous example is, of course, the Alhambra of Granada where can be seen their play of abstract patternings in tile and stucco, and their sport of honeycomb and stalactite. These decorative elements were as important a part of their repertory of ornament as the acanthus to the Greeks. It led them to the intricacies of the *media naranja* or half-orange dome, and to such of their fantasies that are as though bees are forming their honeycombs in the angles of the ceiling. The two halls that lie on either side of the Court of the Lions are no less than masterpieces of the apiarist.

But delicacies of elaboration, scarcely, if at all, less subtle than those of the courts of the Alhambra, are to be enjoyed in the *medersas* of Fez, buildings which have been ignored or lost, and have only returned into the repertory of sensations during the last few years. The *medersas* are sacred schools, still occupied by students. No one who has entered them could forget their enclosed courts and tiled walls, their pierced wooden screens or lattices, archways fringed with stalactites, and cedar beams. It is, particularly, the pungent smell of cedars of Atlas which lingers in the mind, and by obvious analogy with the cedars of Lebanon in the Temple of Solomon gives accent to the Semitic element in Moor or Arab. That, and the sheep-slaughtering, and that they do not eat the flesh of pig or cow. As in all Moslem lands one sickens of the taste of mutton-fat. There is the horror of the food exposed for sale in the *souks*, the sense of disease and poverty and heartless cruelty. None of all such things can be separated from memory of the *medersas* in spite of the music of their names.* But it is true, also, that they resemble one another so nearly that they become confused together in the mind. Having seen each, and all of them on repeated occasions at two separate times, I would now find it difficult to know apart the Bou Inania and

* There are six medersas in Fez: Attarine, Bou Inania, Cherratine, Seffarine, Sahriz, and Sebbaïne. Most beautiful is, perhaps, the Attarine, near the scent-bazaar or Souk Attarine. It dates from 1325. The Medersa Bou Inania in Meknez, and the Medersa Ben Youssef in Marrakesh, and another in Salé should also be mentioned. The *medersas* are described in my *Mauretania*, London, Duckworth & Co., 1940. The mosques in Morocco are forbidden to foreigners. On the other hand it was possible to get some impression of the Kairouiine, the principal mosque of Fez from a roof, near by, whence one could at least see the two stalactitic kiosques or pavilions of the court, recalling those of the Court of the Lions at the Alhambra. But admission is allowed to the Saadian tombs in Marrakesh, with a marvellous ceiling of inlaid cedar wood and arches of honeycomb and stalactite to match any in Granada.

the Attarine. There is little or no structural difference between them. All is arabesque, and stalactite and filigree.

Another work of the first order of excellence is at the shrine of Bou Medine, a mile or two from Tlemcen, the town in Algeria, near the Moorish border, which has beautiful Andalusian buildings. The saint buried at Bou Medine, Choaib Ibn Hussein el Andalousi, for one must not be denied the pleasure of his name, was born in Seville. He studied in the schools of Seville, and in Fez. The porch of the mosque has a most exquisite gilded stalactite ceiling, perhaps the most beautiful of its kind that is anywhere in existence, fully equal in subtlety of execution to anything at the Alhambra, and this could be said of it with little exaggeration, as much as La Macarena or the Virgén del Gran Poder, attached in fact and sentiment to Andalusian Seville.

In order to see the nearest works of art in the other direction it is necessary to take an enormous leap from Tlemcen as far as Kairouan in Tunisia. The Grand Mosque or Djama El Kebîr is so early in date (ninth century) that it has hardly any decoration at all, being simply a Moslem place of worship. The columns, all of different shapes and sizes with classical or Byzantine capitals assembled from anywhere they could be found, have no character of their own. It is only in the planning, in the general whitewashed aspect of the whole, and in wood carvings that have miraculously survived eleven centuries of every peril including the ravages of woodworm, that you feel the hand of Islam. The *minbar* or pulpit of carved and inlaid wood dating from the ninth century must be the most precious existing work of art, in wood, of all the Moslem achievement. The Grand Mosque of Kairouan is very old and impressive, "of much purer style than the buildings of Tlemcen", because, in effect, it is so early in date that it has no style at all, and "purer than the mosques of Cairo, always excepting El Azhar. It has nothing of the filigree or Andalusian style but is in isolation upon itself, without obvious progeny or influence."\* But pleasure is to be had in Kairouan from examples of brick vaulting, in this and other mosques, which are worked out with simple, but wonderful ingenuity. Nothing here resembles the great mosques in Cairo of the Fatimite period, Soltan Qalaun, Soltan Barquq, Qaït Bey, Soltan Hassan, to name but the finest of them, but of these, as of the later Mameluke buildings, some description is attempted in a later chapter.

Let it be said that where the arts are concerned there are five main bodies or divisions of Islam; the Andalusian which includes Morocco; Egypt including Syria; Turkey; Persia; and Moghul India. Of these over the years I have been lucky enough to have experience of four

\* Quoted from *Mauretania*, pp. 219–23.

out of the five. It is only Moghul India that I have not seen. The others form the principal subject of this present book, always excepting the Andalusian upon which by way of preface some remarks have been made in passing.

And so to the main object. For it should not be without interest to compare the illusions of someone whose thoughts and ambitions have turned towards Persia since he was a schoolboy with the reality, once he has been there and seen it. This is, therefore, an amalgam of notes collected over many years and of mental and visual impressions freshly gathered. There can be little question that the Persians were the artists of the world of Islam. Their long history as a kingdom and an entity, even if presented in exaggerated form with its many lapses and inter-ruptions, divides them from the black tents of the Bedouin Arabs who never had an art of their own. At the back of the Persians there is always their hereditary skill in stitching and in weaving, the arts of nomads, or, rather, migrants moving with their flocks and herds from the summer to the winter pastures, arts fostered and made necessary not by the heat, but by cold, and engendered not in barren Arabia but in Central Asia, artifacts, or if we prefer it, artifice of which the Arabs are not capable. The strange fermentation of Islam which has never been properly explained and may have been due to a sudden swarming of the population, as fleas swarm in the dust under old floor boards, carried the Arabs to Spain and Portugal one way and to India the other in the course of no more than three or four human generations, and they imposed a language and an alphabet and a mode of life. But the Persian were the flowering ways.

One has to conjecture for oneself what could have come after the Sasanids had it not been for conquest by the Moslems in A.D. 642, only twenty years later than the Hegira. Even so, they had recovered sufficiently to be producing some of the most beautiful of all ceramics by the ninth century. Their silk textiles and their carpets can have been no less wonderful under the Caliphate of the Abbasids who ruled from Baghdad. But then came the Mongol invasion, and the wonder is that the Persians ever recovered from this. Perhaps their civilization was lighter in structure and they had not the solid conventions of the Romans to go down in ruin, for no worse barbarians had overthrown and conquered Rome. Yet, if devastated by the hordes of Jenghiz Khan they had recovered entirely under Timur (Tamerlane), and Persian building from the era of the Timurids to that of Shah Abbas, that is to say from 1369 to 1630, over a period of some two hundred and fifty years, is something in comparison to which no other colour architecture in the world exists. Perhaps it is not possible for anyone who has not seen them with his own eyes to give an impression of their colours.

The device of Timur was three moons or circles set in a triangle ○○○, signifying that he was Lord of all Three Quarters of the world, and, himself a Tartar or Kalmuck and, until Hitler with his gas-chambers the greatest destroyer of the human race, he, nevertheless, employed the finest Persian architects and craftsmen of his day. All lovers of the rare and curious, and the terrible, alike of the slum kennel and the tent of Tamerlane, should read *The Embassy of Clavijo*, little known, but as fabulous and strange as Marco Polo. Herein we may read of the Great Khanum, or chief wife of Timur, coming from her enclosure "with a thin white veil before her face, which appeared to be entirely covered with white lead or some such cosmetic, the effect being to make it look as though she was wearing a paper mask", reminding me, at the time I read it, of the paper husk of the iris. It made me think of the iris, so lovingly wrapped and veiled, hiding in its parchment integument or covering which, later, is discarded and hangs down like a mask, after the unmasking. This was at the tournament and banquet of *Koumiss* or fermented mares' milk, where the Tartar ladies sat, unveiled, and watched the knights boasting of their war-like deeds, kneeling on one knee. There were jars of wine for the feasting, "and on tripods made of wooden staves, painted red, hung great leathern sacks filled with cream and mares' milk. This the attendants carrying wands in their hands kept on stirring, rocking the milk backwards and forwards while time and again they threw in many loaves of sugar."

For the full and marvellous account of the Great Khanum's dress, with her train held up by fifteen ladies—as of other eight wives of Timur coming each in turn from her enclosure to take her seat at the tournament in his presence, it is necessary to read Clavijo.\* This scene took place at Timur's summer town of tents at Samarcand, which in the description may have been almost more glorious than Samarcand itself.

It is after reading of the tents of Timur in Clavijo that one should consider Persian carpets. At about the time I first read him I worked much upon the five volumes of *The Survey of Persian Art* and have, could I put it so, made myself familiar with the great "Hunting Carpets". In all that mass of wonderful illustration (the colour plates were printed in Vienna and are unsurpassed for accuracy of reproduction) I find I have noted fifteen carpets as being of the very first order. One, out of that number, belonging to the Musée des Arts

---

\* *Clavijo: Embassy to Tamerlane*, translated from the Spanish by Guy Le Strange, Broadway Travellers, George Routledge & Sons, 1928, p. 258.

Décoratifs at Paris, with its birds and cypresses, its peonies and flowering fruit trees, the boughs of blossoming cherry or plum "breaking" against the dark sable of the cypress, is typical of the carpets that can only have been designed by the Persian miniature painters. This carpet was woven in Tabriz. Another fragment of it is in the Cathedral at Cracow. It could be described as having a crimson border and an almond ground.

The Poldi-Pezzoli "Hunting Carpet" at Milan is scarlet and blue, with a great central scarlet panel. Another, once belonging to the Duke of Anhalt and bought by Duveen, is crimson with a yellow-silver ground. A carpet formerly belonging to Baron Hatvany in Hungary has a white fur ground, a pelt like the coat of a Polar bear, and many figures under canopies and pairs of animals fighting, exactly as in a miniature painting. These I find to be the most beautiful of all the Persian carpets; with a "vase" carpet which is an unique instance of colour combination for the identical "lily" forms are shown, side by side, the one being on a white, the other on a green ground. And another "vase" carpet, in which sixty-eight major forms and twenty-two minor ones play in combination against one another. This latter pair of carpets are from Josaquan-Qali, the little hill town near Isfahan where the mountain waters are suited particularly to fine dyeing. It is scarcely possible to decide in one's own mind whether to admire the "Hunting Carpets" more, or to prefer the great abstract patterns. There are the "vase" and "medallion" carpets, so called, but they consist, more noticeably, of rayed flower and pumpkin forms, endlessly diversified; there are others of *millefleur* fashion; and yet another group so perfectly balanced in arabesque and panel that they are the exact counterpart to the mosaic faience decorations on the mosques of Isfahan. In fact, the illustrations of carpets and faience panels are scarcely to be known from each other and could be interchanged.

At the same time I was working on the Persian illuminated manuscripts in the Oriental Department of the British Museum; on the *Nizami*, probably the most elaborate and perfect of all Persian painted manuscripts, with miniatures by Behzad, himself, by Mirak, by Soltan Mohammed, and other painters of the school; the blossoming trees and cypresses, maple or plane trees, flowering oleanders and rockroses, blue irises in pots, tiled pavilions, the wonderful turbans, as diversified as a bed of tulips, some horned, some flecked with gold, or the high turbans wrapped round long sticks which were the headdresses introduced by the Safavid dynasty, further adorned with feathers as a mark of princely rank (it is always a young imberb prince); the glorious tents with white tops and sides, walled and floored with fine Persian

rugs; and with blue and white tent ropes of which the artist cunningly
made use for his perspective; the striped clothes of the shepherds and
their black goathair "lean-to's"; the storks' nests upon ruined walls;
the two kinds of gold, a greenish and a yellow, in Oriental MS. 2265;
and the miniatures in Baber's *Memoirs* (Oriental MS. 3714) by Persian
and Indian painters, with superb bird and animal paintings; a tribe of
green parrots, and a drawing of huge green frogs in a tank of water.

But the coloured architecture which is the glory of Iran, and prime
invention of the Persians, was further enlivened by the most gorgeously
dressed and apparelled figures that have ever been seen by light of
day or night. This extravagance in costume was at its height and
apogee in the reign of Shah Abbas, and is to be found described in the
travels of Sir John Chardin, accounts that can be supplemented by the
few remaining specimens of this supreme sumptuary magnificence.
Shah Abbas, so Chardin tells us, gave away whole chests stuffed with
cloths of gold and silver, in the same manner that even in our day the
late King Ibn Saud of Arabia presented black or brick-red robes and
corded headdresses embroidered with gold to his visitors; and when
thinking of the court of Shah Abbas, "the total effect has to be considered of several hundred courtiers in attendance upon him clothed in
gold and silver and varied tones of grey, scarlet, yellow, green, plum,
and aubergine . . . vermilion, salmon, turquoise, rose, and light green
or pistachio."* "No part of the world", as Chardin says, "can offer
anything more magnificent and rich, or more splendid and bright."

And so on . . . but what is Persia really like? It is certainly true that
no one could form any idea of its beauty from merely visiting Tehran.
I have tried to give a fair description of the capital, a city which is not
without its endearments but they are in the main those of the walled
compound. Any Moorish or North African town is more "picturesque" by far, while the berated Beirut is, in comparison, the city
of Harun-er-Rashid, or of Chu-Chin-Chow. If at this stage we have
yet to experience in person the marvels of Damascus and Aleppo only
more acute still is the disillusionment of Tehran. The inhabitants are
altogether lacking in the art of sitting and lying about, doing nothing,
which is the prerogative of the white-clad Moors whose every attitude
is a revelation of dignity and pose. But it is true that the visual charac-
teristics of a nation can be quickly changed and lost. In the whole city
of Istanbul you may search in vain, or find but one or two aged Turks
behaving with that *dolce far niente* which was the gift of Turkey to the
world at large. So we should not judge of the Persians from how they

---

* *An Introduction to Persian Art*, by Arthur Upham Pope, London, Peter Davies, Ltd.,
1930, pp. 185, 186.

look to-day. It is only necessary to examine an old photograph to see that they have changed.

On first setting foot in Persia one knows, of instinct, that it is not far from Central Asia. And that India is in the near distance. There another Orient begins. It would now be politic to conclude with some remarks on Moghul India, were it not that one finds the conviction borne in upon one that this is the weakest and most facile of those five main bodies or divisions of the arts of Islam. Of the Taj Mahal, a white peacock of a mosque to contrast with the "blue mosques" of Meshed and Isfahan, or even the Green Mosque of Brusa, it would be difficult to find anything new to say. Beautiful, indeed, beyond contradiction, but organically weak and feminine, weak-chested with inability to lift or spread its shoulders which are hunched around it, and meaningless of dome as compared to those other domes that are as war helms or kettle drums. The Taj Mahal is too much of a white rose or a lily; a white peacock, as I say, but not a white rose on fire. I attempt no description in architectural terms, not having seen it. Neither can I find myself drawn with much of admiration to the 'Pearl Mosque' of Agra, of red sandstone, without, but of white marble, blue-veined, within; nor to the red sandstone palaces within the Fort of Agra; nor other mosques there, such as the Djama Masjid "of three great full-bottomed domes, built of red sandstone, with zigzag bands of white marble circling round them". Neither to the reddish ruins of Fatehpur Sikri; nor to the red, or fawn sandstone mosques and palaces of Delhi. The earlier Moslem buildings in India are the great and good ones; but all this is a topic over which personal ignorance cannot be allowed to presume knowledge, or impede the pleasure that they may give to others. They are enough in themselves to form the study of a lifetime.

But this is no longer the Near Orient. Already the limits are overstepped, and it is time to return from things unseen to those we have touched with our own hands and seen with our own eyes. Of these, the more ancient remains apart, there are the ruins of the classical period which cannot fail to strike even the most hardened critic as the relics of a Golden Age. I have tried to write of these as well as I am able, being no professional art historian.

Lastly, there is the Byzantine, of which I wish I could claim a more extended knowledge, outside Italy and Sicily, having neither seen the churches of Salonica, the monasteries of Mount Athos, nor those of Meteora, all of which are surely among the marvels of the Orient. But I know Mistra in the Pelopennese, and have written elsewhere on the mosaic of the Pantocrator at Daphni.* The prospect of the newly

* In *The Hunters and the Hunted*, London, Macmillan & Co., 1947, pp. 31-37.

cleaned mosaics of the Cariye Cami at Istanbul, as mentioned in my Preface, was the original instigation from which the other and longer journey grew. To this it was tempting to add remarks on the Porphyra, and other architectural phenomena of the Dark Ages, which are not without their bearing on the present time. And it is with the vision of skyscrapers of glass and steel in the shape of pyramids, or octagons, or a full circle, towering as high as cliffs above the streets of the only city in the modern world that has the fame of a Babylon and the setting of an Istanbul, that I close the page and invite the reader to this marriage of the East and West.

R

Scale of Miles

0          500

CASPIAN SEA

ARAL SEA

Baku

TURKMENIA

Meshed

Tabriz

Qazvin

▲ Mt. Demavend

Tehran

Veramin

Herat

AFGHANISTAN

Hamadan

Qom

Tabas

P E R S I A

(I R A N)

Isfahan

Yazd

Kirman

Basra

Persepolis

Qazrun

Shiraz

Kuwait

P E R S I A N   G U L F

Ormuz

Bahrein

# CHAPTER I

## BEIRUT

*A look at Naples — Tour of Alexandria — Arriving at Beirut — On waking in the Orient — Taxis in the Levant — Wonderful costumes — "Sapinoie de Barut" — Phoenicians — Lebanon and pre-war Roumania — Boredom of Oriental houses — Horror of the scale model — Byblos — Corniche and* fête *des* orangers *— Silks of Damascus — Quartier Sursock — "Dîner debout" — Night storm and "take off" for Tehran.*

THE sea journey from Genoa to Beirut takes four days and nights, and is nearly as long and expensive as an Atlantic crossing. But we call in at Naples and Syracuse, and go ashore at both cities in order to revive old memories of the Baroque churches. There they still are:

The Gesù Nuovo with its façade of stones cut into diamond points and the *guglia* or "lily" in front of it, a column in honour of the Virgin erected of intent to be seen at any angle against those coruscating squares; Santa Chiara, bombed by Allied airmen who mistook it for the railway station, its cloister of majolica tiles and trellised vines still standing, but the church turned back from the gilded ballroom that it used to be into the original French Gothic of the Angevin Kings, more austere, more noble, less glittering than before:

San Páolo Maggiore with the Corinthian column or two of a classical temple for portico, and the white horses of Solimena in the fresco'd sacristy within; San Gregorio Armeno, another church all grilles and gilded opera-boxes, golden ceilings and tessellated floors; and the sunken courtyard of music-echoing San Marcellino, a hidden masterpiece of Vanvitelli, and it docs indeed resemble stage-scenery and require careful looking for.

There they all are: damaged, more or less: and if not that, dirtier and dustier than of old. The slum streets, slummier than ever, although often the ground floors of old palaces. But all the shops are closed. The picture gallery shuts the moment we get there on that Sunday morning. Vesuvius is hidden in mist. It has begun to rain. Next day it is raining in Syracuse, too, as we drive in a little carriage to the cathedral square for a sight of the graceful façade of golden stone, and behind it the huge Doric columns of the Greek temple. We return on board after half-an-hour, raise anchor, and move out into the misty sea.

Those are old churches and palaces that may mean little to the

I             I

reader. But I had to name them, having seen them again upon a rainy morning. For my own sake, because they were my first subject when I began to write prose. For a long time they were the limits of personal experience. I had been no further. But now they sink into the distance. For all this alters at first contact with the East. Turkey and Egypt and North Africa give one the taste of the Orient which, speaking in the first person, suffered long interruption during and after the War. But it is something that never fades from the mind. Fifteen years away from it make no difference. To imagine it will have changed, essentially or basically, after an absence of a mere handful of years is to flatter yourself into thinking there will be no more fine mornings after you are dead. But the sun will rise and set the same.

The Baroque churches of Naples are far away under the blue, translucent wave. But we will see their counterpart where we are going. At Petra, if we get there, for that is not certain. It may be the eleventh hour, almost the last moment, for a grand tour of the Middle East. But in our troubled time no journey can be undertaken without misgiving. It is better to start in confidence, and see what happens. Plans must be improvised: sudden decisions taken. Petra is only a little part of the journey, to be deferred until the end. The grand object is a view of the blue mosques of Iran. I am determined to see them before it is too late. One may no longer be able to get to them, although, like those golden churches they may still be there. Now they are approaching and nearly in the hand. Another chance may not come and we are on the way.

Next port of call is Alexandria. We are already berthed at breakfast time. Standing at the rail, pandemonium has broken loose below. Dock porters storm up and down the gangway, at once abandoning and boarding ship, like demented souls. They are men of huge girth with handkerchiefs knotted round their heads like pirates, or, incongruously, they wear straw sun-hats. An old negro gentleman, poorly but neatly dressed, with walking-stick, white beard and turban, has pushed past them and offers his services as guide. But he has had no success when we return on board for luncheon and we see him going ashore, sadly, as the last hooter blows. But that is later in the day. And on the way home aboard the same ship, two months later, we see him neater and sprucer in a new grey tweed suit, despite the heat, taking a party of Americans ashore, shaking hands with everyone and announcing that he has been appointed official guide by the Italian shipping company. It was a personal ending to a long and tiring journey.

But we went ashore for a drive round the town, along the parade by the sea, "Down the endless road to Infinity toss'd", past "white lace

houses" and "the foam of the siren's Metropole and Grand", looking
for the "navy-blue ghost of Mr Belaker, the allegro negro cocktail-
shaker", and there could be no closer description of the residential
quarter of Alexandria than in that poem of my sister's. Back at the port,
and coming through the crowd towards the gangway, we hear a
rattle or a shaking as of dice in a box. It is the "galli galli" man con-
juring with his pocketful of day-old chicks; producing them, losing
them, making pretence of pulling off their wings, adding and sub-
tracting them; tearing a length of string to pieces, cramming the bits
into his mouth, lighting them with much spluttering, and pulling out
the string unbroken and entire. His like will have performed at foot of
the pyramid of Kheops forty centuries ago. But after a moment he has
done his act and slunk away. And there are sellers of cheap bags who
send up their wares to the steerage passengers on lengths of cord. But
the hooter sounds. The usual monks and nuns are waving. There is the
noise of the windlass; the gangway comes up slowly. The police and
harbour officials are ashore. We are an inch off Alexandria, and then
an ell, and now a quarter of a mile, passing on the right the huge Royal
palace of Râs et-Tîn that looks all harem and more ennui, and the sun
sets into the monotonous dark sea.

This is the last night on board. The ship is nearly empty and no one
goes to see the film. It is the end of the sea voyage, though the ship
turns round and starts on another journey to Genoa the same day so
that none of the crew or stewards know anything of where we are
going. Nothing is to be seen in the morning; then snow mountains
appear, the sea becomes more blue and Mediterranean, a town shows
in the distance, and at half-past ten we are off Beirut. By which time
Asia looks like some part of Italy and we are in a warm and lovely bay.

Beirut is not a big harbour, but the quay seethes with people who all
swarm on board, and there is no one to meet us because, as it appears
later, we have arrived two days before we are expected owing to a
letter going by the ordinary post instead of air mail. Our friends, however, when contacted, are not perturbed by this and in an hour we are
comfortably installed in the huge yellow Résidence des Pins, looking
on to a race course and surrounded by bougainvillea and stone pines.
There had been an earthquake only a few days before and the chimney-
piece in the Saracenic salon has been badly cracked. Some of the
mountain villages are shattered and in ruins, and our hostess has to
start off early next day with food and medical supplies.

Is it only in imagination that a whiff of the Orient wafts through
the window with the light of morning? It must come, I think, from
the sticks that are burnt upon the fires. Some wood as pungent as

juniper; or could it be twigs of a fig-tree? Certainly it is the smoke of a fire, and I have known it in Moroccan villages and wherever you pass the tents of Bedouins. It has a particular association with the hour of sunset, probably because that is when the fires are lit. Not like the smell of a tramp's bonfire which we know from damp autumn lanes in England, and that smells, always, as if the tramps were burning their old boots. This is the fire, or the embers, underneath the cooking-pot. I have had the strong whiff of it when walking by the old walls of Istanbul where the Gypsies had their huts, for half of them are torn down; and in Brusa. And now in Beirut. Perhaps it is universal to the Moslem world. But there it is again, more evocative than ever, in spite of the loud hootings of motor-horns. The shutters are warm already with the spring morning; there are blue hills and snow in the distance and the stone pines.

Beirut is a town with half-a-million inhabitants that has spread in every direction without plan. The taxi-drivers do not even know the names of many of the streets. Traffic blocks are as bad as in London, and there are so many accidents that they tell you they never know whether they will wake up in the morning in a bed in hospital or in a police cell. Young Levantines, for there is not an old or even a middle-aged taxi-driver in Beirut, and, indifferently, Moslem, Greek Ortho-dox, or Maronite, languid and inclined to fatness, they are only interested in money and in their own low wages, and it is a curious sensation to be driven by them in their shirtsleeves, one hand on the wheel, while they gesture with a whole arm and hand out of a window, apparently contrived for the purpose, and lose, and refuse to ask, the way. It is a town as big in area as Lisbon, and all but as hilly. Perhaps the pleasantest place for living along the whole littoral between Tunis and Istanbul, but with no history and no old buildings except the Grande Mosquée, once a church of the Knights of St John, with Byzantine capitals from a still older church and as you see into it in passing, a place of that calm and repose which are the secret of the Moslems. There they are, sitting crosslegged, or stretched out and sleeping, as though, and it is the truth, there is not much else to do.

Close by, an old arcaded street of shops leads down towards the harbour, and there is a walk by the sea to the Hotel St Georges with the local equivalent of *lazzaroni* idling energetically along the foreshore in front of another and older hotel where Herman Melville once stayed. For the rest, Beirut is little shops and night clubs on steep and hilly streets, leading to villas and better houses, known by the district or quarter of the town, Roumeli, Ez-Zeitoûni, El Ouâdi, El Bachoûra, and so forth. But all over the town, and in every part of it, what are wonderful are the clothes. It must be a legacy from the Turks who in their turn had it from Byzantium. In this respect Beirut may be the most picturesque of all towns on the Mediterranean. Nearly every single person seen is interesting, except the taxi-drivers and the shop-keepers. Now and again you pass a Druze from the hills, in his white turban of peculiar shape, white-bearded and splendidly aquiline. There are Turks, or they look like Turks, who could step straight out of Venetian paintings of the *Banquet of Anthony and Cleopatra*, often in the very striped or light brown *caftans* of Tiepolo. As well, all and every variety of baggy trouser is to be admired. The women are not less wonderful, although few of them veiled, and there are others looking like Gypsies or Bedouins who show their faces and, often, are wearing dresses of dark purple or scarlet, or fiery and bright green. It is not only that the dresses are beautiful in themselves, but one wonders where the stuffs are made and dyed. They do not seem to be for sale in the shop windows. They must be bought in the mountain villages, or are they dyed at home? It is, of course, a truism that if you followed one or other of these gorgeously dressed beings, male or female, to their house you would find them living in rooms with little or no furniture for they wear all their finery and own nothing else. It would be as bare as the room where the old Druze sleeps who passed by now. This has been the case, always, in every part of the old Turkish Empire, and is noticed by every writer in the past. Lear, travelling in Albania, tells of the marvellous costumes of such towns as Scutari and makes the comment that all their wealth and luxury was in their clothes.

Beirut, not old in itself, is bathed in that golden light which pertains to classical sites like Nîmes, or Arles, or Tarragona. You are perhaps first aware of it by the hollowed cliffs of the Grottes des Pigeons, just outside the town. Here, some of the ugliest of the modern villas are building, and I nearly wrote "themselves" after that for it is difficult to believe they have an architect. There is a straight shore of reddish sands and foam; and we are on the road to the airport where we "flew in" or "flew out" half-a-dozen times, seeing it in all lights and at every hour from dawn to sunset. The soil is red and there is a beautiful wood of stone or umbrella pines, the "Sapinoie de Barut" of the Crusaders. Under the trees, here and there, the Bedouins pitch their tents and this wood which may have been here since classical times takes on another aspect, becoming, by alchemy of circumstance, a wood of the Italian *quattrocento*. We see it, by night, with a light or two moving through the trees, and with the addition of torches and running figures and galloping horses it is the wood of Paolo Uccello's *Night Hunt*\*; or,

\* In the Ashmolean at Oxford.

another time, a file of women on their way to fetch water, with vases or amphoras on their heads, glittering in the sun, but the water-jars are empty petrol tins, becomes for that moment Eastern women in a painting by Carpaccio, and it is only later we discover they are not Bedouins but Palestinian refugees. It is a wood that is endlessly beautiful at all times of day. So are the hills beyond and outside the town which at night are honeycombed with lights from all the villas. Everything grows here; in a few gardens there are even the scarlet bracts of the flamboyant tree which flowers nowhere else nearer than Central Africa.

Further hills have monasteries on them which are as likely as not the summer villa of a bishop or a patriarch. There are the Maronite Archbishop, the Greek Orthodox Bishop, the Uniate Greek Patriarch of the Orient, beside the Papal Delegate, the heads of the Jesuit and other Catholic orders, two communities of Armenians, the Syrian Christians, the Moslems, and the Druzes. Much of the time of all diplomats accredited to the Republic of the Lebanon is taken up with paying calls and receiving visits from these different religious dignitaries. Beirut in this respect is only second after Papal Rome, but here the various sects are an integral part of the population, they are not surviving anachronisms given territorial status like the Knights of Malta. The Lebanon is such a mingling of creeds and races as was Roumania before the War, all living in amity and concord and with no persecution of minorities. In fact, the individual you feel certain is Moslem turns out to be a Christian; but is he, then, Greek Orthodox or Maronite? Or Armenian? Not that they mind, being mistaken one for the other. Of course, the person you see fingering a string of amber beads is a Moslem. Perhaps in the Lebanon the most surprising thing to a foreigner is that Arabic is spoken. What language would one expect them to speak? One does not know. The answer is probably Phoenician. With many other descents, as well, they have certainly Phoenician blood in them. It is the commercial instinct they have inherited from Tyre and Sidon that keeps them together as a country, a consideration rising above either race or religion. Nevertheless it is surprising to hear Greek Orthodox and Maronite talking together in Arabic, and it is more unexpected still among the rich Levantines. Less so, however, when a hookah (hubble-bubble) is in use and handed round from mouth to mouth in the hall of the hotel. And among the poorer classes you can tell they are not used to sitting in chairs and would prefer to sit cross-legg'd. There is, as well, a curious flattening of the back of the head among older and even middle-aged natives of the Lebanon, due to their being swaddled when they were infants, and a tendency for the top of the cranium to be peaked or domed. This recalls more than a little— dare we say it?—the peaked scalp of the *Seti* or Abominable Snow Man, on view, and photographed, in certain lamaseries in Nepal. This is to be noted, particularly, with persons who are bald, and when joined to features of Semitic cast it gives a decidedly Oriental look as we understand that in the Occident. These are features that will become more familiar still from early sculptures in museums.

Bargaining is inherent in that physiognomy, and you do not have to stay long in Beirut to know that money is as much the pastime and addiction of the population as are opera to the Italians, bull-fights to the Spaniards, or football to the Englishman. The appeal is, perhaps, less the money itself than the playing with money, and they are not so adept at it as the Israelites. But it is something in the air or in the soil which predisposes the inhabitants towards the clink of coins, and that sooner or later infects every race that breathes this atmosphere. Were the present population to be bodily removed and another settled in its place they would succumb in a generation and become only interested in money. But for all that, and showing in their near relationship as much difference as there is between the Scots and Irish, the Lebanese are lacking in the other talents and do not produce musicians, actors, scientists, as do the Jews. They emigrate in large numbers to South America, as likewise do the Syrians, where they engage in small scale commerce. They do not conduct orchestras, play the violin, or split the atom. It is to be concluded that they are petty traders more than intellectuals.

Arabian princes in yellow Cadillacs are now in place of rich Egyptians. Villas on the harem plan are building for them on the hills, next to the summer retreats of the bishops and the patriarchs. Coming from the Gulf, or from Saudi Arabia, how lovely must seem the snow mountains and stone pines! It is such contrasts that give to the Lebanon a quasi-Roumanian, almost a bastard-Byzantine air, never forgetting that the Lebanon, its Phoenician origins apart, was under Byzantine, then, under Arabian, and lastly for four centuries under Turkish rule. Again, like Roumania, like Moldavia and Wallachia of old, it has rich families and an aristocracy. The Lebanon would seem to be a corner of the world disposed by history for luxury and indolence, except that these are the fruits of hard bargaining. Beirut is the boom town of the Middle East, fated to have more and more hotels and modern blocks of flats. But there are, and will always be incongruities, and in a new hotel on one of our many returns to Beirut looking-glasses had been forgotten in the bedrooms, and the canned music relayed all over the building and in charge of one of the lift-boys had only *Schéhérazade* in

its repertoire which was played over and over again all night and day.
I can hear the opening of the music, as I write this, and am looking
out through the tossing palm trees on to a rainy sea.

For it rains sometimes in Beirut, and when it does the modern
villas are uglier than ever with the hopelessness that besets the interiors
of all Oriental houses, and one looks up at the grey clouds in dread
of the "take off" from the airport at six o'clock next day. And yet . . .
Beirut with all its steep hills and motor-horns is more like that than any
other sort of music. There is a private house in the town into which
the interiors of old houses in Damascus have been fitted where, again,
we arrived one evening when it poured with rain. I can hear the rain
dropping from the palms and am trying not to slip up on the marble
steps. The owner has bought some thirty old houses in Damascus and
removed rooms, bodily, or bit by bit, to Beirut.  Damascus must be
quite gutted by him. There can be little left. He has old Korans in
vitrines on the walls, and superb rugs and carpets. Some of the Korans
are in that early Kufic writing which is so great a work of art in itself,
and of such visual importance, that one wishes the manuscripts of the
B minor Mass or Bach's organ fugues could have been written in it.
The old rooms have been rebuilt there with tact and delicacy, and at
vast expense. There are hanging lamps, inlaid floors of marble, and
much of the seventeenth century panelling is painted by hands that
suggest a school of Oriental children copying the "Douanier"
Rousseau, huge bowls of flowers and views of Damascus that could be
inspired by him, but everywhere there is the Oriental ennui. It is the
stupidity and boredom of the women, their shuttered and imprisoned
listlessness, that makes the air of the rooms infect and uninteresting.
Wherever Moslems have set foot it is the same; at its least bad in the
Alhambra at Granada, but even there the beauty is in the fountains and
the bees'-work ceilings, and in looking from mirador-windows over to
the Gypsy hill of the Albaicín. One soon tires of the rooms, however
delicate the arabesque, the stalactite and filigree. They are materially or
intrinsically boring in themselves; which is not the same thing as
some detail in a church or monastery of whatever date, Baroque or
mediaeval, where the known boredom of the lives the monks led, and
their ignorance and superstition, do not detract from, and even enhance
the effect. The best work from Damascus is as fine as anything from
Cairo or Istanbul, and it is only that the Moslem genius lies beyond its
interior rooms. It is not to be judged by the insides of houses. This
collection from Damascus is more like a museum, and as with all
museums it is a delight not to be living in it. The tiled hotel bathroom
is a work of our own age with its own shortcomings, and as the water

runs out of the bath, once more, and not for the last time, *Schéhérazade* is playing.

A few days in Beirut go by quickly, but prolong themselves in the memory. More particularly if, owing to the exigencies of the journey, you return there, as we did, five or six times for base. And the day must come when you go to the museum. Here on the sarcophagus of a King of Byblos is the first alphabetical inscription, and in the dark and depressing cellar-basement are a score or more of ugly sham-Egyptian coffins in white marble of the Phoenician Kings of Sidon. This is no place for works of art. But there are wall-maps, painted in fresco, of the Kingdoms of the Ancient East, and it was interesting to look for Persepolis, where we were going, and compare Susa, Babylon, and Ecbatana. There is, also, a model of the temples of Baalbek, interesting in itself to the lover of architectural forms if only for the hexagonal forecourt leading to the great temple, but the aesthetic content is that of a plasticine model of the Madeleine at Paris, and the trouble with scale-models is that they so often throw doubts which nothing will ever dispel afterwards upon their original. A scale-model of the Acropolis, it is true, hill and all, would be no better; but then, again, how beautiful was the Parthenon, when new? Or is it that, like waxworks of human figures all models of buildings are hideous, and that much worse because they are in scale. We should be pleased, by the same token, that there is no authentic waxwork figure of Cleopatra, or of Mary, Queen of Scots. A model of Chartres Cathedral is on the same dead level as models of the cathedrals at Coventry or Guildford. But all miniature buildings are not hideous. There are not attendant and unavoidable horrors in the lilliputian. It must be that the Parthenon was ugly and tasteless, new; and if that be so, what of the temples of Baalbek, belonging to a classical decadence six centuries later than the Parthenon? Is it true that their architecture is that of the motor-sales' room, and that the Temple of Bacchus is like Selfridge's in ruin? Or is it only that Beirut, the "Paris of the Middle East", has nothing in it that is a work of art? But let us think of London. The Coronation procession upon its long route did not pass a single building worth looking at, except for the Horse Guards and Inigo Jones' Banqueting Room at Whitehall. Even in the scale-model you can see that the temples of Baalbek are more magnificent than anything in London. So many classical buildings are lying in heaps of ruins, where we are going; and will the mosques be any better? It is a day when all, and everything, is doubtful. Coming away from the museum, there are some columns of a Roman temple re-erected in a little garden opposite the entrance, and it is here that American sailors are brought at great expense by taxi-drivers to visit "the ruins of Baalbek" while the fleet is in.

In the afternoon of that same day we went to Byblos, and the road there is more beautiful than the excavations. A *corniche* road with hairpin bends and tunnels, and an inscription on the rock face, at one point, to *Napoléon III, Empereur des Français*. This was set up after the Druzes had massacred the Christians and a French army corps was sent to Lebanon in 1860, but there seems to be no more chance of a massacre, now, than at Nice or San Remo. For many miles we drive through orange groves and the smell of the blossom is an intoxication. As well, there are banana palms growing on the shores of the tideless and blue sea. The ancient Byblos is one vast midden, a paradise for the excavator with its prehistoric, Phoenician, Roman, and mediaeval cities, one next to the other and as near as allotments or kitchen gardens, with still more to dig up for sure under the modern Djebail, but it is muddling and confusing and there is but little above ground. Happier moments are in the Maronite church of St John Baptist, a twelfth century building where we were shown round by a monk, stoutly shod, with a hood to his gown and a walking-stick, a monk like a wandering friar from *Boris Godunov*, and we watched him hurrying away with a firm tread. On the way home the sunset was nearly incredible, particularly where it caught the terraced salt pans that are so many trays of water, lobster tanks we thought, at first, but there could not be crustaceans in that number, turning the waters to fire, and now going down in incandescence into the purple sea. In the twilight the smell of orange blossom wafts in, haunting every breath, while the driver tells us of the *fête des orangers* to be held next week when, it seems, not much else is done than to sit, or lie and picnic, all day and late into the evening, under the orange trees.

By this time we had learned our way about in Beirut. How to get down, by streets running apparently in the wrong direction, in order to emerge on the sea front near the St Georges Hotel. This is about the only "sited" building in the whole of Beirut, and I could not help comparing it in position with the hotel which is as much or more of a landmark in the seaside town where I was born. Shaped like a letter V, with one wing facing the sea and one to face inwards, that was a huge Renaissance château in yellow brick in Second Empire style. Where everything, with the cliffs and the Castle Hill and the double bay, was bigger in scale for better or worse it dominated the town. Were one suddenly to find oneself here, on this sea front near the St Georges Hotel, not close enough to read the names over the shop windows, what would one's guess be? Not Egypt, not North Africa, with the snow mountains and the blue sea. Perhaps an entirely imaginary land, with the *lazzaroni* lying on the sea wall pretending to be bootblacks, and Orientals of so many different sorts wandering on and off the "set"! Big American cars as taxis are waiting in front of the hotel, but instead of climbing the steps we go into an antique dealer's in the basement. Judging by the little objects carved in olive wood and mother-of-pearl we cannot be far from Palestine, but bales of silk that could only come from Damascus give a clue to where we are. They are among the more beautiful textiles woven in our time and age, with the technique to accomplish anything asked of them, so why stop short at little figures or animals taken from Persian miniatures, and in the newer designs descend towards nursery humour and comic fairy stories? Why do they not copy and put on sale silk brocades from the Imperial workshops of Byzantium? It is the difference between the Basileus driving a four-horse *quadriga*, or a combat of lions and elephants, and Walt Disney. Even so, brocaded with gold and silver, and in multitude of design, they make a gay display. We know where we are, now, not far from Damascus, and it must be Beirut. Perhaps the most beautiful things on sale in the shops are the sleeveless, loose fitting women's shifts, in unpatterned silks of magenta-pink, or green, or heliotrope, or white silk, flecked or rayed with silver. This is the indoor dress of the Lebanon, in this semi-Orient which is more Eastern than the Orient itself.

For there is something eternally, ineradicably Turkish or Byzantine about the Lebanon. Only sumptuary laws of a draconian severity would alter it. Or is it Phoenician, and in descent from Tyre and Sidon? Where else along the shores of the Mediterranean are there dervishes, as among the olive groves of Tripoli, a little to the north of Beirut? And was not Byblos the centre of the cult of Adonis and Astarte? But it is the Orient, not the Hellenic past; and in the distance lies, not Sicily, but Carthage. For Carthage was a colony of Tyre, and you can feel that as far away as Cartagena (Nova Carthago) which is in Spain. There could be Greek colonies to north, or south, or east, or west, but this is a Semitic land. A little of the blood of Tyre and Sidon, there is no doubt, has lingered here. At Carthage, where none of it is left, it must have mixed with African. But the Carthaginians have vanished from the world. There is only the Lebanon left; and who knows what there may be here of the Hittites, Sumerians, and other races, who bore, certainly, some physical resemblance to the Phoenicians as we shall find, later, when looking at statues from Mari, on the Euphrates, in the museum at Damascus? This is a Mediterranean civilization with, not Provence or Castile, but Mesopotamia for hinterland.

The traits that go with it have had longer survival with the upper classes. And it is probable that those revert to it after becoming rich in a generation, or even arriving from abroad. It is something endemic that in their time affected both Arabs and Crusaders. That earth and air and water have an influence is unarguable, or the North American Indians would have remained flat-faced like their forbears in Siberia and never become copper-skinned and aquiline. This is a Semitic begetting-soil with the temple of Solomon nearer at hand than the pyramids of Egypt. How innocent and harmless are our early Kings, Alfred, Edgar, or Ethelred the Unready, beside Nebuchadnezzar! That was a millennium before our Saxon kings, when Tyre and Sidon had long been famous. And eventually Phoenicia, or the Lebanon, formed part of the fifth satrapy of Persia! If that is not Eastern, then Celts and Danes and Saxons do not pertain to the West. So we conclude that it renders Eastern whom it touches, however much it may like to play at being the New York or Paris of its own corner of the Mediterranean. It is a Christian culture where French is spoken, bilingually, with Arabic. The women are like Italians, with non-Italian voices; not those voices for calling down from a window into a courtyard. There is that, always, in the voices of Italians. And you can hear in them the noise of a shutter being thrown back on a hot wall. They are siesta voices. Perhaps it is that these have stayed indoors for centuries and spoken, therefore, in low tones. For, once more, this was a part of Turkey for four centuries. With a Christian governor, or *mutessarif*, since the Druze massacres of 1860, "who was directly responsible to the Sublime Porte, a regime that came to an end in 1915" but that is not long ago. When not Phoenician, we could say, a Persian satrapy; and when not Arab, a Crusading Kingdom, and then a Turkish province. Such is the history of the Lebanon.

What is unique in Beirut is the *Quartier Sursock*, a living survival from old Byzantium, disguised under the name of rue de l'ancien Archevêché Grec. Here live families who have been rich for two centuries or more, and who under Turkish rule had exactly the position of families living on the Bosphorus in the time of the Greek Emperors. Rich Byzantines may have had little or no Greek blood, but they were landowners in Asia Minor, and probably as far as Egypt, and here are the homes of their equivalents and, it may be, their descendants. If you see a portrait of a Victorian ancestor he will be wearing a red fez. For again, as in Roumania, there is little of earlier date and personal possessions, in order to be quickly removable were, mainly, valuable rugs and jewels. The perils attendant on riches must have been identical with those in force at the other end of the Turkish

Empire, at Bucarest and Jassy in the Danubian Principalities. It is remarkable, in itself, that any families could have prospered so long in these conditions which lasted, Janissaries, executioners, and all, until so short a while ago. A character of local renown like the Bosnian, Jezzar Pasha, who defended Acre against Napoleon in 1799, was as cruel and infamous and as much of a monster as his contemporary, Ali Pasha of Joannina. These are satrapies and pashaliks; it is an Oriental world far removed from the High Sheriffs and Lords-Lieutenant of our English counties.

The old houses in this high lying quarter of the town are few in number, but enough to give it character. For example, a house with a pair of jacaranda trees, just coming into flower when we left Beirut for the last time early in May, growing above twin, one-room pavilions to either side of the entrance gates, which in pre-war Bucarest would have been lived in by Albanian doorkeepers. But the marble steps are only a few feet away, and when the door opens we are in a house the like of which we have not seen before. It has a large hall, the whole width of the building, and in effect two floors high, advancing by Moorish-looking or Saracenic arches to windows giving on to a terrace and down on to a cypressed garden. It could be the work of Italian scene painters of 1830 for a production of Rossini's *L'Italiana in Algeri* or his *Turco in Italia*, but is more probably by Armenian, not Italian architects, and rather later in date, perhaps between 1850 and 1870. It is not contemporary Turkish taste; neither is it like the Egyptian palaces such as the delightful little painted Palais Bijou near the Citadel in Cairo. It must, then, be typical of the Lebanon.

The cypresses may be nearly a hundred years old, and in the evening you look down as on to a dark amphitheatre with the sea beyond. Dinner is semi-Oriental, with Arab rice dishes, Eastern ways of cooking fish, and cakes compounded of dates grown in the garden. The servants speak Arabic, and orange-flower water is dropped from an ewer into the Turkish coffee. A feature in these houses are the staircases in a side hall rising in little flights through the non-existing mezzanine into the upper floor where there are more drawing rooms. Another house, near by, has old interiors from Damascus, but not importing with them a museum air, exquisite rugs, and beautiful brocade dresses which are hung upon screens. It is an Oriental house, and its owner who has the vermilion hair and aquiline profile, less of Roxelana, herself, who was a Circassian, than of a sister of the Renaissance Soltan Süleyman the Magnificent in a portrait by Titian, would not pretend to be anything other than Eastern in race. Again, it is surprising to hear persons dressed by Dior speaking Arabic; and once more like the Roumanians they belong probably to the Orthodox church. But Roumanian is a Latin tongue, and one cannot get it out of one's head that Arabic was spoken by Harun-er-Rashid, and Saladin, and King Ibn Saud. Entertaining in these houses is upon a grand scale, and it is clear that the spectres of income tax and death duty have not yet crossed the doorstep. Salmon, turkeys, sucking-pigs, and delicious sweets which are a speciality of the Lebanon, sustain the spirits of a hundred to a hundred and fifty guests at what is not an exceptional entertainment in point of numbers. It is a *dîner debout* which means you stand up, or try to find a chair, but there are no places laid, and this is tiring to our stolid habit of sitting for hours at dinner and staying longer still in the dining room drinking port and brandy. No one here would have the patience; and further East still it is even suggested that they do not like a "sit down dinner" because that means, precisely, sitting next to someone, or, in fact, between two persons, and they never know who is "getting at" them. But this is a race who are ultra-suspicious of each other and everyone else, and who have proved over and over again in history that they are past masters of subtlety and intrigue. In the Lebanon they are no less quick but lighter in the hand, and if they wish to finish dinner it is in order to begin their charades and games. But all through the Orient there is one commodity to waste, which is in endless supply, and that is Time.

It is an element which works its own alchemy, and one easily falls victim to it. Already, at no long distance, it is difficult to sort out in one's mind the events and impressions of so many short stays in Beirut. Always on the way somewhere, having only just got back from somewhere else. In consequence, perpetually tired because these journeys whether by road or aeroplane start, invariably, at six o'clock or earlier in the morning. To recapitulate, we were to leave Beirut in a day or two by air for Tehran. After travelling in Persia for some weeks we were due back in Beirut about the end of April only to leave there again, almost at once, for Petra and Jerusalem. We had, then, to return once more to Beirut in order to go north to Aleppo, seeing Kalat Seman and Krak des Chevaliers on the way, and coming back to Beirut for the last time so as to catch the boat home. Beirut is the inevitable base for all these journeyings. We stayed twice in the yellow *Résidence des Pins* looking over the racecourse among the umbrella pines, and three times in different hotels, earning for ourselves a reputation as hotel nomads from so many changes. At intervals, therefore, over two or three months we saw Beirut from many angles and looked out on it from many different windows. If it changed at all during that time it was that there were more and still uglier new villas.

But, in order to keep to some degree of chronological pattern, visits to the temples of Baalbek and to Beit-ed-Din will be described, later, in the order in which they came. We spent a day in Damascus but that, too, will be sublimated into the impressions of a stay in that city on our way back from Persia.

During this first time in Beirut there was more than enough to do in making plans for the rest of the journey, and in discovering once again that in the East it is no use trying to decide on anything far in advance. Circumstances make their own arrangements, which are often negative. Events settle things for themselves and it is useless to inter-fere. For the moment one had no idea whether there would be any question of going to Meshed, which was one of the main objects in coming to Persia, while the possibility of getting to Petra on our return was, if anything, remoter still. Decisions can only be taken on the spot and at the last moment. *"Ensha' allah"*, that familiar and much worn interjection has a meaning, by ignoring which you only call down delays and disappointments upon yourself. It *does* all depend a little, upon what? Or whom? And the Persian answer is as sensible as any other.

Meanwhile, in Beirut it is at least the Orient again. In proof of which it is only necessary to look in at the door of the Mosque while passing. But the day of departure draws nearer and nearer, and now it is to-morrow. On our last day we went all over the town to buy baskets for our extra luggage. There is the eternal question of what clothes to take, and what to leave behind. It was spring weather in Beirut, although in some connection with the recent earthquake there were torrential rains. In Persia we were told it would be winter still. Tehran is four thousand feet above sea-level, which is higher than Avila. One had memories of how cold it could be in Avila in April, and it might be colder still in Tehran. As for Isfahan and Shiraz they are five thousand feet up, the height of Davos or Zermatt. It could be very cold indeed. And then at any moment it might be very hot. And although it was hot in the daytime it would be cold at night.

For myself, this was the longest journey I had ever undertaken. North America may be further in miles, but this is more far away. The sunset had been stormy, and before long it had blown up into a howling gale. It was of threatening appearance because of the ragged clouds crossing in front of the moon. How the doors and windows rattled when I went to bed! Screws of paper were of no use to deaden them. And then it began to pour with rain. Was another earthquake coming? A fortnight ago it had come like this with a downpour. The safe place was to stand in a doorway, or get out into the garden. And one was warned not to stand below a chandelier. There was a chandelier in the bedroom.

We were to be woken at four o'clock, and I was awake by half-past two, having come back after midnight from a *dîner debout*, prodigious in numbers and in loaded sideboards. My guess would be that there were two hundred persons present, a few of whom in high spirits and out of friendliness wanted us to stay up all night and suggested coming with us to the airport. It had been necessary to escape them by a subterfuge. Now they were shaken off, and so was everything else. One was alone with oneself, as always in a sleepless night. And while it was still dark we began dressing, and just as we were dressed the telephone rang from the airport to tell us there was two hours' delay. So the only course was to get back into bed again. And then the dawn came, and it was so wet that everything was dripping and so foggy that one could not see the mountains. Visibility was no further than the nearest umbrella pine. The bus from the air terminus had been coming to fetch us, but another message came to say that now it would not be passing by. Were there taxis on such a wet morning? A further delay of an hour and a half was announced. One felt lost and disembodied, no longer in Beirut and not yet in Persia. But, at last, it grew lighter. It was the morning. The taxi waited at the door. And in a moment we were driving through the pine wood on the way to Tehran.

# CHAPTER II

## TEHRAN

*Over the desert — Arrival — The* chador *— Silver plane trees — Embassy compound — Nau Ruz — A cut-glass stage for marionettes? — Drive to Varamin — Seljuq tomb tower — First Persian mosque — Picnic in the mountains — A pavilion of Nasr-ed-Din — "Alfredo" the tame pelican — Persian dinner party — Anecdotes of Fath Ali Shah — His wasp waist, black beard, and diamond bracelets worn on the elbow — Mr Hannibal — To Qazvin in a day — Children and onlookers — Droshkies of Qazvin and the Dies Irae — Museum of Tehran — Golden foundation stone of Persepolis — Bronze statue with trousers and long hair — Rayed plates of Zenzan — Street scenes — Reception at Golestan Palace — Luncheon at farm of General Arfa.*

AEROPLANES of S.A.S. (Scandinavian Airlines System) take some three and a half hours to fly from Beirut to Tehran, and cover nearly a thousand miles during that time. The take off is almost imperceptible after the dizzying, intoxicating gathering of speed along the runway, and now comes that sensation of being lifted, up, up, as we climb through the mist that has been torn into little puffs and ragged edges by the storm, are over the foam-flecked Mediterranean and its red shore for a moment and back again, and after twenty minutes or half-an-hour are across the mountains of Lebanon and out high over the desert in full sunlight, now. Large and leprous patches below seen, literally, to have been sown with salt. Only now and again is there green along the course of a river, or some squares of scratches in the sand that show a village.

The pale hair of the Norwegian air crew and air hostesses puts them into a race apart of Nordic beings, a Varangian Guard to whom one has handed over one's life for those few hours. Otherwise, the only way to go to Persia is by road which could take weeks or months; or by tramp steamer to the Persian Gulf. One is in their charge and already half-way there, drinking coffee. Before it seems possible we are over Baghdad; but all we can see of it is the yellow waters of the Tigris, and a muddle of flat-roofed houses, and of the golden domes and minarets of Khazimein, in a suburb, there is no sign. Half-an-hour later come mountains, more mountains, some covered with snow which are the Elburz range, and in midst of them the snowy cone of Demavend, higher than any peak in the Alps or to our side of the Himalayas, but from here it is unimpressive, and not making the most of its height. Then we fasten our safety belts over an enormous far spreading town,

17

which comes nearer in the moment we are aware of it, come down
steeply, touch and make contact, and are arrived in Persia.

After flying one is too dazed for a few moments by the forced
journey to take in many impressions. There are too many preoccupa-
tions with counting luggage and having passports stamped. But what
one remembers is the long and immense line of snowy mountains to
one side, driving into the town, and the spotted *chadors* which are the
first sign of Persia. Nearly all the women wear these blue *chadors* with
the white dots, garments which envelop their heads and come right
down to their feet. They hold a corner of the *chador* in their hands to
hide their faces; or if their hands are full, carrying a parcel, they put
that corner of the *chador* into their mouths. There are open gutters down
both sides of the road, running with dirty water, and there are wide
streets with houses and shops built of a dingy and unpleasant yellow
brick. And that is all there is time to see before we come to a long and
high wall with an arched gateway in the middle of it, and are in the
compound of the British Embassy at Tehran.

We were staying in a yellow brick house, one of the five or six
behind the high wall, built like the Ambassador's residence by Indian
Army engineers about a hundred years ago. Built, that is to say, less
than a decade after the Mutiny, and it has been said that they are a little
like the detached houses in a mid-Victorian lunatic asylum. That
portal, it is certain, is not unlike the entrance arch at Hanwell. But by
this time we are upstairs being shown our bedrooms, and delighting in
a wood fire with the sudden realization that it is, indeed, very cold.
These brick villas are all as charming as possible inside. They are
English homes, more English than ever because they are so far away.
The compound, itself, is full of character. And what are strangely and
perfectly beautiful are the trees. They are immensely tall, taller than any
limes or elms, perhaps eighty or ninety feet high, and the same age as
the houses. They are a kind of tree one has not seen before. Persian
plane trees with silver stems, now leafless because it is the last week
in March, and making a wonderful silvery pallor of tracery in the cold,
cloudless sky. One will never forget the silver plane trees which will
always remind one of Tehran.

Later on, before we left, there were the flowering Judas trees, but
that was at the end of April. They do better here, even, than along the
Bosphorus, and are more healthy and luxuriant in colour. Their full
beauty was something one had been told of, but not seen. By which
time the flowerbeds were full of pansies, but now we were only
emerging from winter and it looked and felt as though there was still
snow to fall. Whenever one walked through the compound one

looked up into those silvery, pale trees. They are as much an expression of Persia as are the green poplars of the Île de France, and in reminder that it is neither an Arab nor a Mediterranean country but tending to Central Asia and lying between the Caspian and the Persian Gulf. It was somehow implicit in those pale boughs that this would be a land, less of the turban, than of the lambskin cap. Meanwhile there were children, who could be nothing but English, playing on carefully tended lawns around a swimming pool, and one could guess they seldom went outside the compound except for picnics in the mountains. The high wall gives a feeling of security and at the same time a sensation of being half-besieged, both of them rather pleasant in retrospect and more still at the time. The compound seems to be self-contained and provisioned as though it could hold out until rescue came.

For the first day or two we led the lives of convalescents, a condition partly enforced on us by the feast of *Nau Ruz*, which is the Persian New Year, whene very Persian must spend the day picnicking in the hills, near running water, a feast that is an obvious survival from pagan and pre-Moslem times, and in origin a *Sacre du Printemps*, or celebration of the rites of spring. It was held during the first week end after our arrival. But, also, we were tired and exhausted after the journey, and it was enough to stay in the compound and look up into those trees. What a sensation to wake up the first morning knowing one was in Persia! This had been a personal ambition for how many years! With Mexico, its flowers and volcanoes and golden churches, for the other goal. Four years ago I had seen the rose-pink shagreen towers and gilded altars of the Santuario de Ocotlán. And now, how marvellous to be waking for the first time in Tehran! But, again, as though con- valescing after an illness, our first expedition beyond the compound walls was to Golahek, which is the summer compound of the British Embassy in the hills four or five miles from Tehran, a replica of its parent, with more streams of water and more of the silver plane trees, and summer versions of the villas, with verandahs, some dilapidated, others lived in, and the summer residence of the Ambassador, where we looked down at grape-hyacinths and cyclamen and picked white lilac. On the way home, passing carts drawn by horses that had their manes and tails dyed with henna, and a long string of camels, we had not to remind ourselves we were in the Orient, and in a part of it not far from Central Asia. That is the difference of Persia. It is not an Arab country. The worse the roads—and they can be bad!—they all lead, in imagination, to Bokhara and Samarcand.

Next day we were to have a taste of Persian architecture for the first time and drove to Varamin, through a part of Tehran where the shops merge into the bazaars after passing a strange cut-glass balcony like one of the attractions of a fun-fair looking over the street. It is a balcony of the Golestan Palace, which is used by the Shah for receptions and audiences and has the Peacock Throne in it. But the balcony looks as if it had been intended as a stage for marionettes, and passing under it one turns back and listens for the squeaking voices of the puppets. We meet a wedding procession; or, at least, a file of men carrying cupboards and armchairs and bedsteads and piles of bedding on their heads, which is the prelude to the wedding; and now we notice that while most of the women wear the blue and white *chador*, the majority, if not all, of the men are either wearing striped pyjamas or more often bicycling in long nightgowns. Of their national dress there are no traces left in Tehran, unless we except a *molla* or two and a few countrymen in round caps like the berets of the Spaniards, but without the umbilical stalk of the beret, and the caps are not blue in colour but dirty brown. There is something a little horrible about these round caps when we see them in process of manufacture in the bazaars of Isfahan or Meshed.

We are now out of the town and looking at the landscape for a first view of Persia, and in spite of what one is told it has no more than a superficial resemblance to Spain. I had thought of it as being like the landscape round Córdoba, or, indeed, like the Spanish landscape, generally, one of the magnificent open landscapes of Estremadura or Old Castile, a limitless plain with snowy mountains unutterably distant and aloof, like the ramparts of another, a lunar world, apart, and often in stark simplicity to be expressed, in drawing, in a single line but this is as open and big in scale, though different. In this direction towards Varamin you do not see so much of the mountains, and though as large in scale and as open there are rocky hills and outcrops in the foreground, and it is not so tawny. It is not lion-coloured; in the jungle country between here and the Caspian there are leopards, and even tigers. But neither could one say it is tiger-striped or leopard-spotted; nor, although leopards and tigers have an Indian connotation, could one see in it a possible resemblance, real or imaginary, to any part of India. At which moment one was passing a group of little domed buildings round a court with a collapsed archway leading to it that must be a *Khan* or *caravanserai*, where travellers drove in their horses and camels, lit a fire and spent the night in one of the domed rooms or alcoves, not indeed a motel, but a camelotel, and built on the same timeless principle.

At Varamin the curiosities are of two kinds. There is one of the fluted grave-towers of Seljuq origin, in the pattern of the famous tower at Gonbad-i-Qabus, which climbs a hundred and fifty feet high on the edge of the blue Turcoman steppe, where Robert Byron met "riders on horses and camels, and high-wheeled gigs ... all Turcomans, the ladies in red chintz covered with flowers, the men in plain red or more rarely ... in multi-coloured silks woven with lightning zigzags. But there were not many fleece hats" (the Turcomans wear hats like black woollen busbies); and he proceeds to rate the Gonbad-i-Qabus with the great buildings of the world, which must be an exaggeration although with its great stature, infinity of long thin bricks, and the shadows thrown from its flutings, standing on a mound above the blue plain it must beyond doubt be romantic and splendid in its kind. The Gonbad-i-Qabus is aged a thousand years, all but, its functional-factorial impressiveness derived from old age and height and isolation, on an edge of the world, and from the huge scale of its flutings, ten in number, and looking as though they would open or shut like wind-vanes, but they are, in fact, triangular buttresses, self-supporting, and helping to hold up the tower.

The grave-tower at Varamin rises to not much more than a third of that height and has the appearance of a thing more of utility than beauty. I would hesitate before denigrating in any way a building of the Seljuqs, knowing of what they are capable at Konya and having seen the green-tiled, pyramidal *turbéhs* at Antalya (both places are in Turkey), but if many of the Norman castles in England and Wales look like toy-forts then the grave-tower of Varamin is not far removed, aesthetically, from a gasometer. It is not beautiful just because it is old, and it has not that scale which is a quality in itself and gives majesty to many of the temples of Ancient Egypt. It is only exceptional because it is Seljuq, a race who were original in their architectural forms and needed but to build in order to display a masterhand.

The mosque at Varamin is another matter. Its dome could be seen but a moment ago before we were lost in a maze of mud-houses flecked with straws, were walking beside contaminated pools and duck ponds, and pursued in good temper by a gathering crowd. We reach the mosque at last, and it is built of brick which is the colour of unbaked clay. It is surrounded by a wall and we climb a breach in that, watched by a crowd of men and boys. The momentary impression is of how achingly cold it must be in winter, and what a furnace heat in summer, in and out of the mud houses! The inhabitants are all ill fed, and have nothing to do but wander round staring at us. And at the moment of climbing the wall there was some invisible stone-throwing, but done half-heartedly as though by a poltergeist who was not really interested or concentrating on his work.

The first time one sees a Persian mosque of the grand epoch must always be a moment in the life of a lover of architecture. The first of the domes of Persia, and a little of a disappointment for it lacked all colour. A dome raised on an octagonal drum above the prayer chamber, the whole in terrible dilapidation, as dust to dust, and as if in any direction there could be bones protruding from the soil. The enfilade of arches fine and noble but, as it were, touched with India, or in another emphasis from the pointed arch of Gothic buildings. What there is of Indian in it being only that one knows more of Indian than of Persian buildings of the date from books and photographs. This brick mosque of 1320–1330 is really its own origin at the fountain head. There is nothing Indian about it. But the stucco arabesques on the walls and archways owing to the colour and consistency of the brick look as though stamped or incised into the unbaked clay. There is a stucco *mehrab* of much richness and intricacy, but this again is of stamped, mechanical finish and appearance. The design seems to lose its thread of argument and becomes mixed and muddled. We have to take into account that no Gothic churches or abbeys, even in Spain, are seen in just this dust, or quite this glaring heat and cold. But the flatness of the ornament is monotonous. There is nothing either solid or soaring about the building. It is settled down in its maternal dust. And we drove back towards a stormy sunset that had no sign in it of spring.

Another day we went up a river valley into the mountains. It was the feast of *Nau Ruz*, the Persian New Year, and already most of the inhabitants of Tehran were making for the hills. The road led up at first over some high shoulders with Demavend in the distance, now revealing itself as a former volcano, and becoming isolated in stature and position, though never, I was to think later, seen to such advantage as from an aeroplane when it really takes on some of the attributes one imagines for Mt. Fujiyama. This valley of the Karaj river is beautiful, and it was only sad that there were no flowers. After a time certain mountain tops had isolated coniferous trees growing on them, of curious effect, for they were dwarfed and stunted by the wind, and there were great rifts or lateral valleys to one side. Just when one thought human habitation was out of the question there was a mountain village built of loose stones, the windowless houses all crowded together on ledges and the smoke, if there was any, escaping so far as one could see between the stone tiles, as in remote villages in Trás-os-Montes in Portugal. What could life be like in winter in such houses, fit only for a cat-leap from roof to roof! There could be no warmth or light of any kind. What could they eat? They grew a few vegetables on terraces not much bigger than window-shelves. Down by the river there were blossoming apricot or peach trees. One wondered if there were trout or crayfish in the river, and immediately another, and yet another village came in view. Along the river bed were willows which were dark red or even crimson in colour, obviously other varieties from those growing in Europe. In parts of Persia, it seems, these coloured willows are admired and grown purposely. Higher and higher the road climbed but it became too bad to go further and we had to turn back, probably an hour or more short of the watershed. From that other side the rivers flow down into the Caspian through country which becomes luxuriant and subtropical, and driving home we could flatter ourselves that there were leopards and even tigers the other side of the mountains.\* A few months earlier a snow-leopard, probably the most beautiful of all fur-bearing animals, had been caught in that jungle country and was on show in the local zoo. One had thought in ignorance that snow-leopards were only found in Manchuria and Chinese Turkestan. Coming back, *Nau Ruz* was in full celebration, and in every direction driving down the hills into Tehran there were *fêtes champêtres* and picnic parties by the side of running water underneath the trees.

A little Royal pavilion was the object of an afternoon's excursion. It had belonged to Nasr-ed-Din Shah, the monarch who visited Europe on two occasions and was the guest of Queen Victoria. In the interior this pavilion was surprisingly, and even captivatingly pretty. There was none of the cut-glass work, but the stucco ceilings in their own mid-nineteenth century version of the stalactite decoration were most fanciful and there were coloured tiles of mythical heroes of ridiculous aspect. A central hall with little rooms or alcoves leading from it, some of them having pretty painted decoration, all in this Oriental Rococo of the fair ground, and obviously but one male inhabitant and a number of females. Could it have been here among all his other pavilions and palaces that the Shah dressed his women in short ballet skirts in memory of an evening at the Alhambra Theatre in London? Persian *houris*, recognizable at once from their joined eyebrows, are to be seen in this guise in paintings on glass and other pictures. If lightly built which, alas! is not probable, they must have looked charming enough in this pavilion that so nearly resembles one of the old peep-shows on a seaside pier.

* In his book of memoirs *Escales de Ma Jeunesse*, Paris, 1956, Prince Matila Ghyka describes a journey to Persia in 1905, and on his way remarks that there were, then, tigers in Europe in the Russian province of Azarbayjan, and lions in the Persian province of Luristan. As pendant to this, Mr Julian Huxley tells us there were lions in the foothills of Northern Syria until well into the second half of last century, and crocodiles until an even later date in the Dog river which flows into the Mediterranean close to Beirut.

The life of a visitor to Tehran is a constant round of entertainment, and this in spite of the fact that during a month on and off in the capital we never once entered a restaurant and only caught sight of a hotel on the day before we left. Perhaps a clue, amounting to a new discovery of how to solve one of the most pressing problems of diplomatic life, being demonstrated by the presence of "Alfredo", a tame pelican who lives in one of the Embassy gardens (not the British, less still the Russian), eats most of the letters and papers and has been known to swallow passports whole. The Russian Embassy, where Stalin and President Roosevelt stayed during the Tehran Conference, is in a compound as big as that of our Embassy and just across the road. And the tablet embodying their good resolutions, now framed on the wall of the dining room of our Embassy, and signed and worded by the three chief protagonists, is as unlikely in action and as despairing in the execution as are all such pledges and promises which by their nature can never be fulfilled. The surviving signer of that document in his wisdom will have known this when he wrote his name.

To dine in a Persian home must be an ambition with everyone who comes to Tehran, and we were invited to dinner by a member of the old reigning dynasty, the family of the Qajars, in direct descent from the philoprogenitive Fath Ali Shah, who is credited with three hundred sons and daughters, and reigned from 1798 till 1834.* Here one tasted fresh salmon from the Caspian, and our host who had been educated in pre-Revolutionary Russia at the *école des pages* showed us family portraits and pictures of his renowned ancestor, not to be confused with paintings of Nasr-ed-Din Shah, that monarch's grandson of Victorian times, pictures which will be mentioned later in this chapter. Those are by a painter of very considerable talents. These earlier portraits are, however, curious enough, and I am tempted to enlarge upon their subject. For this purpose it is necessary to quote from Sir Robert Ker Porter, a traveller who gives a lively, if obsequious account of Fath Ali Shah.† He describes a portrait of the Shah, "seated in all the blaze of majesty upon his throne, and ranged about him twenty of his sons", and concludes "the figure of the King himself, though executed in so tea-board a manner, was fine".

* Prince Firouz is son of the Fermen Firma, head of that branch of the Qajar family who were Princes of Shiraz.

† The passages quoted are from his *Travels in Georgia, Persia, Armenia, Ancient Babylonia*, etc., 2 vols., 1827. His Highness the Aga Khan is descended through his mother from Fath Ali Shah. His family hat, which takes the place of a crest or coat-of-arms, seems to derive from the Qajar crown as shown in Sir Robert Ker Porter's frontispiece to his first volume, just as there can be little doubt that Bakst's drawings for the Shah's costume in *Schéhérazade*, which marked an epoch in theatrical history, were derived from portraits of Fath Ali Shah.

A few days later, after describing the feast of *Nau Ruz*, he had audience of Fath Ali Shah, who was surrounded by his sons: "Each one of whom wore a robe of a sort of gold stuff, lined, and deeply collared, with most delicate sables, falling a little below the shoulders, and reaching to the calf of the leg. Around their black caps they had wound the finest shawls. Every one of them, from the youngest to the oldest, wore bracelets of the most brilliant rubies and emeralds, just above the bend of the elbow. . . . To the clangor of trumpets, and the appalling roar of two huge elephants, trained to the express purpose of giving this note of the especial movements of the Great King", the Shah appeared, "entering the saloon from the left, and advancing to the front of it, with an air and step which belonged entirely to a sovereign. I had never before beheld anything like such perfect majesty; and he seated himself on his throne with the same indescribable, unaffected dignity. . . . He was one blaze of jewels, which literally dazzled the sight on first looking at him. A lofty tiara of three elevations was on his head, which shape appears to have been long peculiar to the crown of the Great King. Several black feathers, like the heron-plume, were intermixed with this. . . . His vesture was of gold tissue, nearly covered with jewellery; and crossing the shoulders were two strings of pearls, probably the largest in the world; I call his dress a vesture, because it sat close to his person, from the neck to the waist, showing a shape as noble as his air. . . . But for splendour, nothing could exceed the broad bracelets round his arms; they actually blazed like fire. And when we know the names derived from such excessive lustre we cannot be surprised at seeing such an effect. The jewelled band on the right arm was called *The Mountain of Light*; and that on the left, *The Sea of Light*." These were diamonds looted from the Moghul Emperor by Nadir Shah.

And there was the beard of Fath Ali, "black and bright, and of a peculiar form. . . . A beard black as jet, and of a length which fell below his chest, over a large portion of the effulgent belt which held his diamond-hilted dagger. This extraordinary amplitude of beard appears to have been a badge of Persian royalty from the earliest times." Then, "His Majesty spoke. It was like a voice from the tombs so deep, so hollow, and at the same time so penetratingly loud. The same awful voice, though in a lower tone, welcomed me to his Dominions." After which, Sir Robert Ker Porter and his party were instantly served "with bowls of a most delicious sherbet".

On 11 April he saw Fath Ali Shah at the horse-race, attended by his camel-corps, in a red uniform "something like the fashion of our British regimentals about twenty or thirty years ago". But their brass caps, of a cone shape, with a bunch of cock-feathers stuck in the pointed top, excited the "risible faculties" of Sir Robert Ker Porter. The Shah was "preceded by a long train of *tchatters*, or running footmen, clothed in light blue. His Majesty rode quite alone, mounted on an eminently beautiful steed, naturally of spotless white; but, according to a particular badge of sovereignty, the creature was stained of a gaudy orange colour, all along the lower part of his body, in a direct line from the swell of the chest to the tail." He continues: "I did not exactly know how it happened, but the Shah's horses generally won", and he concludes his personal account of Fath Ali Shah with a view of the *agréments*, as he terms them, of one of the Royal palaces near Tehran, with its rose-trees, "roses standing in the garden filled with flowers, of a beautiful fabric, in wax, that seemed to want nothing of nature, but its perfume", and swimming-pool where the ladies of his harem "so fond are they of this luxury, remain in the water for hours on end; sometimes when the heat is very relaxing, coming out more dead than alive . . . the Royal master of this *Hortus Adonidis*, frequently takes his noonday repose in one of the upper chambers which encircle the saloon of the bath; and if he be inclined, he has only to turn his eyes to the scene below, to see the loveliest objects of his tenderness, sporting like naiads amidst the crystal stream and glowing with all the bloom and brilliancy which belong to Asiatic youth." And turning back to the dedication page of Sir Robert Ker Porter, we see it is inscribed to His Most Excellent Majesty King George the Fourth.* In all this account of Fath Ali Shah the salient features being his black beard and wasp-thin waist, of which he was inordinately proud, and perhaps the bracelets "worn just above the bend of the elbow". But

---

* A note on Sir Robert Ker Porter (1777–1842), and his travels, may not be amiss. His early ambitions were aroused by seeing a battle-piece belonging to Flora Macdonald, and he secured an introduction as a student to Benjamin West. By 1800, besides executing various religious works, he had obtained the post of scene painter at the Lyceum, and shortly afterwards exhibited a panorama 120 feet long, containing 700 life-size figures, of the *Storming of Seringapatam*. He sent thirty-eight pictures to the Royal Academy, and then took up appointment as historical painter to the Tsar. His life in St Petersburg was "varied with a love affair with a Russian princess", and after travelling in Sweden "a meeting with Sir John Moore ended in an invitation to accompany him to Spain", where he was present at the battle of Corunna, and made many sketches of the campaign, now in the British Museum. His *Letters from Portugal and Spain* contain many aquatints after his drawings. In 1811 he came back to Russia, married his princess, and on his return to England was knighted by the Prince Regent. He started on his Persian journey in 1817, and "following the course of Xenophon's *Katabasis* returned to Scutari". He, next, accepted the post of British Consul in Venezuela, which he held for fifteen years, "painting large sacred pictures and exercising great hospitality". He died in St Petersburg in 1842 on a visit to his only daughter, who had married a Russian officer. Cf. *Dictionary of National Biography*, and *Aquatint Engraving*, by S. T. Prideaux, London, Duckworth & Co., 1909, pp. 225–227.

his white horse, dyed or stained with henna, brings us back to the streets of Tehran where, it is true, the shrimp-pink or pea-green motor-buses are scarcely less curious.

A complement to a Persian dinner party should be a visit to the museum of which Mr Hannibal is the director. Here, in an old palace with early nineteenth century Persian, which means pantomime-Rococo staircase, are gathered collections of folk lore and waxwork figures in the costumes of every province. There are Turcomans from the steppe in their red gowns and shaggy black busbies, and wild looking dervishes, a series ending, horrifically, with the articulated waxwork figure of the Royal executioner dressed in his original red clothes. Nor is there lacking a motionless male figure standing among the others, one of the museum custodians, and Mr Hannibal's little joke. There are the camel litters in which brides were carried, and lanterns, and displays of native and Bohemian glass. Glass painting, also, for which Qazvin was famous, depicting *houris* in ballerina skirts with eyebrows all in one piece, and others more voluptuous still of undetermined sex. There are clocks and keys, and prodigies of carving in the form of wooden spoons, all due to the collecting mania of Mr Hannibal, a person of much learning, and if it may be said so, a collector's piece in himself for he is the descendant of Peter the Great's Ethiopian page. The giant Tsar slept with his head on the Ethiopian's stomach for a pillow and if he moved in the night, it is said, would get up and kick him. The poet Pushkin, too, was descended from him. How Russian are those two nicknames, become surnames, Hannibal and Pushkin! Mr Hannibal escaped from Russia at the time of the Revolution, came to Persia, and has become Moslem. He is a mine of information on all things Persian; has been, so he told me, everywhere in Persia except to Kerman, and it was from him I heard of a mountain region as healthy and beautiful as any valley in Switzerland, and for the first time of the oasis of Tabas.* He was disposed, too, to tell us we had not seen everything in Qazvin.

We had been there a day or two before, on 1 April, and to Qazvin and back is a long day's journey. Mile after mile you go parallel to the snowy rampart of mountains, due west, practically, and in the direction of Tabriz. It is, in fact, about a third of the way there over a desolation of stones and sand. At times the road is just a river bed, and a ghost railway runs beside. There were no flowers and no birds, either, but several illusory Qazvins heralded by big orchards which dwindled like mirages as one got nearer. If it had not been for the railway one might

---

* From all accounts the oasis of Tabas is something quite exceptional, a Persian Ghadames or Timimoun, about two days' journey south-west from Meshed.

have lost the road, but all we saw was an engine running backwards with a van coupled to it. Outside a town, half-way, nomads were encamped in their black tents of camel hair, and as amateurs of Gypsies we came up for a nearer look. They had baby camels with coats of grey jaeger tethered behind their tents, and there was Persian lamb galore in the form of kids of every colour, grey, black, brown, or white, bucking or gambolling around. But these were poor and solitary nomads not belonging to one of the great nomad tribes. Qazvin, when at last we reached it, was like a shabby prolongation of the Mile End Road, and immediately certain characters attached themselves to us as though ordered to do so in their horoscopes. They even seemed to be hanging about waiting for us when we arrived. There was a young man with cropped hair and an idiotic shape of head, dressed in a smart grey suit as from the "forty shilling tailor", and wearing a pair of new brown boots. They looked very thin, with blunted toes as though in deference to football, and as if their material was not leather, but paper made from bright brown autumn leaves. Later, we were to know such shoes are worn all over Persia. This young man never left us for a moment. He held himself well, and at times we wondered if he was a member of the secret police told off to follow us. He was on good terms, we noticed, with the smiling big policeman who long ago had climbed, uninvited, into the box-seat beside the driver as our self-appointed guide.

The children of Qazvin, in what can only be described as their misery, could have occupied a painter for half his lifetime. One little blue and nondescript girl, in particular, dressed in rags, with an aquiline nose that could be nothing but Oriental, and clever, but hooded or veiled eyes, by which is meant they had an opaque film, like a piece of talc, over the iris. She, too, followed us everywhere, poor little thing, a little bird-like or beaked phantom from Picasso's "blue period" of fifty years ago. And we climbed down some steps into the bazaars, which were shut because it was a Friday, and saw an old man with a beard, in a white turban, imperturbably warming his hands at a little brazier in front of his shop which, too, was shut for the day. He would be sitting there, one supposed, all day long, perfectly happy and content in the bitter cold. There were piles of snow in the corners of all the courtyards of the mosques. And to complete the picture, the poor wretch who came shuffling with his hands in his sleeves, bringing the key, begged continually in a high voice, and little as we knew Persian we could understand that he was asking for money to buy pistachios. It was a meagre diet in cold weather but in all probability it is the only luxury of the poor. That, and a little fruit, melons, more particularly, in summer.

The monuments of Qazvin take second place to the living Persians, the incident over the pistachios having occurred while we waited at the smaller of the two mosques. The light was bad owing to a leaden sky which held promise of more snow, and it was difficult to make out much of the stucco wall panels of the interior. Their flatness and drabness of colour, and condition of eternal and hopeless dustiness are deterrent to appreciation. One has to go on telling oneself over and over again that they are twelfth and thirteenth century work and relics of a golden age. The Friday Mosque is much larger, with every necessary feature but a lot left out. That is to say, it is lacking in just those qualities one looks for in a Persian mosque. It has got them all, and yet they are not there. It has the colour, but it is too sparsely applied though a good deal of the tilework, I fancy, is of early nineteenth century date. In the prayer chamber or sanctuary are the Seljuq frieze and panels with "those graceful trailing flowers, roses, tulips, and irises", admired by Robert Byron, and as he remarks, "generally thought to have been invented by the Safavids four centuries later", for their date is not long after 1100. They are strange indeed when we think of our own twelfth century, or even of the Romanseque churches and abbeys then building in France. It is like putting a leaf from *The Tale of Genji* into the Lindisfarne Gospels. There is the same contrast between an age of poetry and of flower lovers, and an age when all imagery was apocalyptic and of the wrath to come. I am afraid the answer is that ten centuries is too old for stucco. It cannot last so long as that. The Friday Mosque at Qazvin is now in the condition that what is early in it is too old, and the smallest touch of restoration would but make things worse. But there is some beautiful brick arcading of the thirteenth century, brick arches leading to an ablution chamber which is like a *hammam*.

The other monument is a tomb, but our smiling policeman escort after conferring with the young man in brown boots took us to the wrong one. This had an ugly iron railing round it, and was certainly not twelfth century. We left just as the little hook-nosed "blue" girl and the others of our entourage caught up and came upon the scene. We next found ourselves outside police headquarters, by far the most imposing building in Qazvin, where it was suggested we might take coffee and rest awhile (in a police cell?), but declining the invitation we drove out of the city by way of a tiled town gate, perhaps a hundred years old and an epitome of bad, bad taste. In one of its alcoves on the town side were huddled a family of nomads, the men gaunt and aquiline and tall. The little girl who came up and begged persistently in piteous, professional voice, interspersing that with laughing and talking to the women, was now frightened off by the King Charles spaniel accompanying us, "Tadpole" by name, as if to the roaring and springing of a full grown lion, giving point to the ridiculous lions in tilework upon gateways in Persia that must really be put there to frighten people. Whether, or not, there are lions upon this gate at Qazvin, here were living a nomad family in the shelter of the town gateway from which in imagination one could not but hear strident fanfares blowing. From a little mound just beyond it we had a clear view of the town, mosques, orchards, and all, and I could not pretend to myself I was sorry as we drove away. Was this all there is to see in Persia? And if so, was it worth it to have come so far? Taken together, Varamin and Qazvin were a disappointment. The most interesting things in Qazvin, children apart, were the cabs or droshkies, harnessed to a pair of nightmare horses, and so ragged and tatterdemalion that they made a "subject" in themselves. There had been a line of ten or a dozen of the cabs drawn up in the square, all alike, but as different from each other as the Kings and Queens of the beggars. What novels could be written about them! There is the whole of the *Comédie Humaine* contained in them; one could think of a great draughtsman spending years in drawing them, just as a musician might find material in them. Coming away over that endless stony plain, where the "ghost engine" played, I was wondering to myself if the droshkies and horses of Qazvin were not as formidable a theme for variations as the *Dies Irae*.

The corrective for depressed thinking is a morning in the museum at Tehran. This is in the neo-Achaemenid quarter among hideous banks and parliament erections built in "Darius" style. But now, at last, we are to know the artist in the Persian and need have no more forebodings about Meshed and Isfahan. Even the postcards at the door are an excitement of anticipation; domes and minarets, and views of the great platform at Persepolis. The museum is of recent date and most admirably installed, except that in a mood of xenophobia there are not sufficient labels in French or English to explain the objects. On the ground floor are cases with wonderful bronzes from Luristan which could be the inspiration of much modern sculpture, but the comparison is almost unfair because in a single show case there may be works of several generations of bronze-age craftsmen who had not to force their talent but in ignorance of all else worked naturally in abstract form. Through various cultures the nationality of Persia emerges and takes shape, reaching its culmination in a sculptured panel from Persepolis, one of the only pieces not *in situ*, showing Darius, King of Kings, enthroned, with his son Xerxes standing behind him.

A bronze scent-burner rises at his feet, and a turbaned figure is salaam-
ing to him with a gesture that is familiar in every country of the Orient.
Near by is an extraordinary historical relic, the golden foundation stone
of the palace at Persepolis, found buried in a stone box some twenty
years ago after its probable location had been calculated mathematically
by the archaeological expedition working there. It is now a much
venerated national treasure, bound with ribbons in the Persian colours,
and with reason for there is probably more of the ancient Persian in his
modern descendant than there is of classical Roman in Rome to-day,
or of ancient Athenian in the figures engaged in endless argument
over money and politics in the Athenian cafés. Darius, King of Kings,
is the Clovis or the King Alfred of the Persians, and nothing will alter
the fact that he was King not far short of a thousand years before they
reigned. The golden plaque is also a thing of beauty in itself, and it
must be a torpid and dull soul that does not feel a thrill when this
sheet of gold with that inscription is put into his hand.

A capital and part of a column from Persepolis give indication of the
scale of the giant palace, as do sundry objects in a show case which on
nearer inspection are the detachable ears off huge statues of bulls. One
is beginning to connect this taurine cult in one's mind with the tauro-
machia of Crete and Spain, and at the same time determining that one
knows the Persian type from these sculptures, from the curled hair
and scented beard of Darius, of Xerxes, and from their soldiers and
followers who imitated them in this as much as the *zouaves* or the
*cuirassiers* of the Second Empire followed the waxed moustaches and
"imperial" of Napoleon III, when all ideas and notions are shattered
by a statue. It is a thing unique and outside experience, though, yet,
familar in a strange way. A bronze figure, rather over lifesize, of a
moustached man, in peculiar, but obviously, riding clothes, and unmistakably not only Aryan, whatever that is, but even Celtic in physical
type. Whoever he was, most certainly he did not belong to one of the
barbarian races with Mongol blood in them, still less was he Semitic in
the sense of Arab, nor, with the Russians so near, has he the high
cheekbones of the Slav. This tribal, or minor king, for we do not know
his name, could have come out of Gaul to Persia. The only way to
discover more about him being to look closely at his clothes, when it
is apparent that his wealth must have derived from herds of horses.
He is a horseman-king, wearing woollen or linen over-trousers which
are like leggings pulled on over his ordinary trousers, as though for
riding bareback over the steppe. But, as well, he is no Parthian, nor
Turcoman. Neither is he a fair-bearded Kaffir from the far corner of
Afghanistan.

This mysterious statue of a man with hair done in the fashion of the Italian *quattrocento*, as at the court of the d'Estes in the frescoes of Ferrara, dates probably from the second or third century A.D. Is it a portrait? Remembering that the portrait effigies on tombs in our own country only essayed to be likenesses in about the reign of Richard II one is nervous of arguing this, but until the coming of the Moslems it could be said that, as in the classical world of Greece and Rome, sculpture more than architecture was the art form of the ancient East. It may even have been the multiplicity of statues all over the ancient world, hundreds or even thousands of them in one town alone such as Palmyra, that made the Arabs coming out of the desert into luxury forbid themselves the graven image. This statue is in all probability a portrait; and if not a personal likeness it must be a rendering of the tribal type. Their kings or chiefs were of this appearance. But what is it? This statue could have been dug up in Gaul and labelled Vercinge-torix. It is thus, we might think, we would have seen that Celtic chieftain walking in the Roman triumph. Perhaps it is true that just as the Persian Kings wore their hair and beards in the fashion of the Great Kings of the Assyrians, two centuries earlier, and affected the royal garments that they wore, so, falsifying to a little extent their own physical type, thus, also, this horseman-king of the steppes may have imitated something of Parthian or ancestral-Cossack dress. The truth being that he is really a typical true-blooded Persian, in reminder that the race of Iranians, in essence, have nothing of Slav, or Mongol, or Semite in them. As to his curious, pre-Islamic dress, with its accent on his being a horseman, we shall see the same riding trousers on bas-reliefs of the Sasanian Kings. In their accoutrements, as on the carvings at Naqsh-e-Rostam, so strong is this accent that they have something of a circus pride. This statue of a horseman on foot marks the Aryan in the Iranian, a context in which it should not be forgotten that the word "Eire" in derivation is of the same roots as "Iran". It is for its racial affinities that this statue, here, far away near the shores of the Caspian, is familiar in a strange way.*

Textiles and ceramics are on the upper floor of the museum, and here is all the evidence of an age in which the hand of man could not go wrong. In this respect Persians of the eleventh and twelfth centuries were greater artists than the Chinese. A figure of a blue peacock is a

---

* This statue was discovered in 1934 in a village called Shami in the province of Khuzestan, in South-Western Iran. It was found by peasants in what is supposed to have been the basement of a Parthian temple. It is recorded by the late Sir Aurel Stein, who happened to be visiting the site, in "An Archaeological Journey in Western Iran", *Geographical Journal*, Vol. XCII, for October 1938, and in *Old Silk Routes of Western Iran*, London, Macmillan & Co., 1940.

Portrait of Nasr-ed-Din Shah by Sani-el-Molk Ghaffari (1812–1866).
(In the collection of M. and Mme Moghadam at Tehran)

Beggar woman in dog-kennel at Meshed

Street scene at Meshed

miracle of beauty, and the potter had only to draw a group of human heads with slant Mongol eyes and crisscross garments to achieve a work of art. They had brought the firing of their pots and plates to a fantastic degree of sensitivity, and were as sure of their results as the most expensively equipped of research chemists. There is pottery from the newest and most recent excavations, with a show case of striped and rayed plates from Zenjan that are quite exceptional in their impetus and sureness of touch. These wonderful studies in the force to be obtained out of thickening or dimishing a pattern of converging lines are so much of a conducted experiment that they could be, and pro- bably are, the work of one man. They are what a personal taste liked most in the ceramics. Among the silk brocades and rugs there are beautiful things, if not on the scale of what might be anticipated in Tehran, but the best Persian rugs and carpets of fabulous and mounting value are mostly abroad by now. There is, however, a marvellously subtle and beautiful silk rug of "polonaise" type in tones of rose. And the museum comes to an end with what amounts to a broadside or bombardment of the myriad sons and daughters of Fath Ali Shah.

The curiosity shops of Tehran are full of dug up jugs and plates, real or spurious, at low prices, cheap, that is to say, when compared to what they would fetch in London, Paris, or New York. Good carpets are almost unobtainable, and so are Persian miniatures. Painted pen and pencil boxes, some of them exquisitely painted in the style of miniatures, are about the best objects on sale, even if the earliest of them are not more than a hundred years old; and there is painstaking and hideous inlay in ivory and mother-of-pearl and what looks like, but cannot be, pistachio. The slower and more painstaking the uglier, till a point is reached at which such work should be prohibited, and not only because of its danger to the eyesight. But the best shops are not in the bazaars; they are in the wide streets near the Embassy, and most of the shop owners are either Armenians or Jews. The bazaars are disappoint- ing; and so, indeed, are all shops other than curiosity shops though, in spite of their mean appearance, it is a popular saying in Tehran that you can buy anything you want if you know where to look for it. There would appear to be but one bookshop, and there are scarcely any restaurants. A Russian restaurant where the caviar is nearly as expensive as in London, and another near the railway station frequented by taxi-drivers where slices of swordfish from the Caspian cooked on skewers are the favourite dish, are the only exceptions. And there are *kebab* stalls in the streets which will be avoided by the squeamish. The average shop is like a bicycle shop or small grocer in a Midland town in England, if you substitute a dingy yellow for red brick, and people

3

the purlieus with men in striped pyjamas or nightgowns and a few women in *chadors*, with now and again an old man walking past with a henna'd beard. Changing money in a bank is a slow process taking most of the morning, but made exciting on one occasion by the wildest looking tribesmen drawing out money in a feverish whirl of yelling and gesticulation. They had the most aquiline features ever seen, real vulture or eagle beaks, carried long sticks, and wore ragged white or green gowns and turbans. It seems they were Baluchis from one of the poorest provinces of Persia, near the frontier with Pakistan. How, then, and why, were they drawing money from a bank in Tehran?

The Persian Crown Jewels are near by in the National Bank of Iran, in a specially designed strong room. Unfortunately we missed seeing them owing to arriving back a day late from Isfahan, and so were unable to contrast them with the collection in the Old Seraglio at Istanbul, but it seems they would hold the second place compared to those. There are heaped bowls of pearls and emeralds and rubies in the taste of the Indian rajahs, and perhaps there is still visible the globe of the world carried out in precious stones, which was the work of art and plaything of Nasr-ed-Din Shah.

We were in Tehran at the time of the Baghdad Conference, and one night were invited to a party given by the Prime Minister in the Golestan Palace. It took place in a huge room at one end of which is the Peacock Throne, really a bed more than a throne, of rubies and diamonds and gold and enamel, glittering like fire, that night, under all the electric lights. Whether it is the authentic Peacock Throne looted from the Moghul Emperors at Delhi, or not, it is neither very valuable, nor a work of art. But it showed to greater advantage in a room full of brilliant dresses and uniforms than it had done when we saw the palace, privately, a day or two before. Even the Royal servants now wear ordinary suits of clothes and look like workmen. The palace is consequently seen under the worst possible conditions. There are interesting but gloomy Qajar portraits on the ground floor. Of the cut-glass balcony looking on the street there is no sign, but the staircase and several entire rooms are done in cut-glass work, and one is told again and again that it had its origin in looking-glass ordered from Europe, and arriving broken. This is supposed to have been the inspiration of the glass mosaic, but that is altogether too fortuitous an excuse for a thing so typical of Persian taste and mentality. A little of it has half the charms of a fun fair, but at the Golestan Palace it is all hammered and fitted together with too childish a taste and flair. How well I remember coming away from the party through the palace garden, all lit by lamp standards with candles burning in them in midst of the flowerbeds, as opulent as chandeliers, while a military band was playing!

Another day we were invited to luncheon at a farm in the country where lives an Englishwoman who was the first British ballerina to dance with the Russian ballet of Diaghilev. Her life is devoted to good works, and her husband is a Persian general and politician. Their farm is in the foothills a few miles from Tehran, and in that landscape facing towards Russia it was not inappropriate to hear talk of Nijinski and Pavlova, and to hold in one's hands a silver christening bowl inscribed with circus drawings by Picasso.* On the wall of the dining room hangs a large scale map drawn by the general with the migrations of the nomad tribes, a map which should be the prize of any geographical magazine. The farm is conducted upon military lines; the farm hands milking the cows spring from their stools and give a military salute, while the cows, a few humped ones among their number, seem inured to the word of command. We went into a labourer's cottage with henna-haired children playing at the door, and saw the spotless interior, whitewashed, and the heaped mattresses which are spread upon the floor. As we emerged, a man appeared carrying in his arms a baby donkey that was too young to stand. The pastoral scene is part-garden, with tall poplars and little channels of water, and wild flowers growing on the banks. Spring had come at last. It was beautiful looking up into the hills and into the distance. The wistaria on the terrace at the Ambassador's residence was in flower, we were told, and with this reminder of Florence and of the villas at Fiesole and Settignano during May we drove back to Tehran, half in mind to see Brunelleschi's dome hovering above the town.

Almost on the last day of our visit we went to one of the only old houses that are left. The door was opened by a girl, for once not wearing a *chador*, but baggy trousers and some kind of a turban'd headdress. The interior garden is delightful with flowering trees and fountains and tiled courts. This house contains one of the best art collections in Tehran, and it is particularly interesting because of its

* This must be an only item to have escaped the documentation of every smallest scribble, dated to the day and almost to the hour, by the Proteus of our century. And not certain of the analogy, on consulting Dr Lempriere's *Classical Dictionary*, with preface dated, Pembroke College, Oxford, November 1788 (the year Tehran became capital of Persia) it gives: "He had received the gift of prophecy. and from his knowledge of futurity mankind received the greatest services. . . . Like the rest of the gods, he reposed himself on the seashore, where such as wished to consult him generally resorted. He was difficult of access, and when consulted he refused to give answers, by immediately assuming different shapes, and eluding the grasp, if not properly secured in fetters." It seems an apt comment on the anarchist-sage of Paris-Antibes.

pictures by Sani el Molk Ghaffari (1812–1866), court painter to Nasr-ed-Din Shah. There are a full length portrait of the Shah, which is probably by his hand, and a number of drawings. The full length portrait, exuding a strange and poetic melancholy, is remarkable for the black clothes of the Shah and for a distinction which is near to that of full length Elizabethan portraits with an attribution to Nicholas Hilliard, particularly that of a knight in white armour.* And the drawings, it could be said, pertain to the school of Holbein. There are coloured drawings of young princes, a wide field for an artist when we consider that many of them, if of the Qajar dynasty, had forty or fifty brothers. Persian ladies, of course, never sat for their portraits; but there are drawings of princes and nobles in black astrakhan hats if, in some instances, imbued with a dullness that may have been due to the subject's natural gloom, or hauteur, or lack of conversation. In brief, this is one more painter to be added, when one might have thought the lists were closed. Coming away from the house in the evening light, Tehran had never looked better than on this day before we left. For it is a town that grows upon one though there is almost nothing interesting or beautiful in it. More than all else, one had become fond of the compound for its own sake, and because of happy times spent in it. But, also, more often than not, it is sad to leave somewhere one will never be again.

* Belonging, formerly, to Mr Henry Harris.

# CHAPTER III

# THE HOLY CITY OF MESHED

*Prospect of Meshed — A gold and a blue dome seen from the air — Drive into the town — An old palace with modern comfort — First walk in Meshed — A street cry — Trumpets at dawn and sunset — Marvellous human types — Golden dome seen from a window — Pilgrim scenes — Terrace of the turquoise merchant — The blue dome — Bakers and felt cap makers — Dr and Mrs Shadman — Grand dinner party — British Consulate falling to ruin — An imitation lion — Tus, and tomb of Ferdausi — Shrine of Khajeh Rabi — Beggar women in dog-houses — Macabre tea party — A street in Central Asia — Clerical tenor — Ribbed domes — No hope of the Shrine — Climbing the minaret — View over tiled courts — Ivans like card houses or film sets — In flower with tiles — The blue dome alters in colour.*

THE absorbing topic on the day or two immediately following on our first arrival in Tehran was whether, or not, to go to Meshed. This holy city lies nearly six hundred miles due east, almost on the remote frontiers of Soviet Russia and Afghanistan. *Ramazan* was fast approaching, and it was certain one would see little or nothing of Meshed once it had begun. From the few accounts, and there are not many persons who have been there, the Shrine and Mosque of Meshed are the most beautiful of Persian buildings, more beautiful, even, than the more legendary Isfahan.

A number of people, Persians included, were anxious we should make the journey. In part, because both buildings are inaccessible to infidels, which gives to Meshed some of the interest attaching to all things that are forbidden. In the end it was decided we should go there at once before the beginning of *Ramazan*, and we set off armed with letters of introduction to both the Keeper of the Mosque and the Mutavali Bashi or Keeper of the Shrine.

It was one of the excitements of a lifetime to be thousands of feet over the desert and flying to Meshed. Again and again in the aeroplane I was asking myself if it could be true. And now, returned from seeing the wonders of the Middle East, I know that no expectation was ever better fulfilled, even at Petra, or Palmyra, or Isfahan.

By road it is two days' backbreaking ordeal with a night in the middle in a nondescript hotel. But it is only three and a half hours' flight over the lunar landscape in an aeroplane. Why not fly on to Lhasa, or to Bokhara and Samarcand? We could be in either or any of them in a few hours' time. Meanwhile, not a town or village anywhere, nor a patch of green, and impossible not to wonder what would happen in a forced landing. Wherever could be the nearest human being, let alone an ambulance, or a mechanic? For the barren mountains and salt desert show no sign of life. Then, suddenly, only some three or four minutes before the scheduled time, we come close over the shoulder of a mountain and see a town below. And in the middle of it, no bigger than pinheads, a golden and a blue dome. Lost sight of while we come down to land and are met by a friend from that instant, the American Consul, but appearing again in a moment of indescribable excitement as we drive into the town.

For this is a first taste of the blue mosques of Iran. I shall never be able to forget the moment of sighting that blue dome again, losing it, and seeing it once more near enough to catch the china gleam of light on it. And now, while one holds one's breath, the golden dome appears. A wide street or boulevard has been cleared in a circle round these two buildings, the Shrine of the Imam Reza and the Mosque of Gauhar Shad. The Shrine has a golden dome shaped like a helmet and a pair of minarets plated with gold; while the dome of the Mosque is blue—but what shade of blue is it? For it changes colour. It alters with the hour. As well try to fix the blue of the air or the ocean in one word. The pilgrims are as wonderful as the golden and blue domes. But this is only the first view of them. We will come to look at them again and again. One could, and does, walk round that boulevard for hours on end.

We are by now guests of the American Consul in his old house with several courts like houses in Marrakesh or Seville. The fruit trees are in flower, but only yesterday there was a fall of snow. Like the old Moorish houses the entrance is in a narrow side street, holding little promise of how charming it is within. Upstairs there is a large drawing room with raftered ceiling, and our host who was previously Consul in Seoul displays his taste by charcoal rubbings of Madonna-like Boddhisattvas from the Diamond Mountain in Korea, every conceivable art book, and pictures by modern painters from Haiti. Sunlight comes in through the windows and one has the feeling of a flowering land. A little later we are walking through the narrow alleys, passing Moslem ladies who not content with being veiled wear a black mask or visor in front of their faces, on our way to another and lesser mosque with a blue dome.

The days, and not only the days, pass like a delightful dream. For one is woken early in the morning by an abrupt and peculiar street cry, of unmistakably Eastern accent, intending always to look out of the window and find out what it can be; having already long before this heard the strange orchestra of drums and horns which plays at dawn and sunset in a kiosque or open pavilion above one of the tiled courtyards of the Shrine. This is a rite, probably pre-Islamic, and dating back to the sun worship of Zoroaster (Zarathustra) and his sages. But the hour to listen is at sunset when you can climb on to the roof of a kindly turquoise-merchant—at Meshed even the donkeys wear necklaces of blue beads!—and the drums and trumpets and their players are outlined against a golden sky. Then, one dome and its minarets glitter so that you can hardly look at them; and the other, swelling heavenwards and subtly dimishing, is the colour of the blue empyrean.

But this is to anticipate. I first heard that peculiar street cry, which breaks off abruptly as though cut short, during my afternoon siesta for that first day it was warm enough to start summer habits. One was overwhelmed now by the human types, the more marvellous because in Persia "gents' suiting" is more generally the striped pyjama and one collides with men bicycling frantically in long nightgowns.* Here are mollas, models of dignity with walking-sticks and henna'd beards; hook-nosed Afghans; ragged Baluchis; and Mongols with slant eyes and high cheek bones in little round caps. Unimaginable, incredible as a spectacle; Orientals worthy of Rembrandt or Tiepolo. I must explain that all the entrances, and even the passages leading to the Mosque and Shrine, are forbidden to Christians. Both buildings are inaccessible to infidels, this is the beauty of it. You can stand in the opening of an alley, and delay there for an instant to look in a shop window, then turn and get a momentary glimpse of Mosque or Shrine, but that is all. And even in that time there may be mutterings and angry looks.

On that first afternoon we were taken to the Shrine Museum. Here is one of the most splendid of Persian sixteenth century carpets, which came over to the Persian Exhibition in London in 1931; and among other treasures the golden frieze from the tomb of the Imam, a wonderful masterpiece of calligraphy and pierced goldwork from the hand of Ali Reza, calligrapher to Shah Abbas, inscriptions by whom appear on some of the Safavid buildings in Isfahan. There are beautiful illuminated manuscripts, as well, but the real purpose of the visit was in order to look out on the golden dome from a window in the upper floor as this was the nearest view one could get of it. Certainly the

---

* As I write this, Mossadeq is released, weeping copiously, and still wearing the striped pyjamas and grey dressing-gown in which he was arrested and began his imprisonment three years ago (5 August 1956).

ladies of the party would never get so near to it again, though it was possible that men might have other chances. It all depended upon a number of things, which is why we had been given letters of introduction from Tehran. So a window was opened and we looked out on the golden dome which was about fifty yards away.

Opinions differ as to the date of the dome for its helm shape is of an earlier form. But the dome as it stands, though it may have replaced a previous one of the same design, was the work of Shah Abbas and was built by him in 1607. Later, it was damaged in an earthquake and in 1672 the traveller Sir John Chardin watched new golden plates being made to repair it in the workshops of Isfahan. So the golden tiles were brought here over the desert on camel back which is more romantic than if they had come by lorry, and Harun-er-Rashid, more important to us than the Imam Reza, lies buried underneath the dome.* From this distance one can see the joining of the golden plates which, one would guess, are hammered in with golden nails, but it was not possible to be certain of the process by which they were fixed in place. But the domes of St Mark's at Venice are sheathed in copper while this is a dome of plated gold; and it is impossible not to mention the domes of St Mark's in this connection because they hold that wonderful hint or suggestion of the Orient. When one first sees St Mark's one has dreams and visions that there could be such domes as this, a foretaste or promise which is fulfilled, here, to an unimaginable degree. But it is a helmet-shaped or warlike dome, no "pleasure dome", as the sunlight strikes and dazzles on that gilded casque, moving slowly round its surface and brushing it, if we like to think so, with the hand of time. The court between the dome and our balcony is planted with flowerbeds, and coming down into it we go to a gateway where one may stand for a moment and look into one of the courtyards of the Shrine. But that is all one can see of it, and after a moment or two one has to come away.

* Who was the Imam Reza? He was the eighth Imam of the Shiah Moslems, living at Medina, next to Mecca, and summoned here to Khorassan by the son of the Caliph Harun-er-Rashid for the purpose of proclaiming him his heir. Two years later in A.D. 808 the Imam died at Tus, "of a surfeit of grapes", and the Shiahs believe the Caliph poisoned him. He lies buried beside Harun-er-Rashid in this Shrine at Meshed, second only in holiness to the tomb of Ali at Kerbela, in Irak. There were twelve Imams descended from Ali, son-in-law of the Prophet, and his daughter Fatima. They are the venerated saints of the Shiah Moslems, who almost prefer Ali to his father-in-law Mohammad. The twelfth Imam vanished mysteriously, and in expectation of his return to earth the Safavid Kings of Persia kept two horses bridled and saddled in the palace stables at Isfahan, one for the twelfth Imam, and the other for Christ by whom they believed he would be accompanied. The Shiah faith became the established religion of Persia in 1492. There have been many impostors claiming to be the incarnation of the twelfth Imam, including the Mahdi in the Sudan, and that other Mahdi in Somaliland.

The Golden Dome at Meshed

The rest of the afternoon was spent in wandering in that circular street around the Mosque and Shrine. Now and again there would be a stir in the crowd as a blind beggar came by, singing on his round in guttural voice. There was a fanatical note in him which cleared his way. But there is another side to the picture. Disease and poverty are terrible in Meshed. A beggar woman feeds her baby at her withered breast. There are children with sores which they insist on showing; there are scrofulous heads and diseased eyes. It gives a sort of fury of poverty to their rags and blains. There are more scowls than there are smiling faces. But the bearded mollas and the pilgrims are wonderful beyond words. Characters with nothing more than the clothes they walk in but how many centuries of fanaticism in their tread and gaze! The mollas of the Shrine of the Imam Reza must form a corporate body of stick-in-the-mud diehards without their equal in the world of living beings unless it be in some ancient rookery or haunt of ravens. There is an unlimited number of them, coming in and out of the Shrine like bees at the opening in a beehive, and you know that at a moment's notice they could swarm and sting. The late Shah Reza Pahlavi fought and vanquished them, resorting to such stratagems as ordering a factory outside the town to build its chimney higher than the minarets of the Shrine, and on occasion arresting and even shooting some of them, but they are in force again. There must be several hundreds of them. The fiery aloofness of their approach making them the more interesting, for never twice do you see the same individual, and as they pass you must put away your camera and may not stare. There is the feeling that you could spend a lifetime in Meshed, and on the last day see a molla who had lived his life here but whom you had not seen before. During my few evenings in Meshed I used to wonder where the mollas were, and what they were doing, for like moths in the daytime they move off and hide away.

But we are tired out, having been on our feet all day, and go up on to the terrace of the turquoise-merchant. A motor-bus revs up its engine, annoyingly, just below, for it is the moment when the drums and long horns take up their station. Strings of lights go on, up and down the minarets, and along the open kiosque or pavilion. You can see them beat the drums and blow their horns against the sunset, but the motor-bus drowns all the sound. And then a horse and cart come noisily upon the cobbles, and this curious orchestra only plays for a few minutes and one will miss it all. It is as if the wind blows in our direction and the sound suddenly carries, and comes to us, faint but distinct upon the sunset air. Not music, exactly, but an ancient fanfare, a blowing of shawms and trumpets, and now nearer at hand the light

catches the blue dome and one sees its pattern of yellow arabesques or
tendrils growing bigger as they descend upon its swelling form.

Who built this blue miracle? She was one of the few women, other
than Fatima, in Moslem history, Gauhar Shad Begum, wife of Shah
Rokh, and daughter-in-law of Tamerlane. The date is early in the
fifteenth century, and the architect a native of Shiraz. The sister
mosques of Herat and Samarcand are falling to ruin, or already in
heaps upon the ground. These are, it seems, the most beautiful Moslem
buildings left in the world for the mosques of Isfahan in their perfection are touched with decadence. These are the buildings of the
Timurids, the family of Tamerlane, conquerors of half the earth, and
the greatest architecture *in colour* there has ever been. And it is dark
now, and we come back to the Consulate, sated and tired, but scarcely
believing what our eyes have seen.

In the middle of the night, at half-past four in the morning, the
music of Zarathustra played again. Of weird effect, knowing they had
gone up into their kiosque to welcome in the dawn. I asked who they
were, and they are servitors of the Shrine, not professional musicians.
The Shrine employs two or three thousand servitors and has properties
the size of a kingdom, in fact as big as Denmark. So the Keeper of the
Shrine informed me.* It is a court appointment made by the Shah, and
the present intendant is Dr Shadman, who administers the revenues,
maintains the Shrine, and directs the various charities. The Mosque is a
separate entity with its own organization and the office of Keeper has
been hereditary in the same family for two hundred years. Thus are the
two buildings, the Shrine of the Imam Reza and the Mosque of
Gauhar Shad, that stand side by side at Meshed.

Next morning we walked by that lesser blue mosque among the
bazaars. It, also, is a building of the Timurids dating from the middle
of the fifteenth century, with a broken blue dome and stumps of
purple and blue minarets. Near by, the bread making is fascinating to
watch. There are the loaves shaped like a saddle or a lifebelt, a loaf, in
fact, to wear round your neck if sinking in water, and there are loaves
like cornucopias, the bakers' ovens being deep firepits and their
apprentices like blackened devils armed with long rakes and grappling
irons. A furious activity as of some satanic boiler-room possesses them.
And the bazaar of the cap makers is no less diabolical as they scoop up
the embryo skull-cap from the oozing scum. But the Meshed bazaars

* Robert Byron writes that the revenues of the Shrine amounted to £60,000 a year.
That was in 1933. Cf. *The Road to Oxiana*, London, Macmillan & Co., 1937, p. 218.
Estates in different parts of Persia have accrued to the Shrine through legacies over the
course of many centuries.

are not sensational. They do not compare with those of Damascus, or Aleppo, or Tunis. Too much must have been pulled down when that new street was made. Yet the old habits are inveterate. The inhabitants can make a new building look as though in use for centuries. There is one street or back alley where they carve the local soapstone, and all down to the smallest apprentice of eight years old are coated with grey grit and dust. It must get in the eyes and lungs and be dangerous to health. One wonders what are their figures of mortality in that back-yard where so readily they could be carving gravestones.

By this time we had met several of the leading inhabitants and had delivered our letters to the Keepers of the Mosque and Shrine. Dr Shadman and his wife, whom he met at Cambridge, between them have lived twenty-five years of their lives in England. At the time of our visit she had just published the first translation of Caesar's *De Bello Gallico* into Persian; while the edition of Proust which I had noticed in the Library of the Shrine had been the gift of her husband. Their home is in a beautiful garden two or three miles outside Meshed, and the property of the Shrine. It is what we would call an orchard more than a garden, with its long lines of fruit trees. Meshed is, apparently, famous for its apricots, one sort being of huge size, and all of them unknown here. They, also, grow delicious cherries; and the pride of the garden is a huge tent-shaped greenhouse banked with begonias and cinerarias and geraniums up to the roof, the pots packed as closely together as in a seedsman's stand in one of the marquees at Chelsea Flower Show, and all ranged in order by two or three of the forty gardeners who move up and down the stages, barefoot, as nimble as cats or the powder-monkeys of old naval battles. In the house lying in this garden we talked of London and of the poets, and out of the many topics touched on it was perhaps only surprising that neither of these cultivated and informed Persians, nor apparently any of their countrymen, had read *The Embassy of Clavijo*. Later, after conversation with them both ranging from Chaucer to Ferdausi, and from Seville to Isfahan, we dined on dishes of rice, chicken cooked in pomegranate juice, and glasses of sour milk (mast) mixed with salt, the only dis-agreeable note in a long drawn and delightful evening.

On the night following our host gave a huge dinner party attended by all the *élite* of Meshed; the Keepers of the Mosque and Shrine and their wives, the general commanding the district, and many more. For one or two of the ladies present it was their second sortie into the world; the first having been some weeks or months previously, and again at American invitation. There were present some of the young American Point Four doctors and their wives. They and their trained assistants, who are often young Persian women going from village to village on their bicycles, have vaccinated seventy-five thousand in Meshed alone and a quarter of a million in the countryside. The value of this work, and of American participation generally, is not to be exaggerated. There is an amount of misery to be relieved among young and old that is scarcely credible. It would be easily understood if the doctors said they did not know where to begin. There are the old ending their lives in agony, the young born to blindness or other infirmity, and the mothers many of them still reluctant to be examined by a doctor. The sad part of it is that an inevitable result will be a swarming of the population in the next generation, and less food for all.

Another sad memory of Meshed remains. It is of the deserted British Consulate, which stands in a beautiful tree-shaded compound nearly as large as that of our Embassy in Tehran. But it would be impossible to exaggerate the mournful and shaming impression that it gives. On a rainy evening we were met at the gate by the kindly caretaker, Mr Raj, who looks after the place like his own child. We had met him before when he came to greet us at the airport. Two or three bearded and handsome Sikhs stood there and salaam'd, and one watched them with a little catch in one's throat, for they are a last surviving relic of the British Raj. We had tea in a dilapidated room with a hole in the ceiling and plaster falling from the walls.

Mr Raj, according to the degree of collapse, has to camp out from room to room in his little house. But it is the Consulate itself which is pitiful and disgraceful; holes in the floor, half-fallen rafters, but the pictures of our Kings and Queens lovingly dusted and still upon the walls. All round lie orchards and lawns, two houses for the vice-consuls, tennis courts and kitchen gardens. Deserted only a few years ago, but now fuller of ghosts and more haunted than I could ever say. The British Consul used to live here in great state for this was the most important of some five or six Consulates and Vice-Consulates spreading out in a line along the Afghan frontier. He only rode out, we were told, with outriders and the garden parties are a legend. The collapse came when the Consulates were closed at the time of Abadan, and now nothing can be done because, legally, the Consulate is the property in equal parts of Great Britain, India, and Pakistan.

Our American friends have now a bright and glorious Consulate of their own which brings the better points of the new world into the old city of Meshed. And have we nothing left to say where we have been famous for three hundred years? One would think it is the worst form of propaganda to allow this "Fall of the House of Usher" state of affairs where we have still so many interests. After this, even the sight of a ridiculous imitation lion outlined with electric lights and standing in a bed of potted geraniums, part of the decorations in the square, near by, for the coming visit of the Shah, could not cheer me!

There is not much to see outside the town of Meshed. Tus, the earlier capital of Khorasan, is a ruined city in the desert such as Isaiah wrote of; but it has not even a branch for the owl, or a shelter for the satyr! It is completely shattered and broken, though clambering across the débris, over the moat and up the mound, you have only to look down to your feet and there will be bits of pottery and broken shards. Why has Tus, a great city, vanished from above ground with not a wall standing, when so much is left of desert cities a thousand years older, like Jerash or Palmyra? It must be that the Mongol hordes came here. And yet those same barbarians in the space of a generation or two produced the Timurids who, still fresh from their massacring, directed the Persian genius to its greatest buildings. Just beyond Tus there is the tomb of Ferdausi, who died here a thousand years ago, a work of the late Shah Reza Pahlavi in Persepolitan-cinema style, with a nice garden, all the greener because it is so near to Tus.

And lacking the time to go to Nishapur where Omar Khayyam is buried, we took the short road to the shrine of Khajeh Rabi. This is a saint's tomb built by Shah Abbas with much tilework and a blue dome, I would imagine, but it has been stripped for repairs and is covered up with scaffolding. Outwardly, with its elaborate octagonal form and tiled alcoves and recesses, calling aloud to be walked round on that rainy Friday, it seems more Moghul than Persian, and even to be the poor dark relation of the Taj Mahal. In the interior the tomb of the Saint was the object of fervent bowings and prostrations. Being a Friday, the Mohammadan sabbath, there were huge family parties driving to the shrine, a dozen or more veiled women and children sitting in rows on a cart drawn by a single wretched donkey. These sabbath scenes are the occasion of nearly as much cruelty as in a Sunday bull-fight, and they occur in every Moslem town from Marrakesh to Meshed. We had a sickening experience of the same nature in Cairo a few weeks later. They are carts hired out for the purpose so that the donkeys have their ordeal every Friday afternoon, except for a merciful month or two in winter when there is deep snow, and while they pull their cartloads along lengths of road which are no better than a river bed there are scenes from which it is wiser to avert one's eyes.

That same afternoon we first saw the beggar women of Meshed who live in dog kennels. Driving along one of the narrow streets near the American Consulate, a quiet street with no shops in one of the cleaner parts of the town, there was a wooden dog kennel on the cobble stones with a woman coming out of it with bowed head. The Armenian chauffeur, noticing our surprise, told us the woman lived in it and slept there, adding that there was another woman who lived the same way in a street nearby. The kennel, for it was exactly the shape of a dog kennel, was the size of a large crate or packing-case, in fact big enough for a mastiff or a St Bernard. But the woman could have room neither to stand up nor lie down. It reminded me of horrible photographs I had seen in some book, of a prison at Urga in Mongolia where the prisoners were kept locked up in large wooden trunks or boxes on the floor, and in the photograph you saw their hands protruding from a hole in the box to beg for food. Some had lain for years in those wooden coffins. This seemed to be something horrible and peculiar to Central Asia. Are there not the Tibetan hermits who have themselves walled up alive? But this beggar woman, this was not the least peculiar part of it, was tall and well built and must once have been handsome.

Coming back from the Shrine of Khajeh Rabi we drove past again. But she was asleep in her dog kennel. One could see her huddled inside it, sitting on her heels, which must be how she slept at night. How terrible it must be in winter with winds blowing out of the ends of the world, out of the cold heart of China and Siberia! She cooked her food, we were told, on a little charcoal brazier on the pavement.

Her kennel stood outside quite a respectable looking house and we had seen her talking to her neighbours, laughing and joking and on good terms with them. She was alert and in her right mind; neither an old hag, nor a half-wit; and I began to wonder if she was some sort of holy woman. But when we stopped for a moment she slammed her door, as much as to say beggars had their rights as much as anyone else, and how dared we stop the car and stare out of the window at her. We felt sorry, and not a little ashamed of ourselves.

The other beggar woman lived a few streets away but in the same quarter. They were back streets with little traffic, and some distance away from the Shrine. But what happened now was more peculiar still. For we stopped the car and got out to walk, and coming nearer heard laughter in the dog kennel. Its occupant was "at home" having a friend to tea. We could see them sitting there, side by side, but not their faces which were hidden by the top of the door. Again, the sensation was not one of poverty. We had seen worse beggars in Meshed by the hundred. But what were they doing in this quiet part of the town, in these by-streets? There was nothing whining about either of them. They were not begging.

My mind was much haunted by these beggar women. Had one started, and the other copied her? So, one was the "only original and genuine" woman in a dog kennel; and the other an imitation, at second hand? Were they friends, or rivals? Their kennels were exactly the same, at a glance, and must be built by the same carpenter. They must have cost quite a little money. Perhaps each beggar woman was encouraged and given her dog kennel by the house owner, who liked to have a holy woman living at his door. I knew of a house near Tunis where a madwoman, a *folle* or holy idiot, lived in the garden and among other things prophesied the beginnings and ends of both world wars. But it was impossible to find out more about them. A local authority, who must know, smiled cynically and said the Moslems had no "holy women". And to a recent enquiry to Meshed I had the following answer: "All I can find out about these women is that they are not considered mystics or demented but are ordinary beggars catering to the pilgrim traffic. No one seems to attach any particular importance to them here." Probably there have always been one or two beggar women living in dog kennels and it is the tradition in Meshed.

Would one be able to get into the Shrine and Mosque? For myself, I was beginning to relish the idea that one could not. Some twenty years ago a few travellers were allowed to enter, but not one of them has written of it in any detail. Robert Byron went in disguise, and shuffled through the courts at "a quick Persian-looking trot". But reading his accoun closely, the only describes the courts or quadrangles and their tiles. He did not enter either Mosque or Shrine.

The possibility was a daily and nightly preoccupation until I really hoped it would not be allowed. How lovely that there should still be a mystery! And in Meshed, particularly, where mystery is worth while! And we discovered another street, if anything more marvellous than the circular boulevard or Ring. For one could not help comparing it in one's mind with the Ring round the Hofburg in Vienna, if only because it was so utterly different. Not that this street was at all difficult to find. It led out of the Ring, but one might have missed it. For the Ring, mollas and pilgrims apart, held so many attractions. There were the photographers, where one could have a snapshot taken against a painted background of the Shrine and its minarets, with a sky all doves and angels. And there were the carpet merchants with better rugs for sale than we saw anywhere else in Persia, including some from Russian Turkestan which is no more than forty miles away, and a beautiful *ghilim* or two, rugs that are used for saddlecloths and are in most delicate tints of blue and green and yellow. *Ghilims* still go for moderate prices, and in the way of rugs are the best purchases to be made to-day in Persia.

The street had water, or an open drain if we prefer it, running down the middle so that one walked down one side of it, and came back along the other. Here were more makers of felt caps, of that brown skull-cap kind which seems glued dustily to the head. And there was a *Khan* with steps leading down into it where a continuous drama of the weighing and carrying of sacks of grain was enacting. A Tartar-looking man with Mongol features, in a long coat that was, incongruously, the shape of an old frock-coat, wearing a skull-cap and sandals made, it seemed, of rags and feathers, kept running in and out of a subterranean cellar bent double with the weight of each sack, jerking it off his shoulders on to the scales, and creeping back for more. All round was the courtyard of the *Khan* with arched rooms where the merchants stayed. In shops, near by, were some of the pigeons for which Meshed is well known; white, with shell crests and feathered feet.* The birds are kept as pets and were picking grain up off the floor. But it is the drain or water channel which is the hub of life. There were fantastic tents and booths along its banks formed of knitted and twisted rags, as near as one could see; and men in rags strung as thick as cormorants upon a string. As the street continued it got poorer and poorer, and the further it went the more Mongolian or Tartar-looking were the inhabitants till one felt it could be Tashkent or Yarkhand. Who were they? Afghans, Uzbeks, or Hazaras? Hazaras who come from the mountains and are of Mongol stock descended from Timur's armies? We had now a considerable crowd following; being as much a source of interest to them, as they to us. A policeman would come up and disperse them, and they would collect again. They were Callot-like scenes of rags and poles, with men wading, women doing their washing in the dirty water, and even a man fishing.

All the time from a window on the first floor of a brick house, a child of about twelve or thirteen intoned the *muezzin*'s call in fervent and urgent voice, while no one listened or paid attention. He would stop for a moment, come back to the window and begin again. All this in a street that seemed to fade out or die away into Central Asia; that yet had a ghost in it of Aldgate, of Whitechapel, of the Old Kent Road. And as we crossed a bridge in order to turn back, with momentary flashes of the stone footbridges of Bourton-on-the-Water, of Thornton-le-Dale, and other green-duck-villages of England in one's mind, there he stood again in the window with both hands to

---

* In *Fancy Pigeons*, by James C. Lyell, London, 1887, there is a chapter on Turkestan Pigeons, describing some thirty Central Asian breeds. The Meshed pigeons are probably related to them. I only saw white "selfs", no other colour, though told that they existed.

Qom, a few moments before arrest

The Blue
Mosque at
Isfahan

his mouth making the *muezzin*'s call. A precocious youth, with ambition to be ordained and forever practising in his "clerical" tenor! Meshed is a city of fanatics, and this is one who is still in his teens, who aspires to the surplice and the dog-collar for it is the same thing. A student learning the *Koran*, and how to call out the *muezzin*'s cry over and over again till it is perfect. And one heard him calling again and again until his voice died away in the distance.

Whether, or not, one would obtain the twin-permits for that pair of buildings was a problem to which the answer could not, now, be long delayed. The moment was coming, and in the meantime one could think of the impact of the blue mosques. I have since been told by a friend who came here long ago in 1935, and stayed in old hostels where the pilgrims lodged with their camels, that there is some lovely blue tiling on little mosques along the route to Meshed. That being so, the first shock of the blue and the golden dome would be a little lessened. For this coloured architecture is one of the aesthetic sensations of a lifetime. Here is colour in architecture for the first and last time. One must forget Wren's dome of St Paul's, and St Peter's in Rome, and Longhena's Madonna della Salute upon the Grand Canal. We are looking at domes of turquoise or sapphire in the evening sky. While we gaze they go through subtle and incredible changes in the air, and against the distant mountains. Now I am back in England, if I shut my eyes, there they still are, so beautiful and satisfying in form and colour that I can scarcely believe I had the luck to see them. What a fortune to have known the Alhambra and the Generalife of Granada, and now the blue domes of Meshed and Isfahan!

There are but few of them, these two towns apart. The famous Blue Mosque of Tabriz with its fifteenth century tilework is a melancholy ruin. Those persons who have seen it agree it is scarcely worth the trouble of going there. The only peers of Meshed and Isfahan are Herat and Samarcand. The ribbed dome of the Mausoleum of Timur at Samarcand, ribbed, and therefore different from the domes of Meshed or Isfahan, is of the sapphire or turquoise order, but sadly damaged, and, it would seem, wantonly restored. The mosque and the *madrasehs* are left, half in ruins, but of the palaces and pleasure domes of Timur described in *The Embassy of Clavijo* there are no traces left. They are gone as completely as Timur's summer town of tents.

There is only Herat, in Afghanistan, of which Robert Byron has left beautiful descriptions. Gauhar Shad Begum, daughter-in-law of Timur, who built the Mosque of Meshed, lies buried there. Formerly, Herat had the finest buildings in Asia, "adorned with fabulous richness", works of the Timurids which survived until 1885 when all but

4

seven of the thirty minarets were demolished, and the connecting
buildings largely or totally destroyed, probably by order of Indian
Army engineers who were advising the Afghans in an expected invasion by the Russians. It was supposed the buildings might serve for
cover and that the minarets could be used for observation posts. So
perished the most glorious of all Asian buildings. The Mausoleum is
still standing, but the *madreseh* and the mosque of Gauhar Shad are
gone. The dome of her Mausoleum, Robert Byron tells us, is turquoise, and its ribs "like those of Timur's tomb at Samarcand are
sprinkled with black and white diamonds, the ribs", he continues,
"being as fat as a sixty-four foot organ-pipe". But the dome of the
Mausoleum has lost its crown, and been still further damaged in a
recent earthquake when two more of the minarets collapsed.* It is,
precisely, such a ribbed dome that will elude us. This device and
invention of the Persians is something missing in their own country
and only found beyond its borders in Central Asia and in Afghanistan.
We shall see saucer domes and swelling domes, but not the ribbed
domes shaped like a canteloup melon.

    This seems to be all that there is of the blue architecture. One hears
stories of another blue mosque somewhere in a remote part of
Afghanistan. This must be at Mazar-i-Sherif. I was shown a colour
film of it by the American Consul at Isfahan. But it was entirely retiled
in the last century, Robert Byron tells us, who adds that "it might be
described as a cross between St Mark's in Venice and an Elizabethan
country house translated into blue faience". Or is it the ruined Shrine
of Khoja Abu Nasr Parsa at Balkh, a few miles away, where is another
of the fluted or ribbed domes? Of silvery and light blue effect, for
"where the glaze has worn off, at the top, the ribs are white and look
as if they had received a fall of snow". But it is obvious from photographs that there is very little left at Balkh. Samarcand is inaccessible:
Herat lies in ruins: there is only Meshed left.

    It had been made clear to me by now that there was no hope what-
ever of getting inside the Shrine. If one returned, perhaps, to Meshed
in ten years time!... But Meshed alas! is somewhere one will never
go again. It made it no better to be told by Dr Shadman that the

---

    * Robert Byron has a beautiful phrase in description of the minarets. He writes of
the blue towers "rising haphazard from the orchards, grape-blue with an azure bloom",
with "tilework of diamond-shaped lozenges filled with flowers, and bordered with
white faience so that the upper part of each minaret seems to be wrapped in a glittering
net.... From close at hand it seems as if one saw the sky through a net of shining hair
and as if it had suddenly been planted with flowers." Cf. *The Road to Oxiana*, by Robert
Byron, Macmillan & Co., London, 1937, pp. 100, 101. Other quotations from pp. 286,
296.

Shrine is even more beautiful inside than out. But one has to respect their wishes. It is their religion and their Shrine. The Royal Mosque at Isfahan has been disaffected and turned practically into a museum in order that foreigners should see it. Why should not the Persians have their holy places! I was in entire sympathy with them. And after the kindnesses received, and friendships formed, it was out of the question to try and enter the Shrine in disguise. That, if at all, is for the irresponsible and young. So the Shrine is a mystery, enhanced. The Imam Reza and Harun-er-Rashid, we know, are buried there: Harun-er-Rashid, whose ambassadors brought a gift of elephants to Charlemagne, and were entertained by him to a hunt of wild aurochs in the Hyrcanian forest. That seems far indeed from Baghdad, and further still from Meshed.

But on the morning of our last day in Meshed I was taken up on to the roof of the Mosque in order to visit the workshops where the tiles are made. What was practically a lost art has been revived in order to restore the tilework, and the actual process of making the tile mosaic can be watched. The pattern is drawn, and then cut out in paper, after which a man sitting, crosslegg'd, chips away at the tiles with a hammer and chisel. It is the simplest of processes carried out by the traditional two men and a boy, or a technique of great complication performed by ordinary workmen, whichever way you look at it, but at least it is done by the traditional method. This is how the tiles were fired, and tile mosaic made, in the fifteenth century; and no doubt the glass windows of Chartres and the gold mosaics of Byzantium came from workshops of this size. The work has been instituted by the Keeper of the Shrine, at whose invitation the men of our party had assembled after climbing several ladders. It was a flat roof like a terrace with rows of little cupolas rising on it. In one of the workshops an immensely long section of something in wood and plaster, hollowed out so that one wondered, at first glance, whether it was a drain pipe or a canoe, was the model or section of one of the minarets. It is in this manner that the tilework on the minarets is repaired. They make a model to study it, and then assemble and integrate the design.

It was an exhilarating and marvellous sensation to be standing on the roof of the Mosque of Gauhar Shad Begum. For the moment one could not see much more, and did not want to appear too inquisitive. The tile workshops came in for more than their share of attention because we were hoping so fervently to be allowed a step further. But it would be impolite to show any curiosity. At the same time one must not be too disinterested. One must express that it was wonderful to have got thus far without presumption of anything more.

I did not even like to lift my eyes to the blue dome that was just above
me. We were longing to be invited to look down into the court. Then,
suddenly, he sent someone forward to step down under a little archway
giving on to the parapet directly above the court, and it was translated
to us that this was in order to see if any of the mollas were looking.
We moved near enough to look down for ourselves, but the next
moment a message must have come back that it was better not.

However, there was an alternative plan. We were to be allowed to
climb a minaret. On Easter Sunday, a week before, when it was snowing
heavily, my friend Wilfrid Blunt had been taken through the court
of the Mosque, and allowed to pass through the sanctuary or prayer
chamber. He was the first non-Moslem to have seen it since the War.
And now we were to be allowed up the minaret, which in a sense was
more interesting still for one could take one's time there and not be
hurried.

We had to scramble up over part of the roof where there were
stepping-stones, with a man to hold on to us in case we slipped. This
was immediately at foot of the drum of the blue dome. Then, we
crawled through a low door into the minaret, and it was like climbing
up, up, inside a factory chimney.

When one emerged it was on to a little covered balcony with a roof
overhead, and a railing, and the stalk or stem of the minaret behind one.
What lay below quite took one's breath away. There are three courts
or quadrangles, from one of which you could see the pilgrims passing
directly from the Mosque into the Shrine. Each of the courts has four
porches or *ivans*, which should make twelve in all, but I am certain
I counted either fourteen or sixteen. The *ivans* give the peculiar
character as they do, indeed, to all Persian mosques. They are like so
many giant scaffolds, or hoardings, or stage-sets. Or as, when playing
as a child at card houses, one had to put a building of bigger cards in
the middle of each side of the house in order to prevent it falling down.
You might take them for some part of a huge film-set, particularly
when they have no backs.* There is an *ivan* in every direction you look,
and always in the middle of a wall of a court, never in the corner, or
at one side. All the *ivans* have their inner side covered with tilework,
while some, so to say, are double *ivans* with two faces of tilework, in
and out.

We were, ourselves, almost astride the top of an *ivan*, with our twin

* The Friday Mosque at Yazd has an *ivan* or portal over 100 feet high, with a pair
of minarets growing from it. Yazd has the best architecture in Persia after Isfahan and
Meshed, and in *The Road to Oxiana*, p. 202, Robert Byron extols the "sanctuary of this
mosque whose walls, dome, and *mehrab* are covered with fourteenth century mosaic in
perfect condition."

minaret at the other end of it, looking thin and shaky and undergoing repairs. Behind, till one moved round the balcony, was the blue dome. All three courts were full of the faithful, prostrating themselves, or listening to sermons, or just sitting in lines along the walls; but, luckily, not looking up. Others were too intent moving from the Mosque into the Shrine, or the other way round. But the dizziness of the height and the roundness of the balcony, turning in a circular movement of its own above the huge courts, themselves alive and buzzing with the fanatic crowd, as well, the flashing of the gold minarets and golden helm-shaped dome, made it difficult to grasp the plan.

It is the court immediately under our feet which has the best tilework. We are standing just over the *ivan* leading into the domed prayer-chamber, with the blue dome of it at our back but a few feet away. Therefore, we cannot see its tilework, or that of our minaret, but we only need to look opposite. It is a two-storey cloister or quadrangle of open arches. The effect of the tiles is as though the whole court of the Mosque is in flower; in tones of gentian and sapphire and lapis lazuli, with a running text all round the cornice of the entire quadrangle composed of flowering and interlacing letters. Another inscription round the edges of the *ivan* beneath us, which leads into the prayer-chamber, is from the hand of Baisanghor, a famous calligraphist, son of Shah Rokh and Gauhar Shad, and grandson, therefore, of Timur. It is in white and yellow on a ground of sapphire; while the frieze round the whole quadrangle is in white *suls* alphabet upon darker morning glory (*ipomaea*), blue, with Kufic interlacing. The flower patterns are those of the finest and most intricate of Persian carpets, and may be the work of such miniature painters as the famous Behzad of Herat.

Over on the left above an *ivan* is the balcony for the musicians, the open kiosque or pavilion in which they play their drums and horns. And every way you look are lesser courts which must be mollas' or students' lodgings, or offices of the Mosque and Shrine. But now we must look round for a last time and come away. There lie the three courts, the most glorious of them being right under our feet, and all the *ivans* with their surfaces as flat as cardhouses, and more than ever like huge stage-sets. Or they have become screens to show off the tiles. One looked for a last time from higher than its own level at the golden dome, and turning, stooped down into the minaret, and climbed down the stairs.

Coming down over the stepping-stones I was so near that I could touch the blue dome with my hand, and picked up a chip or fragment of it to carry away in my pocket. I could see the subtlety of its swelling shape and the almost mamillary or Paphian beauty of its curve; admire the black Kufic writing upon its waist; and the yellow arabesques or tendrils that are so simple in pattern as they grow bigger from the apex and descend the swelling sides. Back again on earth, looking up at the minaret a moment later I could scarcely believe I had climbed it for the most exciting experience I have ever known. But the dome had changed colour. The blue which I had been comparing to turquoise was now sea-green in the midday sky. By evening, at the hour of the horns and drums, it was a shining turquoise again, but darkening in the twilight to a cornflower blue.

# CHAPTER IV

## ISFAHAN

*Desert Road — Holy City of Qom — Cut-glass proscenium arch — Under arrest — Breakdown — Arrival by lorry late at night — Breakfast in Isfahan — Blue vision of the Madraseh Chahar Bagh — Maidan or Great Square of Isfahan — The "blue mosque" or Masjed-e-Shah — Courts of turquoise and lapis lazuli — Mosque of Shaikh Lotfollah — What colour is its dome? — A china kiosque — The Friday Mosque — Two brick dome chambers — Ali Qapu and Chehel Sotun — Avenues of the Chahar Bagh — Jolfa and its Armenian church-mosques — Last look at Isfahan — The blue domes of Persia — One more look, and never again.*

THE grand object of our journey was to get to Isfahan. How can I ever forget the excitement of lying awake knowing that in the morning we would be on the way! One can fly there in an hour and a half, but in order to see something of the country we thought it more interesting to go by road. This would take, we were told, about eleven or twelve hours.

We were brought cups of black coffee at six o'clock in the morning when it was too early to eat anything, and after the customary delays over luggage it was seven o'clock, and then half-past seven, when it occurred to us with appetite returning that the shops would be open soon and this would be the day of all days to buy a pot of caviar to eat upon the way. Caviar had so far been one of the disappointments of the journey for only once had we tasted it, and the best caviar in the world comes from the Caspian. This entailed further delay and was entirely fruitless. That morning there was no caviar to buy in all Tehran, where, incidentally, when found, it is nearly as expensive as in London. Neither could we buy a loaf of bread to eat with it, if we had bought the caviar, being offered instead a bar of chocolate at the equivalent of twelve shillings. But it was only the delay that mattered for we had been given a hamper of food, so we thought, and bottles of gin and whisky to last us as far as Shiraz.

In the end at nine o'clock in the morning, and two hours late, we started off from Tehran. It would be impossible to exaggerate the desert nature of the road. There are stretches of it that are like a switch-back a dozen miles long with the ends looped upon the hills, and salt lakes and the salt desert in between. Now and again a ruined *Khan* with arched entrance and rows of little domed cells stands beside the

55

road, and there are a surprising number of petrol lorries coming up from the oil wells in the south, or returning empty. Away in the distance a black nomad tent or two, and a row of camels against the skyline. And as the morning grows hotter always a play of mirages at the illusory and shifting shores of the salt seas. It was after some couple of hours of this monotonous and uninhabited waste that we decided to stop and eat something, having had no breakfast. It was then we discovered that they had remembered the gin and whisky but forgotten to give us any food. Worse still we had no water. We would be all day on the road, and it was imperative to buy food and water.

At about midday a town in the distance became the holy city of Qom, or Kum, but it is pronounced Gum. It is a place of pilgrimage second only to Meshed, Fatima, sister of the Imam Reza, being buried here.* In consequence it is full of pilgrims, and infidels are no more popular than in Meshed. From the river bank, near one of the bridges, there is a view of the Shrine of Fatima with its golden dome and four blue minarets. It looks Oriental and beautiful from this distance; one of the tall leek domes or shallot domes, of another type altogether from the saucer domes, and giving its date immediately from its shape, the period being early nineteenth century in the reign of Fath Ali Shah. Nothing can make the grouping of it anything but beautiful seen over the water. The golden dome of Qom and its four blue minarets are one of the visions of Persia that remains in the memory, just because they are so Persian, even if the tiles on closer approach when you are across the river and in the town are in the patterns of the inlay on a cigarette box.

All roads and alleys in Qom lead to the Shrine, and nowhere could we find anything that we dared to eat. Most of the shops have fly-blown heaps and piles of a pilgrim's holy biscuit or cake for sale, but they are too dirty and too much handled. A bottle of mineral water was as unknown as a tin of sardines, and after much searching all we could buy was a loaf of bread. It was at about this point that we first drew the attention of the police upon ourselves by innocently walking along a street that led towards the Shrine. Walking ahead, feeling certain that we would be turned back, I just managed to get as far as

* The four great centres of pilgrimage for the Shiah Moslems have all got golden domes. They are the Shrine of the Imam Reza at Meshed, and the Shrine of Fatima at Qom; the other two being Najaf, the burial place of Ali, and Kerbela, both of them in Irak. Kazimein, another pilgrimage shrine in the suburbs of Baghdad, has its two main domes, and the balconies and soaring tops of the four chief minarets, "all covered with gold, of a truly fabulous gorgeousness. Indeed, it is a demonstration of the marvel of gold!" Cf. *From an Antique Land*, by Julian Huxley, London, 1954, pp. 180, 181, and a colour plate opp. p. 220.

the main entrance where I caught the glitter of the cut-glass archway of the *ivan* leading into the Shrine. It must be the best example in Persia of their fun-fair style, of which the first hint was that cut-glass balcony in the Golestan Palace at Tehran; a high porch of three arches like an open pavilion at foot of a pair of minarets, with cut-glass proscenium arch behind it leading into the Shrine. The glitter is quite remarkable, and of a kind one associates more in imagination with the pagodas of Bangkok. It is the last and ultimate invention of the Persians, a hundred human generations after the sculptures of Persepolis.* But I was only to see it during winking of an eyelid for the Qom police force were active and on the trail. We were taken in charge for having a camera and escorted to the police station where much time was wasted. Cups of Turkish coffee were brought while I tried to explain I was a writer and not a journalist. Later, I felt sorry that I had refused the cakes and biscuits when we stopped for a frugal meal by a stream, and all we had to eat was the soft inside of our loaf of bread, for we dared not eat the crust, dipped in gin.

Continuing on our journey over a road that got worse and worse, about sunset our car broke down. First a broken spring, and then something more serious; and there we were, luckily in a little village, but right out in the desert, and about a hundred miles from Isfahan. Buses came past, but every seat was taken; and I thought we would be that night, or several days and nights in the desert. Huge petrol lorries came thundering by, while loudspeakers in the inns on both sides of the road blared out loud. It was like a continuous, ghostly performance in an Oriental music hall, while we sat on a bench outside one of the inns and a sound of distant hammering was the blacksmith trying to mend the car. One would have to sleep here on a table with a rug thrown over it, unless one preferred to sleep in the car with the broken spring. But, eventually, after we had started again, and broken down once more, a Point Four lorry stopped to offer help; and so, on the roof of a lorry, sitting on tyres, we arrived at midnight. But I am not sure that this is not the best method of all by which to reach one

---

* It was irritating to be told much later that we had missed another mosque with cut-glass decorations in fun-fair style, at Qazvin. The Shrine of Fatima at Qom, in spite of its late date, has some works of art of a better period in the form of carpets made for the tomb-chamber of Shah Abbas II, who is also buried there. They are a set of silk carpets woven at Josaquan-Qali in 1671, "the last great demonstration of the Persian art of carpet weaving", according to Mr Upham Pope, who has counted up to as many as twenty tones or colours in them. They are of the "polonaise" type; and one of the finest of the set with a design of formalized cypress trees, as far as I remember, on a silvery-yellow ground, was exhibited at the Persian Exhibition at Burlington House, in 1930. Cf. *An Introduction to Persian Art*, by Arthur Upham Pope, London, 1930, pp. 121, 123, 141, and pl. 68.

of the most beautiful cities in the world. Because we arrived there
tired and hungry after a little of an adventure I think we reached it in
the right state of mind.

There could be no better preparation for what one beheld next
morning against a blue and golden sky. For one must and should come
out of the desert in order to taste the poetry of those blue domes and
minarets for an eternal and first time. To have fasted for a day before-
hand put one in the mood of getting there after ten days or a fortnight's
journey over the rocks and sand. This was how it was intended that
these paradisal buildings should be seen. The white plane trees which
are so particular to Persia were scarcely in leaf, their pallor but one
more preparation for what we were to see floating in luxury and
indolence in a sky of deep lapis lazuli. The first impression of this
fabled city is a vision that can never fade from the mind. How can one
communicate the marvel of waking, and knowing one is in Isfahan!
One does not know whether to hurry over breakfast, or enjoy every
moment of it, it is so good to be alive under the blue sky, which
threatened to rain at one moment, but luckily kept fine.

The first and incredible revelation of the Persians as great architects
and a race of artists comes in the wide, tree-lined avenue only round
the corner from the hotel. But how can one describe it? Once again,
it takes one's breath away. One can scarcely believe or take in what one
sees. It is a blue dome, blue upon the blue. A few days before this, in
the Holy City of Meshed we had seen a blue and a golden dome—a
dome plated with gold, an astonishing sight as it flashed in the sun—
but the blue dome of the Mosque at Meshed is blue like the sea, while
this is sky blue, or could one say turquoise. It is the Madraseh Chahar
Bagh, or College of the Mother of the Shah, late in date, built after
1700, but I can only say that it is scarcely credible that a mosque should
be so "Persian". It is in the perfection of what one would imagine
the Persian style to be, and after a day or two of misgiving I came to
admire it as much as anything in Isfahan.

The curve and swell of the turquoise dome are beautiful if anything
in the world is beautiful, and to deny that is to reject the beauty of the
blue bird or the lotus. It is especially lovely if you contrive to get the
swell of the dome outlined against a minaret and curving heavenward
on the other side. Moreover, it is subtly patterned or inlaid with
arabesques in yellow, aubergine and lapis blue upon the turquoise
ground. That is how I remember it, and I have looked long and carefully at a superb colour slide, and this is the nearest I can get to it in
description. The court of the sacred college or *madraseh* is lined with
students' cells, and the vaulted exterior or alcove of each has its "nerve

lines" picked out in one tone of blue or green or red or yellow upon the white, all in formal pattern, but not unlike what it would be were there a race of spiders that spun their webs laterally, and not in a circle, or they are like the membranes in bats' wings. The great portals, as well, offer one masterpiece after another of abstract patterns in faience, while the interior of the dome, itself, is azure blue with golden arabesques and there are windows in it formed from a trellis or lattice work of tiles.

But this is only a beginning. Better is to come. A few moments later we are in the arcaded Maidan or Great Square, which is about twice the area of the Square of St Mark's at Venice, or the Place Vendôme at Paris,* with the Royal Pavilion or Ali Qapu to one side of it, and the Masjed-e-Shah or Royal Mosque at the far end. The Ali Qapu is a many pillar'd porch for coolness, and a grandstand from which to watch tournaments and games of polo in the square below. It has little fresco'd rooms of utmost beauty. But it is the Masjed-e-Shah, the Blue Mosque, that holds our eyes. In aspect, in music, in poetry, in detail, being all covered, every inch of it, inside and out, with blue tiles. Here we are in the heart or centre of Iran, as much so as any beetle that has crawled into the rose. This is the final blossoming or culmination of Persian art, so full and beautiful that it can go no further. Beauty, indeed, begins to lose its meaning and be nearer to abuse or surfeit. Some writers, Robert Byron among them, are a little nauseated and will not brace themselves to describe it. But that after all is a gesture like, shall we say, being thrown from your horse at seeing the Taj Mahal. The Masjed-e-Shah is blue, blue, blue, as much as the Taj Mahal is of white marble, but it is true that it is given additional point and interest by being built askew. The mosque "leads off" to the right hand from the main portal owing to the complication of having to face in the direction of Mecca, which gives an added and oblique mystery to it for it has more than a few of the elements of a stage-set. That is to say, the technique of the tiled panels at the Masjed-e-Shah is in two manners, a leisurely and a hurried. There are panels of pure mosaic, a most lengthy process; and there is the other type, the *heft rengi* or seven colours, which is the quicker method, tile-fresco, as it were, compared to tile mosaic.

All the interior of the Masjed-e-Shah is done in tiles of the latter kind, but the entrance archway is in pure mosaic. The reason for the more rapid work is that the great builder Shah Abbas wanted quick

* It seems that the Maidan at Isfahan is seven times as large as the Square of St Mark's, almost a third of a mile in length, and "appreciably larger" than the Place de la Concorde in Paris. I can only reiterate that it *looks* about twice the size of the Square of St Mark's. Cf. *Pietro's Pilgrimage*, by Wilfrid Blunt, London, 1953, p. 124.

and dramatic effects which he could see finished in his lifetime. That is why some of the results are like stage-scenery. The prevailing colour is a pure cobalt blue, but the great dome above the prayer-chamber is a paler blue. Even now I am not sure I am right about the colour, for Arthur Upham Pope, the American authority on the art of Persia, tells us of Professor Herzfeld actually comparing a turquoise with the spandrel over the entrance to the Masjed-e-Shah and finding that the china tile had a decidedly clearer and more saturated colour. But the dome, certainly, is paler and early in the morning it is a pale cornflower blue.

In another moment or two we are under its blue vaults, bluer than anything imaginable, more blue than the Blue Grotto. Overhead are beautiful arabesque panels in tilework, the patterns resembling those on the finest and most precious of Persian carpets. Coming out from this cloister of sapphire and turquoise, we are in the great court of the Mosque, in dazzling heat, with the blue "sets" or "drops" all round us, for this is how the flat sides of the court appear with a blue mist or sheen upon them from their china surface. Now we come into the prayer-chamber of the Mosque, itself, where the magnificence of the tile panels of lapis lazuli blue is almost overwhelming, but the lower aisles or chancels to each side of it are more restful and we can look out through their columns upon this prodigy of formal pattern and invention. All round us are blue meadows in blossom, or blue skies seen through a network of flowering branches, all in china tiles. The rigid geometrical patterns, so dear to the Moslems, are in flower.

What are lacking are figures dressed as in the reign of Shah Abbas from this blue set-scene. But what a city it still is! One of the first towns since classical times, laid out on formal lines. Avenues with channels of water down them, arcaded bridges, bazaars with vaulted aisles and doorways like cathedrals! One could wander here for days on end. There was no square to compare with the Maidan anywhere in Europe until Louis XIV built the Place Vendôme. And this is to speak of the Maidan without its mosques, for there is another, the Shaikh Lot-follah, just across the Square. It is smaller, much smaller than the Blue Mosque, and still subtler in colour. In comparison to the Blue Mosque this is an Amalienburg or Petit Trianon. It is small in area, with portal askew like the Masjed-e-Shah, no court in front of it, and approached by a winding passage. For the Mosque of Shaikh Lotfollah, as a building, is full blown and on the decline. How difficult it is to define the colour of its dome which is a flat casque or helmet in shape, not one of the swelling domes! Robert Byron writes of it as "A flattened hemisphere made of tiny bricks and covered with prawn-coloured wash, on which a bold branching rose-tree is inlaid in black and white."* And he speaks of "ornaments of ochre and dark blue" to soften the harshness of that rose-tree pattern, and bring it into tone with the "soft golden pink" of the background; and beneath it all "a pervading under foliage of faint light blue". But I looked at the dome of Shaikh Lotfollah long and often during the few days we were in Isfahan, and never once saw the ground of the dome as "prawn-coloured". Rather, it is *café au lait* but with a tinge of another colour in it. Or it is the colour of a *mousse* of coffee and I can see the exact colour, now, in my mind's eye but scarcely name it. More, still, like the colour of *marron*, like the *marron* in a 'Mont Blanc' but without the cream in it, and with a drop of strawberry or raspberry juice added. And it certainly has that undercurrent of light blue, that faint blue lustre from its china surface, which is in counteraction to the tinge of the red fruit in it. It is difficult, but illusive, as difficult to define as the gorget of a humming-bird, or the colours of a dove's throat. For being ceramic it has the slightest touch of lustre in it. The inlay is glazed, as Robert Byron noticed, but not the stucco wash, and it is to this he attributes what he terms "the broken highlight", whose "intermittent flash", moving with the sunlight, "adds another and a third texture to the pattern". Yet, when you look again, that dome of china is quite matt, with no lustre on its rounded surface.

The interior of Shaikh Lotfollah is disappointing to the verge of being uninteresting, because it is so perfect. All the light comes into the chamber through double latticed windows or traceries of china, high up in the drum. A huge formalized peacock, all eyes and lozenges, is inlaid in the dome, covering its whole surface. In order to make its effect it should seem to rattle and shake its feathers which grow bigger and bigger as they descend. But they do not move, but are still and static. They are frozen and have no movement. And the panels of white calligraphy on the blue ground are lifeless, too. They do not write themselves. They are not far removed from the gold lettering on a Turkish cigarette. Far gone are all the force and strength of Kufic lettering. It is, of course, of utmost splendour as a scheme of decoration. Yet the interior of Shaikh Lotfollah in spite of its miraculous perfection is but a thing of china, and once that point is reached which is no more than the statement or affirmation of its own material then we are nearing the statutes of Carrara marble in a *campo santo*. The Mosque of Shaikh Lotfollah, to which I had looked forward as to a

* Cf. *The Road to Oxiana*, by Robert Byron, London, 1937, pp. 199, 200. Shaikh Lotfollah was "the saintly father-in-law" of Shah Abbas. Cf. *Pietro's Pilgrimage*, by Wilfrid Blunt, London, 1953, p. 124.

San Vitale or Cariye Cami of the art of Iran, disappoints and palls in
its perfection. It is the more surprising that the still later Madraseh
Chahar Bagh should be so beautiful and such a work of art.

There remains the Friday Mosque, but it gains from the delay and
from being seen after the more obvious mosques and other buildings
of Isfahan. For this city presents almost a surfeit of polychrome
architecture and painted tile. In respect of colour Isfahan is incomparable, but from the aesthetic picture a more solid substructure is
lacking until we see the Friday Mosque. It is of the twelfth and
thirteenth centuries, begun in the time of Malek Shah the Seljuq,
work of an epoch of fervour and fanaticism, and in a truer sense the
golden age of Islam. This was content to express itself in plain brick,
putting little reliance on colour, or not yet having grasped the possibilities of that. Once comprehended, these became a fever and then
a weakness. But it is a different spirit in the Friday Mosque of Isfahan,
more in the vein of the Cluniac monks who were contemporary, and
of Cistercian monasteries in France and Spain. Not the soaring giant
hand of Durham, less still the spirit that inspired the sculptures and
stained glass of Chartres, both for the same reason that the Friday
Mosque is puritan, not a shrine of mystery but of plain thinking,
yet the work of a race of deeper aesthetic aptitude and sensibility than
any other that has raised temples with no altars, or altars without a
statue, in any other land. In the centuries before the Mongol invasions
the Persians were creating one of the great art epochs of the world.
The evidence is left to us in a few miniatures, in their ceramics, and in
their brick buildings; in the buttressed cylinder of the Gonbad-i-Qabus
climbing to a hundred and fifty feet over the blue Turcoman steppe,
in the Towers of Victory at Ghazni, and in this Friday Mosque at
Isfahan.

Here the best vantage point is the roof, and this is nearly always
accessible except during Ramadan. The minarets are entirely typical
of the Persian style. It could not be mistaken for any other; neither the
capp'd needle or pencil minarets of Turkey, due to the great architect
Sinan; the Mameluke minarets of Cairo that seem to be in imitation
of bronze ewers or scent burners to a like extent to which Wren's
steeples to the City churches follow or inspire the silver sugar-castors
of the Carolean age; nor one of the green-tiled minarets of Fez. It is
wholly Persian; the rows of cupolas below, not so much so because
they may revive North African memories and remind one of the
hundreds of similar cupolas at El Oued. But the court is one of the
typical tiled courts of Persian mosques; and from the roof we see what
is more typical still and indeed that feature which is unique to Persia,

the tiled *ivan*, a portal or entrance arch which as we noticed from the top of the minaret at Meshed need, or need not, lead into a domed chamber. If not, it has no backing and stands erect by itself, resembling therefore a built scene for the theatre seen from behind. At Meshed there is that astonishing view over three courtyards of the Mosque and Shrine with fourteen or more *ivans* rising above them like frontispieces to card houses, or even premature suggestions for the Lever or United Nations Buildings in New York City. When, as often, there is a minaret at either end of an *ivan*, the thinness of their structure is still further accentuated and with its patterned tiles it looks more than ever like a house of cards.

In spite of its austere brick exterior there are magnificent examples of tilework in the Friday Mosque. The abstract repertory is endless, but we could not look here for companion pieces to these other blossoming fruit boughs or blue meadows of spring flowers. They are to be seen in the Blue Mosque and in Shaikh Lotfollah. These are rayed suns or sun-motes, and all the limitless phases of the hexagon and octagon as in sublime patchwork. As for the inscriptions in Kufic lettering they are miracles of compact invention and of becoming gravity and import, although they may seem at first to the uninitiated to be some form of maze or puzzle. Especially grand are the Kufic writings in the interior of one of the *ivans*. Here, it has from its re-petition almost the aspect of a heraldic cognisance or crest, as though it is some emblem repeated over and over again *ad infinitum*, in reverse and sideways and upside down.

Later ages further embellished the Friday Mosque. There is, in particular, its *mehrab* dating from about 1310, a marvellous work in stucco, not inferior to the decorative art of the Moslems in any part of their world, and a peer to the stalactitic marvels of the Andalusian Moors. It has the look of Córdoba or of Tlemcen, that is to say, and is not specifically of Persia. But with the interior vaulting of the *ivans* that is another matter for they exhibit the bat-wing segments that are peculiar to the Persian style, less laboured and later in date than the Andalusian stalactite and honeycomb and of a different meaning, as though the segments would fold or shut up. It could be the fanciful interpretation of the inside of a tent, and one may not be far wrong in guessing the date as near 1700.

The supreme merit of the Friday mosque, however, are its two dome chambers, both dating from before 1100. Some authorities would see in these, and in the smaller one in particular, the summit of Persian art. The shape is peculiar, the smaller being some thirty feet square and sixty high, which relates it in form to the stone tomb-chambers of Soltan Qalaun at Cairo, and to the stone tomb-mosques of Soltan Barquq and Qaït Bey in the desert outside that city. Having lately had an opportunity, such as does not occur to everyone, of seeing the mosques of Cairo and of Isfahan within a few days of each other I would not concur with this opinion. The smaller dome-chamber of the Friday Mosque is impressive enough in its austerity and "pure cubic form". It is a lesson in the strength and dignity that can be achieved in brick, not red brick as we know it in Northern Europe, but mud bricks of a uniform mud-brown. But this instance of Spartan puritanism in the enamelled air of Isfahan is not enough to make a simple brick chamber into one of the aesthetic wonders of the world.

What is superb in the Friday Mosque is its ensemble of pride and age. Sufficient of colour in its courts to put it on a par with the painted mosques that are its neighbours, and under that a solemnity and seriousness of purpose as befits a building that is more than twice their age. Isfahan would be given over to gaiety were it not for this solemn note of warning. Without the Friday Mosque Isfahan would be as the Rome of Bernini without the early basilicas. Inside its brick vaulting we recall the fervours of the Moslem religion, and the later mosques however beautiful are in comparison but so many china kiosques or pagodas, meant only for sensual gratification of the eyes. The appeal of the Friday Mosque is to the faith and mind, and those are the virtues of the earlier years. In its origins and early history Islam was a reforming or puritan religion. They permitted no altars, no idols, and no priesthood. Nevertheless, indolence and the laxity accompanying it, are attributed by the Occident to the turban'd East. But this opinion can be contradicted at every turn and nowhere more so than in Isfahan, because in this city both extremes are present, tiled courts and domes of turquoise, and the plain brick Friday Mosque. How often have I longed to hear the call of the *muezzin* of those days! In his phrases, chanted at dawn and sunset, there would be all the militant spirit of early Islam. If one listens now in the middle of the night, it is like comparing the screech of an eagle to the note of a blackbird or a nightingale. And in the same imagery the brick dome of the Friday Mosque is a war drum or a kettle drum, while the other domes of Isfahan are but painted or enamelled tiles.

In any event one is entirely sated after seeing the three mosques in a single morning. Instead, we will have one more look by evening light at the domes of Isfahan. But that need not be to-day, or even the day after. There is so much else to see; and how pleasant a palace, or even two palaces, after the *mehrab* and the *minbar*, which is as though one might say a pleasure dome is to be enjoyed after the prayer book and

Mosque of
Shaikh Lotfollah
at Isfahan

Detail of the Blue Mosque at Isfahan

the pulpit. For myself, I see no resemblance whatever between the Ali Qapu and "a brick boot-box", the term that Robert Byron uses to describe it. Rather, it is a pavilion of a delightful fancy with a not unwarranted touch to it of the interior of Bolsover Castle. First and primarily a grandstand, with little retiring rooms leading off it for no uncertain purposes of feasting and love-making, the pillars of the open, grandstand portion of it being magnificent stems of cypress or cedar, with an incomparable view from the balcony over the Maidan to the dome of Shaikh Lotfollah opposite and the Blue Mosque. There is always the light and sparkle of china on those minarets and domes. From upstairs the view is more beautiful still because it takes in the mountains, and there is little room after room, some with alcoves pierced to receive wine jars and cups of porcelain, others painted with arabesques of flowers and pheasants, and some with fading Jacobean frescoes of figures wearing European clothes, probably by the hand of John the Boor, a mysterious Dutchman. The little rooms are exceedingly pretty but there have been exaggerated accounts of them as works of art. Whether Persian or semi-European they are exactly in the mood and of the aesthetic value of little Jacobean rooms in England.

The other relic of the palace of Shah Abbas is the Chehel Sotun or Hall of Forty Pillars. There can be no question that this pavilion is influenced by the Hall of the Hundred Columns at Persepolis. It has immense wooden pillars made from the single stems of trees, some of them with stone double-bodied lions for bases, again in the Achaemenid style, Persepolis being so nearly on the road from Isfahan to Shiraz that almost every Persian traveller must have seen its ruins. In the water tank in front of the Chehel Sotun are stone maidens from another palace garden, but neither lions nor maidens are, aesthetically, anything more than curious, the lions if we like to think so being belated cousins to those in the Court of the Lions at the Alhambra in Granada. On the sides of the Chehel Sotun are other frescoes by a European hand that are more faded still, and in the interior there is an audience hall with bearded Shahs, galore, engaged in battle, or with the bottle.

Both Chehel Sotun and Ali Qapu are beautiful as pavilions, if no more than that, but must have been more lovely in midst of blossoming orchards and rose gardens. Shah Abbas, and later Shahs, had little palaces in pavilion form scattered all over the city, no doubt with delicate interior decoration of stalactite and painted arabesque,* enlivened by the silk and brocade dresses of Safavid times which were among the most varied and gorgeous that the world has ever known.

* Like the little throne palace of Shah Soltan Hassan described by Arthur Upham Pope in *International Studio*, December, 1930.

5

The Grand Turk and the Great Moghul were contemporary to the Safavid, and there may have been little in magnificence of apparel to choose between the progresses of the Sultan at Istanbul and the retinue of Shah Jehan or of Aurungzebe at Delhi or at Agra. Yet no other Oriental city, not Cairo, not Delhi, not Istanbul, could offer such a spectacle as the Maidan of Isfahan on a spring evening, or after nightfall. Now there is scarcely a figure not dressed like a worker in Huddersfield or in the Belgian coal mines, all in the cause of nationalism. Further, the beauty of the Maidan is wrecked by the flowerbeds and silly railings where it should have had cypresses and tanks of water. Planning as simple as that could restore it to its rightful position as one of the beautiful places of the world.

The other formal beauty of the city was the Chahar Bagh, the avenue leading into Isfahan, with four rows of poplar and plane trees and a canal in the middle "interrupted at intervals by large square or octagonal basins and overhung with rose hedges and bushes of jasmine". A balcony of one of the Shah's palaces overlooked this down its whole length. The Chahar Bagh has still its plane trees and a trickle of water, in gutters to both sides and a canal in the middle, but there are no roses and no jasmine though these could be put back for less than it costs to buy a motor-bus or lorry. The great arcaded bridge of Shah Abbas is another of the wonders of Isfahan, carrying the Chahar Bagh over the river past country houses and so in the direction of Shiraz, ending in a public garden or orchard "whose fruit was at the disposal of the inhabitants of Isfahan". This Allahverdi Khan bridge is, still, more imposing than any bridge in Rome or Florence, arcaded on both sides, with an outer arcade for foot passengers, and even alcoves where they can talk or make coffee. Below are stepping stones for crossing the river in the shade at low water. It is only sad that the crowd crossing the bridge are on their way home from a factory. Loud and appalling sirens blow at six and even five o'clock in the morning in order to assert that this is the century of factory man, and there are wails like warning voices through the night and day.

Jolfa, the Armenian suburb of Isfahan is the other side of the river, imparting quite another sensation if you walk about in it. For the women are unveiled and wear shawls on their heads like peasant women, while the blue sky and domes of the churches might cause one to wonder if it is the south of Russia. There are cypresses growing in courts and a rumour of vines. In fact the Armenians make a red wine to which with little alteration one might apply a patronizing phrase to be found in Baedeker where, talking of some typical French or German town, he observes "tolerable French" (or German) "is spoken here".

It is a palatable red wine to be preferred infinitely and on all occasions to the treacle-wine of Shiraz.

But the curiosity of Jolfa is its church-mosque built in the time of Shah Abbas, who encouraged the Armenians and induced them to settle here. From outside except for a cross it entirely resembles a mosque, while in the interior one might wonder for a moment if one is looking at oil paintings of a Shah and his three hundred sons feasting and battling, but instead it is one long string of gory martyrdoms.* The interior of the dome is entirely Persian in style of ornament, being given a peacock-eye decoration subtly beautiful of its kind. Silk needle-work curtains of an exceptional execution in the way of flowers hang by the altar steps. All in all, to a European the Armenian cathedral of Jolfa is a beautiful and touching thing; while at least two or three other Armenian churches are of the same date and worth entering. Under that blue sky it is as though some lost corner of Provence had been inhabited for three hundred years by Russians.

Nothing could be more different from the Armenian quarter than the bazaars of Isfahan. These, too, are due to the planning of Shah Abbas who built archways leading into them that could well be the entrances to colleges or *madrasehs*. There is beautiful brick vaulting for their ceilings, much of it as good in detail as if the aisle of a mosque had been converted into a bazaar. Amid so much talk of the *souks* in Damascus and in Aleppo those of Isfahan are little mentioned though incomparably better as architecture, while the few inhabitants who still look and dress as Persians should, and used to look, are generally gathered here as though in search of protective colouring. The printed cottons of Isfahan are the best things sold here for the typical em-broidered cloths are on sale along the Chahar Bagh. Some of the interior halls in the bazaars are more picturesque even than the long alleys, but the climax is the moment of coming out on to the Maidan which is as much of a sensation as that first time, or any other time, of walking out under the porticoes into the Piazza of St Mark's. This is at the northern end of the Maidan where, of old, from the upper galleries musicians played at stated hours, "some after the Turkish, others in the Persian manner". We are left to conjecture for ourselves exactly what this means, and to wonder whether like the café bands in the Piazza both sorts played at once. The French traveller Thévenot in the seventeenth century says that among the instruments were

* Mr Julian Huxley was appalled by the paintings. Cf. *From an Antique Land*, 1956, p. 223. But they are less horrific, by far, than the frescoes of martyrdoms in the Roman church of San Stefano alla Rotonda, a circular building with little chapels all round it, where, as Mr Michael Ayrton put it: "You can enter, and dial your favourite saint."

copper trumpets eight feet long which could be heard all over the town.*

It is now evening and we will have our last look at the domes of Isfahan knowing that never again will there be opportunity to see them. A few days later flying back from Shiraz to Tehran the aeroplane touched down for a few moments at the airstrip, which is a stretch of desert near a little tomb with a blue dome. It has the impact of the broken arch of an aqueduct in the Roman *campagna*, for the domes *are* Isfahan as much as those broken arches lead to Rome. As the aeroplane came in to land, and climbed again, the domes were far away in the distance like turquoise points of light, the long avenue of the Chahar Bagh swung into place, the domes still shone for a moment with the light of china on them, and then were gone. That last sight of them was but in reminder. One knows this is the last time we will really see them.

The *ivans* of the Blue Mosque look more than ever to be screens or shutters, frontispieces to card houses, or scene-sets which may be shifted one day, and either moved to new positions or stored and put away. It is even a question whether the *ivan*, once evolved, has not become a kind of clothes-line or towel-horse on which the Persians hung their tile panels. That extraordinary vision of fourteen or sixteen of the *ivans* seen from the balcony of the minaret at Meshed now has its explanation. It is a functional necessity turned into an excuse, in the same way that the Japanese used screens to divide up their rooms and then took to painting them; or that the great height of the Perpendicular Gothic churches first necessitated huge windows, and later made a point in having them. The *ivans* are display screens. By now they have no other purpose. That is why there are so many of them giving such a peculiar impression at Meshed.

Of all the Persian domes, not taking into account those of Shiraz which are of a different shape and later date, perhaps the most beautiful and the purest in colour is the little Royal Mosque or Masjed-e-Shah of Meshed, seen that first morning when we started walking to the Shrine of the Imam Reza and the Mosque of Gauhar Shad, and neglected in the excitement of what was to follow. It has a wonderful

* There must be a connection between this and the "Royal Music" of the Shrine of Meshed performed from the pavilion or "music-house where, according to an old Persian custom found in other Royal cities, sunrise and sunset are greeted with music", Cf. *Encyclopaedia of Islam*. "Royal music" of this nature used to be, or still is, performed daily under the arch of a government building at Tehran, but I was only told this on my return from Persia and never heard it. Mr Gerald Reitlinger in *A Tower of Skulls*, p. 31, heard the "Royal" music at Kermanshah. "At sunset, five or six respectable looking citizens climbed to the top of a ruined tower and banged drums, beat cymbals, whistled on flutes, and tootled upon horns for about half-an-hour."

intensity of turquoise—turquoise, so to speak, of the purest and first water, without blemish, but beside those more sensational buildings it may be overlooked. The dome of Gauhar Shad, we have said, is sea-green, changing again into sky-blue, or to paler cornflower blue, though it will be agreed that in Meshed, the town of turquoises, one's understanding and appreciation of a turquoise is enlarged once one has seen a collection of the blue stones unwrapped in different bundles on a merchant's counter and the many variations in colour of which it is capable so that "turquoise", ever after, becomes a name with new meanings.

Now we are in the Maidan of Isfahan looking at the Blue Mosque which has a turquoise dome, paler in colour than the courts and screens of sapphire and lapis lazuli that surround it. The curving of its dome is calculated to a marvellous nicety, and one does not know whether to admire this dome most, or that of the Madraseh Chahar Bagh, that later building not in the Maidan but in the long tree-lined avenue. These three domes, the Gauhar Shad at Meshed, and the Blue Mosque and the Madraseh Chahar Bagh in Isfahan, are the beautiful and inimitable things of Persia. One had the preconceived idea that the Persian domes might look like turbans. But this is not so. In respect of which, it is surely the Moghul domes, the domes of Delhi and Lahore, that resemble turbans, and the Persians with their cold winters, despite the magnificent turbaned headdresses worn in the Safavid miniatures, were as apt to wear fur caps or pointed hats of astrakhan.

Climbing over the roof of the Gauhar Shad I had been so near to its blue dome that I could touch it with my fingers. At this distance from the eyes the whole dome looks as though it has been thrown on the potter's wheel and moulded with the hand. The domes of the Renaissance are impersonal compared to this which is so clearly made and finished by hand. The domes are geometrical inventions that are as full of complications and contradictions as the apples of Cézanne. One could never tire of looking at them. They swell towards the eye, and then away from it, with a ripeness that makes the mouth water and that satisfies. In another sense they are like sun-clocks or astrolabes; and they are ceramic objects held up or exposed in the sunlight for the sun to move round them so that there is always a mock-sun or parhelion reflected and burning there. Airy sculptures to be admired from any angle and in the round, but they are abstract forms and not sculptures. It is a physical architecture calling almost for sexual admiration, but is it pre-eminently feminine? Where all the women go veiled, are the blue domes of Persia so many abstract emblems of femininity? Was the feminine look and feel of the dome in the mind of the architect and potter while they worked? The domes of Istanbul by contrast are military of impact. They are essentially masculine. It is no surprise on seeing them to learn that the Turkish architect Sinan was a military engineer. Nevertheless the secret of Sinan in his mosque architecture is repose, but it is masculine repose. One could say that it is the repose of a victorious warrior at a time when Turkey was a great military power, while the Persian if not wholly feminine—for their history makes one wonder about that—is an architecture of luxury and lassitude. There is perhaps an excessive flowering or abnormality in the architecture of Isfahan to the extent to which there is a drugged or narcotic excess of repetition in the temples and sculptures of Angkor. Neither is entirely normal.*

But if this theory is too fanciful let us wonder why this polychrome architecture was not carried a step further. The ribbed domes of Herat and Samarcand appear to be a little top-heavy, and more Northern or Central Asian than Persian of aspect. The Mausoleum of Timur is ribbed like a canteloup melon, turquoise in colour, its ribs sugared or sprinkled, as it were, with tiles in the shape of black and white diamonds. More akin in effect, one might think, to a starry night than to a blue sky. But in Persia everything works out and tends towards blue, as much so as in Baroque churches everything is gilt as though gold is the criterion and pabulum. Why not some other colour? In Portugal, a land which no one would compare aesthetically to Persia, there is hardly an instance of other than blue *azulejos* as though the Portuguese tile makers were tied to that convention by the literal meaning of the word. In the Mosque of Shaikh Lotfollah another ground has been attempted, and one so subtly discriminated that it is difficult to name it. The Persians could have tried and achieved almost any combination of colouring, and one is at a loss to understand why they failed to do this. With their love of roses why did not the architects of Isfahan try for a dome of rose-petal? Of white, like a white rose; or of ivory? Indeed, of any and every colour of the rose? Or of the apricots and

---

* One recalls what the traveller Sir Thomas Herbert tells of the Maidan in the evening, "where the Potshaw (Pasha) and others frequently resort for pastime, as tumbling, sleight of hand, dancing girls, and painted catamites (that *nefandum peccatum* being there tolerated)". Pietro della Valle, the Italian, tells of the Festival of Roses, and how "at nights the ganymedes of the coffee-houses issue forth into the streets near the Maidan, torches in hand, to scatter roses over the passers-by in return for money". The Carmelite Father John Thaddeus accuses Shah Abbas of introducing the vice into Persia, where it was surely known before, adding that his harem contained, besides women, more than two hundred boys. Three contemporary accounts, in fact, agree. Cf. *Travels in Persia*, by Sir Thomas Herbert, Broadway Travellers, London, 1928; *Pietro's Pilgrimage*, by Wilfrid Blunt, London, 1953, p. 129; and *A Chronicle of the Carmelites in Persia*, edited Anon., London, 1939.

nectarines in their orchards? Their potters had achieved masterpieces of ceramic art six centuries or more before the Blue Mosque was built. Those rayed dishes from Zenjan in the museum at Tehran could have suggested and inspired a whole school of polychrome architecture. Compared to those, and to much else, the china domes of Isfahan are conventional and almost dull. They have a fullness, nearly a dullness of formalized pattern, and are not bold and daring. The designs are those on brocades and velvets, and the genius of the Persians could have thought of something more.

But it is not true to say this. If there is anything beautiful in the world it is the Blue Mosque at the end of the Maidan against the distant mountains and in the evening sky. One would love to look once more at its dome of turquoise and sapphire, but it is too late. Nearer at hand, the lattices of china under the dome of Shaikh Lotfollah are like perforations to a casque of many colours. That pavilion of porcelain is locked for the night and its fired splendours die, one by one, in the interior darkness. Coming away, there is only the blue dome of the Chahar Bagh, moon-like, for it has the curve and swelling of the full moon, through the pale stems of the *chenar* trees and near the evening star. Look again! for this is a last view of the blue domes of Isfahan.

# CHAPTER V

# SHIRAZ

*Inside the dragon-fly — Shiraz as a city of the South — Wine of Shiraz — Twins in pale blue pea-jackets and Eton collars — Chemist's shop and museum — The flowering match-box — Giant skeleton, and story in triplicate — Persian gardens are a disappointment — Carte de visite — To Persepolis — The great platform — Man-headed and winged bulls — Rock-carvings of Naqsh-e-Rostam — The Sasanian horseman — His fringed cowboy trousers and huge hair balloon — Passing of the Qashqai at foot of the rock-carvings — The Qashqai come past in the night — Night ride and cortège à la Tzigane.*

IT is perhaps inevitable that one should start off for Shiraz with some expectation of Seville. Because of the promise of wine and cypresses and roses, and more than a hint that this is the Andalusia of Iran. Are not the sherries of Cadiz and Jerez in descent from the vines of Shiraz? Are not the poets Hafez and Sa'di buried here in gardens that are loud with nightingales? Were there an opera with a Persian setting it would surely be in Shiraz, reminding one again of Seville where the scenes of four immortal operas are laid.*

And the reality? We had had our fill of motoring, arriving in the middle of the night at Isfahan, and decided to go on by air. The hotel there, despite its curious plumbing system leaves pleasant impressions, and it was sad knowing one would never see again yet one more relic of former British supremacy, the old hotel guide in his faded khaki coat, who had been messenger to the Consulate and was so proud of being a Bakhtiari tribesman. Harrowing in another sense is the behaviour of Persians at an airport, the way they hold hands fervently and at the last moment embrace as though never to meet again in this life. There were several pairs of mollas in black turbans with beards dyed with henna who embraced furiously before departure, and the usual persons who, surprisingly, have paid their fares. A fat man with folding legs, designed for sitting crosslegg'd on the floor, with a horde of small sons all of an age as though born from different mothers on the same birthday, climbed noisily, toy-laden, up the landing-steps into the insect-body of the aeroplane, and soon their moans and despairing war whoops, but not of battle, and tearful goings to and fro along the gangway, made attention to anything but themselves impossible. A

---

* *Figaro, Barber of Seville, Carmen,* and *Don Giovanni.*

man with hair brushed in every direction and looking like a murderer
fleeing from justice sat with eyes shut for an hour and a half during the
whole journey, but was not of more interest than that he was a molla
without his turban. And an old lady like the great-grandmother of all
grandmothers hid herself in her *chador* and hardly showed her kohl-
stained eyes.

Shiraz is a city of wide tree-lined streets and an excellent water
supply, something unique in Persia, due to the munificence of the same
private individual who at the cost of two million pounds has endowed
it with the best equipped hospital in the Middle East. There are indeed
the roses and cypresses and the tombs of the poets; and from a distance
the domes of the mosques are onion- or leek-shaped and a little
Russian of aspect, while on nearer approach their portals have tile-
panels of pink and yellow flowers that are peculiar to this part of
Persia.* It is the "dew-dropping South" of Mercutio; but not the blue
and golden Mediterranean. Perhaps it is the width of the streets, and
the trees growing along them, and the knowledge that should you wish
it you can drink water from the tap in your bathroom, that makes
Shiraz unlike other Persian cities. Also, it is not much more than a
hundred miles from the Persian Gulf, and that leads past oil-derricks
to the Indian Ocean and to India. It is no longer near to Central Asia.
The early traders came by sea from Portugal and built their fort at
Milton's Ormuz. Samarcand is not over the mountains. The winds
waft to Muscat and Goa and Golconda.

The hotel in Shiraz is comfortable, if eccentric in certain matters,
but not cheaper than the Ritz or Savoy in London. It has an immense
tank of water in front of it, and a garden full of childish statues of white
lions and tigers of the same material, one would think, as the red or
white lions or white harts of English inns, but of coarser, non-heraldic
execution. The garden and water-tank are lit at night with careless
but purposeful extravagance to show the Persians are as fond of electric
lights for their own sake as the Chinese are of fireworks. It is full of
flowers, and there is an invention met with nowhere else; instead of
flowerbeds they have wicker baskets six feet or more across planted
with petunias and pansies. Nights looking on to that garden are balmy
and scented; at dawn the *muezzins* from far down in the city are as the
ghosts of those nightingales; it is only the wine of Shiraz that disappoints and sickens. It is in fact very nasty indeed;† and after one or

---

\* Shiraz tiles of the Zend period, in their delicate pink, yellow, or light blue, differ
from other Iranian *Kashi*—*Kashi* being the opposite of the *Heft Rengi* technique. Cf.
p. 80.

† Robert Byron mentions three wines of Shiraz; a very dry golden wine "preferable
to any sherry"; "a dry claret, nondescript at first but acceptable at meals", and "a

two attempts we drank canned beer from Milwaukee, or even Pepsi-Cola. Food was mainly various rice dishes; or seemingly quadruped chickens appeared which from their tough muscular nature must have fancied themselves to be velocipedes. We were waited upon by a pair of stout middle-aged Persians, probably not more than thirty years old, one of them burly and hoarse as though a drinker of red wine, and with the physique of a *picador*, both dressed by a caprice of the management in pale blue pea-jackets and Eton collars. These unidentical twins did much of the work of the hotel, including making up the accounts in Arabic numerals which we could not read and translating them by sleight of hand into colossal totals.

A day or two went by pleasantly enough in this manner looking down from the terrace and loggia on the first floor, at breakfast time, at the siesta hour, and again at sunset, over the flower garden to distant cypresses and the leek-domes of Shiraz. It is decidedly a town of flowers. The taxi-drivers held a rose in one hand while they drove, and had another in a little vase in front of them on the dashboard which they smelt from time to time. There must be many rich families living here. But there are incongruities: such as a pharmacy, chemist's shop would be the wrong word for it, stocked with every French, German, and American patent medicine, but with a staff of assistants who had little if any idea what it was all about. They handed one the medicine hoping one would be able to read the label, and it was obvious that this innocent corner shop could be the poisoner and drug-fiend's paradise.

Near by—but how far away in a different sense!—is a museum installed in a round or octagonal pavilion presided over by a custodian with a henna'd beard, whom it is necessary to isolate, so to speak, and then chase round and round the building in order to get admission. But the interior has good tilework and a few drawings, and the whole has a curious air of having been bought entire and set up again in a street in Nice or Cannes. It is because of the double contrast, with that up-to-date but casual pharmacy on the one hand, and the paved street and flower garden, not to be anticipated in a Persian town, coming from Tehran. Being Ramazan we did not enter any of the mosques, but had to be content with their characteristic flower-tiled portals with red and yellow roses which, prettily tawdry as they are, have their own word to say of flowers and sunshine, such a message as one used to get on opening a box of Italian wax-matches with trigger-fastening of

sweeter *vin rosé*, which induces a delicious well being". Cf. *The Road to Oxiana*, p. 185. Our own experience of Shiraz wine, both here and at Persepolis, was limited to a glucose, off-gold treacle which not even drinkers of tonic wines would taste willingly for a second time. We were told of one good Persian white wine, a Riesling, to be tasted in a Russian restaurant in Tehran.

elastic, and as likely as not a burnt finger, but on the cardboard lid some Tetrazzini or other human nightingale of the warm South singing among the roses and carnations, and my memory going back to long ago, the *bersaglieri*, hats with curling green-black cocks' feathers on one side tied under their chins, rushing past on their bicycles playing shrill marches on their bugle-band. But back to Shiraz, where the streets may be paved but the bazaars are dirtier than anywhere, though well roofed with high brick vaulting.*

The fame of Shiraz is not its mosques, but gardens. We saw three or four of these. Seed packets, presumably from Carter's or Sutton's, have borne rich results but hardly those to be expected in a Persian garden. Petunias and pansies are the rage, and there is an occasional wistaria arbour. Innumerable roses, too, but to the eye of an amateur none of them either old or interesting, being less lucky in this respect than Miss Nancy Lindsay whose expert and trained hand found four or five unique *damascena* roses in the northern provinces of Persia, near the Caspian, which she brought home and propagated; or than my friend and colleague Mr Wilfrid Blunt who found a most curious rose of two colours, the inner and outer petals different, in an old garden near Kerman, in the centre of Persia. One is a little inclined after Shiraz to think that the beauty of Persian gardens is a delusion. There can be nothing in Persia nearly so lovely as the Generalife of Granada, which is a Moorish garden of the fourteenth century.

As to what Persian gardens were in the past, there is more evidence. Water-filled canals, orchards and cypresses were the mainstay, and the favourite flower was the rose. In the ninth and tenth centuries the

* I was sorry to miss seeing the giant skeleton of the eight foot six beggar which stands, so I was told, at head of the stairs in the medical school at Shiraz. Persons still living remember him begging in the bazaars. And if the reader will forgive twin irrelevances which this is my excuse for recalling, I would mention the beggar-on-horseback of whom there is an account and a coloured plate in *Picturesque Illustrations of Buenos Ayres and Montevideo*, by E. E. Vidal, 1820. The account reads: "To an European, the most remarkable member of the mendicant fraternity is a Beggar on Horseback. There are several here, and the most notorious of them, who always rides a white horse, is chosen as the subject of our sketch. . . . His manner is essentially different from that of the true object of charity. He accosts you with assurance and a roguish smile; jokes on the leanness of his horse which, he says, is too old to walk; hopes for your compassion, and wishes you may live a thousand years. His station is outside the Colegio, formerly the Jesuits' College, to which is attached one of the best churches in the city." The sketch is reproduced in my *Sacred and Profane Love*, London, Faber & Faber, Ltd., 1940, p. 270. Twin to him, or indeed triplet, if we include in this trio the giant beggar of Shiraz, is the subject of the following story. During the seventeenth century a giant Patagonian Indian, nine foot high, with two heads, was brought alive to England, and after incredible vicissitudes, not his skeleton, but his mummified body was to be seen recently, for two pence, in the pavilion on the 1100 foot long iron pier at Weston-super-Mare.

Seljuq Shahs gave audience under a plane tree solidly encased in silver, an image beautiful in itself as poetry and which hints at the Imperial gardens of Byzantium. The gardens of Timur's palaces at Samarcand had low fences of wood palings, painted red, to edge a tank of water, or wall in a plane tree's shade; and at Clavijo's first interview "His Highness was sitting on the ground, by a fountain that threw up a column of water into the air backwards, and in the basin of the fountain there were floating red apples". Wild flowers were much admired, particularly the tulip and narcissus, the latter so much so that "Persian geographers sometimes mention where there were especially fine wild fields of them".* But where flowers are concerned it is ever and always a return to the rose, of which Sir John Chardin mentions four varieties red, pink, yellow, and white: and two bi-colours, one red on one side of the petal and white on the other, and its pendant which was red and yellow. These kinds were called Don Rompe or "two places" in Persian; and he saw roses of three colours on the same bough, yellow, yellow and white, and yellow and red. Of these grafted wonders Chardin writes with as much enthusiasm as did the first travellers at about this time to see orange trees in full fruit only two inches high, and other dwarfed trees in Japan.

Admission to the gardens of Shiraz is not without its comic side. We arrived at one well known garden to find its iron gates padlocked and the house taken over by the army. At once, ferocious military characters came hurrying down the avenue of plane trees towards us, and as they got nearer we could see their bristling moustaches. They waved their arms frenziedly, talking volubly the while in that curious illusion that the foreigner will understand if you shout loudly enough at him, and then, disconcertingly, with much gesture produced card-cases out of their tunics. It was, we were given to understand, absolutely and entirely out of the question for anyone to be admitted into the garden without a visiting card. Unheard of and utterly impossible, with more gestures and shakings of the head. And of course we had no card of any kind on us until I remembered I had in my wallet the name card of the lady who had sat next to me at dinner a few nights before, on which she had written the name of a town on the Caspian where there was a good hotel, and on the card were the Royal arms of Great Britain embossed in gold. They seemed as pleased with it as we were, and at once unlocked the gate, the officer who was senior asking

---

* Quoted from *An Introduction to Persian Art*, by Arthur Upham Pope, London, Peter Davies, Ltd., 1930, pp. 205, 210. Quotation from *The Embassy of Clavijo*, translated by Guy Le Strange, Broadway Travellers Series, 1928, p. 220. *Travels in Persia*, by Sir John Chardin, edited by Sir Percy Sykes, London, 1927.

me, as we left, in supplicating voice if he could be allowed to keep the card, from which one has to conclude that just as there are collectors of spiders and stamps and match-boxes so there must be collectors of visiting cards. But like all the other gardens it was disappointing.

A day or two in Shiraz is enough and it is time to move on to Persepolis. It is a beautiful drive in a flower-decked taxi, beginning over a shoulder of the mountains and so down on to the plain. Here and there, but far into the distance, are the black tents of the nomads, and we pass a small group of them, and then another, more picturesque than any Gypsies, all heading in the same direction towards Persepolis. These are not poverty stricken like the nomads we saw on the road to Qazvin. They are wearing the bright flamingo colours of the Gitanos, two old women, in particular, riding fine ponies with the air of Faraonas or Gypsy Queens. As far as possible they ride on the green banks and keep off the road, and we see more groups of them in the distance, but only in two's and three's.

The last few miles are never to be forgotten, over the plain where Alexander of Macedon passed, which is green at this time of year as the green flash of sunset in a green sea. The road leads on, dead straight, for miles. At last, something like a high platform or dais stands out from under the shadow of low hills, and instinct tells one it is the great platform of Persepolis. In another moment or two we see it more clearly, standing up now as abruptly as the hull of a huge ship when you stand below it on the quay. The first climbing of the stairway is another unforgettable experience, its immense scale making one feel as insignificant in the face of time as the humble lizard that darts to hide in the crevices of that cyclopaean wall. Twenty-five centuries ago this was the Versailles of the "King of Kings", who spent the spring months here,* the winter at Susa, and the summer at Ecbatana, which is the modern town of Hamadan. The standing pillars are epical and terrific for they are nearly seventy feet high, only thirteen of them still erect of the seventy-two that formed the audience hall of Xerxes. Everywhere are figures of man-headed and winged bulls with curled beards, and sculptures of the "King of Kings" giving audience with a parasol held over his head, or fighting with winged gryphon and always winning. In one place only, the stone lintel of a window, is there a trace of the black marble walls which Herbert says were "so well polisht, that they equall for brightness a steele mirrour". The newly excavated processional stairway, however repetitive its sculptured figures, is interesting for the differences in dress between Medes and Persians, for its figures of warriors (as they still do in the Middle East)

* Persepolis is the Greek name. No one knows what was its Persian name.

leading each other by the hand, its carvings of Afghans and Hebrews and Ethiopians, and the two-humped Bactrian camels brought here as tribute from Central Asia. Scarcely less interesting is a case in the little museum full of spherical objects that are eyes fallen from many of the statues, now sightless, if we like to think that, in their old age. Near by, a handful of charred rags, falling to dust, are remains of the curtains of Persepolis, hangings of the Tyrian purple or scarlet, set on fire by Alexander after a drunken banquet. Burned, at least, by his orders.* Myself, I preferred that view from the platform of Persepolis into eternity, or into nothing, over the green plain.

We spent three nights at Persepolis which was ample time for exploring the ruins at all times of day and getting caught in a dramatic thunderstorm as we came down the hill from the Royal tombs. Never could a plain have looked more wonderful than in that thundrous light. It seemed to lie out into the ends of time. Down the hill we ran jumping over the stones and boulders, and took refuge in the director's garden which is built on to the museum. I have had the experience of a thunderstorm at Mycenae, coming out from the beehive tomb and seeing the lightning over the Argolid plain, and such a storm whether at Mycenae or Persepolis is the hour of ghosts. When we could get away the light was more golden than ever on the huge shattered columns and that cyclopaean terrace. Even the village below with its flat roofs looked picturesque enough with women in bright dresses putting things out again after the rain, and the hotel seemed to be the centre of world civilization as one got back into one's room. It has in fact comfortable bedrooms but the prices are excessive, all lights are turned out by a master switch at ten p.m., and on the principle that the second time it is repeated it becomes an offence there was more of the Shiraz wine. But even that ran out after the first night, and for the rest of our stay we drank bottled lemonade. Persepolis on its high platform is unendingly beautiful to look out upon, though like so many other ruins it is lovelier from a distance.

But not far away there is a work of art greater than any of the sculptures of Darius. And as it befell, we saw this in more appropriate circumstances than one could ever have wished or imagined. The

* When at Persepolis, it is of interest to recall the mosaic of the *Battle of Alexander*, found in the House of the Faun at Pompeii, and now in the Museum at Naples. It is a copy of an antique wall-painting by a famous painter, Philoxenus of Eretria, who in 315 B.C. made a painting of Alexander at the Battle of Issus which was fought eighteen years earlier, in 333 B.C. Only four colours are used in the mosaic, black, white, red, and yellow. Alexander, with his helmet fallen from his head, is attacking a Persian officer while Darius prepares to retreat in his war-chariot. There are eight Greeks and fifteen Persians in the mosaic, and as well as being one of the most remarkable relics of Greek painting it depicts the costume of both Greeks and Persians.

Sasanian rock-sculptures of Naqsh-e-Rostam are carved on the cliff face but a few miles away. Long before we came within sight of them we were caught up in a line of goats and camels, and could scarcely believe our good luck. What had been held out as a possibility ever since we arrived in Persia had come true. They were nomads on the way to their summer pastures. These were the Qashqai; the other main nomad tribe being the Bakhtiari, of which the father of the beautiful Queen Soraya is a chieftain.

By now we were below the cliff face. There are six or seven of the Sasanian bas-reliefs and four tombs of Achaemenid kings. Also, a tomb house in exact copy of a stone house of the ancient world. But let us be precise; Darius and Xerxes were Achaemenid kings; the Sasanians are much later, and the rock-sculptures date from the third century A.D. Of one, in particular, the impact is more than tremendous. I would say that it is as though one saw a rock-carving by Donatello in this valley below Persepolis. It is the Roman Emperor Valerian surrendering to the Sasanid Shapur I, or Sapor, who is carved three times life-size riding a giant war horse of Gattamelata or Colleoni breed.* The dress of the Sasanid is fascinating, if not a little frightening. His hair is frizzed out into huge curls; or does he wear a formal wig?—while his crown is surmounted by the enormous balloon-headdress which was the insignia of their kings. His chest, with huge necklace, and his arms look Indian (there is an obvious Indian as well as Roman influence in the sculptures); and he wears some form of fringed or fleece-like riding trousers, relating him to cowboy, gaucho, Red Indian on horseback, Cossack of the steppe, horseman of the puszta, or the feria, any and every kind of horseman; circus-rider not excluded. I want to stress his horseman, circus air.

All round him are other rock-sculptures; of Sasanian knights, nearly a thousand years before the joust, engaged at tournament;†

* The fate of Valerian, if true, is harrowing to read. He was defeated by Sapor in A.D. 260 in Mesopotamia, and in the words of Dr Lempriere of the *Classical Dictionary*, "when he wished to have a private conference with Sapor, the conqueror seized his person and carried him in triumph to his capital, where he exposed him, and in all the cities of his empire, to the ridicule and insolence of his subjects. When the Persian monarch mounted on horseback, Valerian served as footstool, and the many other insults which he suffered exited indignation even among the courtiers of Sapor. The monarch at last ordered him to be flayed alive, and salt to be thrown over his mangled body, so that he died in the greatest torments. His skin was tanned and painted in red, and that the ignominy of the Roman Empire might be lasting, it was nailed in one of the temples of Persia." A tendency among contemporary Persians to deny this history of cruelty as being contrary to the tendencies and character of the race is hardly borne out by the deeds of Nader Shah, or the ferocious conduct of Mohammad Agha, first of the Qajar dynasty, and a eunuch, who had the eyes of 11,000 of his countrymen plucked out after a siege, and, himself, counted them in a gory heap to be sure not one was missing.

† Not the least extraordinary find reported by M. Rostovtzeff in *Caravan Cities*

more kingly scenes with the hair balloon, or whatever it was, much in evidence; and figures that with their fluttering draperies could be Boddhisattvas, and not even Indian but Chinese. Certainly there is a Buddhist influence, too; the great and paramount importance of the carvings being that they are almost the last time the human figure is depicted before Islam put a stop to sculpture. At Naqsh-e-Rostam we see what was lost to the world by this embargo on the Middle East.

And turning round, for as far as the eyes could see in both directions there were the Qashqai nomads on the move, more and ever more of them, right at foot of the carving of the Sasanid in his muslin cowboy trousers and balloon turban, riding like a circus king. To see them go past in such a setting was one of the wonders of a lifetime; more so still for an *aficionado* like myself. Like a circus procession in the Elysian Fields they went by. Tribesmen in their distinctive Qashqai hats; baby camels trotting behind their awkward mothers; beautiful young girls, unveiled, which is a treat in itself in Moslem lands, riding as to the manner born, holding a lapful of baby kids; and matriarchs of the tribe passing like empresses or queens, but in the Gypsy manner, one of them in a bell-shaped, almost a ballet-skirt of peony red, others in green or purple, all with saddlecloths and splendid trappings of tassels nearly to the ground. The men shouting to the herds, and the noise of their camel-bells making a din and a clamour that died away into the dust.

For some distance we drove on, catching up with them, and they did not seem to mind. But there was little point in it. The head of the column must be several miles in front, and it had no centre or main body. It was better manners to turn back and worry them no more; and indeed after half a mile or so their column left the road, straggling endlessly out of the distance over that green plain. Coming up out of it, or so it appeared, but our road led away in the direction of Persepolis, and we lost them.

That same afternoon we returned to Shiraz, to the hotel with the flower garden and the wide verandah, and to the ministrations of the Eton-collared twins. We were to stay the night before flying back to

(1932) are the *graffii* found scratched upon the walls of Dura Europos, the fortress town on the Euphrates. One of them (p. 195) represents a knight clothed from head to foot in armour riding a horse which is protected by chain mail. "Writers", as he says, "have frequently referred to these Iranian knights, comparing them to statues, so immovable did they sit upon their mounts, but until these drawings came to light not a single picture of these early forerunners of the Knights of the Middle Ages had come down to us." This remark is perhaps not quite true, in view of the bas reliefs of Naqsh-e-Rostam. And it is a line which could be continued in direct descent, it may be, down to the quilted and chain-mailed horsemen who still form the bodyguard of the Emirs of Northern Nigeria and the French Sudan.

Bridge of Allahverdi Khan at Isfahan

Persepolis, the great platform

Tehran. Having seen something of Shiraz we did not go down to the town again, but spent the late afternoon in the garden and looking down through the cypresses to the distant domes and minarets.* It is dark early in those southern latitudes, quite dark before it is time for dinner, and after that one sits on the terrace, talking and listening to the fountain, the garden as I have said being lit extravagantly as though for some festival. To-morrow the Persian part of our journey would be nearly over and we would be back in Tehran for a day or two of packing and collecting visas and exit permits. Never again could one come to Persia. It was the one chance of a lifetime. And before mid-night, no doubt delighting in the contrast and in the sense of power, the twins—for surely it was they!—turned out all the lights in the garden and it was time to go to bed.

At about half-past three in the morning while it was still dark I woke up hoping to hear the *muezzins*, and listened for them, and heard instead some curious and confused shouting from down in the town, but there are always such noises at night in Oriental cities. This sounded as though a beggar or two in different parts of Shiraz had got hold of a microphone and was amplifying his complaints and grievances to the night air, and I must have fallen asleep again.

What I heard next was while half-asleep and half-awake, a scurrying and a confused shouting, but not continuously, only at intervals every now and again, and in midst of a murmuring and a busy and a warm vibrating and a clappering, a ringing, that was it, a lolling and a clashing, a ringing of metal and a swinging or a striking of it, now coming louder and louder, and going by, passing by the gate, a per-petual scurry of animal feet and a straying and a shouting that I remem-bered from the morning. It must be the main body of the Qashqai moving by night through Shiraz; and I got out of bed and went on the balcony to listen to it, still half-asleep.

All was dark. There was not even a light burning at the gate. I went back, and came out again to listen. One could see nothing, and only hear the scurrying and shouting when a goat or a camel strayed from the road and had to be run after and driven back into the flock. They were passing the gate of the hotel for two hours at least without pause or intermission, during which time hundreds or even thousands of Qashqai and their camels and goats, riding and on foot, must have gone by, and of course I should have dressed and gone out to look at them.

---

* In *A Tower of Skulls*, London, Duckworth & Co., 1932, pp. 106, 107, Mr Gerald Reitlinger finds the *mot juste*. They are "odd blue-tiled domes, shaped like mangel-wurzels". But he, and other writers, say there are no minarets, though I seem to remem-ber that there are.

6

What nocturnal beauties was one missing? Moth-like empresses and queens, dark and disdainful, crow-faced princesses of the Gypsies; young girls of the green plain and the rocky valleys riding in the night when their sisters of the cabarets and night clubs were tiring; camels, ambling awkwardly, and goats kid-like or saturnine? While I lay awake the goat bells and camel bells were as loud as church bells, like a curfew or a tocsin, different of intent, but a sound like no other sound since I heard ten thousand pairs of castanets played by the women and children of Seville as they walked at sundown to the Feria, playing as they went along.

Still they came past, in silence but for the shouting when a goat or a camel left the road, the noise of their bells even louder and more insistent, now like a droning, a loud and steady murmuring and throbbing, but a soothing and a lulling, for I fell asleep again with the sound ringing in my ears. In the morning there was no sign of them. We tried to follow them by car for some ten miles but they had gone on, or vanished. Our aeroplane, starting from Bushire upon the Gulf, was delayed and we had to sit about and wait. When at last we started, it touched down at Isfahan for long enough for us to see the blue domes in the distance, but no bigger than pinheads or points of blue light, and an hour or two after that we were back in Tehran.

## Postscript

AT the time of writing, a most interesting book has just appeared: *Lords of the Mountains*, by Marie Thérèse Ullens de Schooten, Chatto & Windus, Ltd. Its subject is the Qashqai who, she says, have spelt their tribal name Kashka'i, Gashghai, or Quashgu'ai, but by decision of their Chieftain the Il Khan, Nasser Khan, have quite recently decided to adopt the simpler spelling of Gashgai. The name derives from "Kasha", meaning a horse with a white star on its forehead, or else it implies that they came from Kashgar in the wake of Hulagu. They are of Turkish language and race. Migration always takes place in the early morning, their terrain being country that lies close to the Persian Gulf. Wintering in the warmer regions round Firuzabad and Kazarun, where the country averages two thousand feet, in April when the heat becomes extreme they move by stages, past Shiraz, to their summer pastures, going to graze on the slopes of the Zagros chain, at an altitude of twelve to fifteen thousand feet. The Qashqai is the largest migration of any Persian nomad tribe, and it involves some four hundred thousand men, women and children, and about seven million head of cattle. The saddlecloths which we noticed must be the "gaily-chequered blankets decorated with tufts of wool, called *Jajim*", that Mme Ullens de Schooten mentions, and are not the same as the pileless rugs called *Ghilims* or *Gelims*. Her book is remarkable for its beautiful photographs of the nomads, many of them in colour.

# CHAPTER VI

## DAMASCUS AND PALMYRA

*Farewell to Tehran — A thousand miles in three hours to Damascus — View over the city — Wonderful figures in the souks — Mosque of the Omayyads — Mosaics of kiosques and pavilions along the river Barada — Echoes of ancient Ephesus — Classical entrance to the Mosque — Museum of Damascus — How to get to Palmyra? — Desk and counter-desk — The flag captain — Mosque of Soltan Selim — Azem Palace — Silk brocades — The Ghûta — Apricots of Damascus — Desert drive — Hunting castle of the Caliphs — Palmyra at last — Temple of Bel — Carvings of camel riders — Colonnaded street — Palmyrene tombs — Mummies wrapped in silks from China — A sinister châtelaine and her train of tragedies — Return to Damascus — Night club on the Abana — Frogs' legs of Chtaura — Down the mountains to Beirut.*

IF anything, Persia is more difficult to leave than to enter. There are endless complications to do with exit visas. Perhaps it was our own fault for we had changed our air tickets in order to come down at Damascus instead of Beirut. In order to do this it was necessary to have a Syrian visa. We had already a Lebanese visa in our passports, and Syria and Lebanon are "sister republics" which in theory means that one visa will do for both countries, but as in many human families there is nevertheless a certain touchiness in their relations with each other, and we were warned to be circumspect. It was a Saturday and we were to leave at dawn on Sunday morning. Our Chancellery Office where so much energy and kindness had been shown on our behalf closed at midday, just the hour at which in a mood of southern indolence the Syrians had announced that they would give the visas. And this was the hour precisely at which the police desisted from their duties in the matter of granting exit permits, and the distracted clerks in the air office announced that it might be necessary for me to follow the Chief of Police into the country where he spent the weekend in order to persuade him to give us the necessary permission to go away.

All this, with packing in prospect and the strain of saying goodbye to friends, produced a mood of acute distraction in which I almost forgot to take notice of the tame pelican "Alfredo" in the garden of the house where I was lunching, a bird who—so strong an individuality must be given human rights and not addressed as "which"!—has evolved, as already described, his own method of dealing with unnecessary diplomatic papers and documents, by swallowing them whole. When

84

the storm of anxiety had abated a little, or lulled itself till it broke out afresh early next morning at the airport, it was proably due to hypnotic suggestion from "Alfredo" that we went off in a taxi to have tea with our friend Mme Moghadam in her beautiful old house and were driven instead, by mistake, to the house of the Chief of the Police who is her husband's cousin. He was on the steps of his house and about to "leave for the country", but my nerves were too harrowed to mention the question of exit permits when he very charmingly asked us in to tea, and we drove off leaving him standing at his door in his dashing uniform rather like that of a Spanish general, without telling him how nearly we might have had to come and bother him on business.

Next morning the Consul-General most kindly came in person to the airport and added the weight of his authority in helping us to get away. And almost before we could realize what was happening it was time to shake hands and say goodbye. It was the last of Persia, but only the beginning of other marvels of the Middle East. We flew back in a wonderful Pan-American D.C. Six which went on to Paris and across the Atlantic to New York and Chicago; breakfasting above the snowy mountains, smoking cigarettes over the desert at three hundred and thirty miles an hour, and arriving at Damascus after a journey of nearly a thousand miles in three hours. Before luncheon we are in one of the most famous and ancient cities in the East. In fact, it is often said that Damascus is the oldest inhabited city in the world.

I have to say that the first view of it is more than a little disappointing. There is a terrace with Arab cafés from which you look down on the town, but it cannot compare with looking down on Fez, with its old walls, white houses climbing up and down on hills, green-tiled minarets, and flat roofs where women in bright dresses take the sunset air. Neither does it compare with the spectacle of Marrakesh, a huge African city in an oasis of date-palms, or even with the green-tiled roofs of Meknez. But the Arab music from the cafés is persistent. There are mosques down below with Turkish minarets that are shaped like needles, and we see roads leading for miles straight out of Damascus, to Aleppo, to Jerusalem, and back over the desert to Baghdad. All round lie the orchards of the Ghûta where we will go in the evening, a living paradise in these parched lands, with its little running streams, where the walnut trees are in leaf, the apricots were in blossom only a week or so ago, and now the pomegranates are in flower.

What is marvellous in Damascus is the great Mosque of the Omayyads, and it grows the more wonderful with every step you get nearer to it. For the way leads through the bazaar or *souk*. Here you have humanity as you may never hope to see it again. One wonders in astonishment where they all come from for there is little sign of them in the modern town. There are Druzes from the mountains in white turbans of peculiar shape. With their beards and fine aquiline noses, and from the way they sit or stand, they call for a painter of the stature of Carpaccio all to themselves. And now at our elbow there is a group of Bedouin women, more picturesque than any Gypsies, with earrings and necklaces of golden coins, dressed in smoky black as though dyed in the smoke of their own camp fires, with under-garments showing, of smouldering, then flaming scarlet, or bright green, and all of them with tribal tattoo marks in light blue or purple on their tawny faces.

At this moment a motor, hooting loudly, comes down the middle of the street pushing pedestrians on to the pavement. We dive into a dark tunnel leading off it, and hung from end to end and roof to floor with tinselled slippers, emerging from that into the goldsmith's *souk* where we are jostled by veiled women. Arabs in black or brown *burnouses* with corded headdresses wander along, holding each other by the hand. Here are more women in white sheets, cowled like nuns, and with frilled pantaloons showing above their slippers. Arabs from other villages have black and white tartan headcloths trailing over their shoulders, and there are women of a particular group of villages in apricot-coloured mantles with black stripes. All and every sort of baggy trouser is to be admired. There are fezzes and turbans, and now again a molla in black headdress, bearded, and leaning on his walking-stick. All in the striped sunlight, and we look up and notice that the roof is made, incongruously, of corrugated tin. And now appears a magnificent contrast for as we come to the main entrance to the mosque, a white and classical vision of cornice and architrave carved in stone with leaves and garlands hangs above us, of Greco-Roman architecture, either a fragment of the Roman Temple of Jupiter, or part of the church of Theodosius I which stood upon the site. This relic of Roman splendour is of wonderful effect, traversing the centuries as though nothing lay between, and bringing to that Oriental scene, as it were, a touch of the Venetian Renaissance and of Palladio.

And now for the Mosque of the Omayyads, which entails the tying on of slippers or *babouches* over our shoes in midst of a seething crowd of German tourists. The court is great and glorious beyond words, with two-storeyed arcades round it, but we must turn and look up immediately above us for here are the mosaics recently uncovered under the plaster. There are remains of them elsewhere under and on the face of the arcades, but this is where they are best preserved. There is nothing else like them. They are unique. The Greek craftsmen of the eighth century working to the Caliph's orders could not make use of the human figure. There are no saints, or soldiers, or Virgins. Instead, the mosaics are an architectural fantasy of bridges and kiosques and pavilions, and villages or individual houses built on rocks or crags, all in an umbrageous valley of plane trees and date palms which may, perhaps, portray the surrounding plain or Ghûta of Damascus. A certain bridge in the mosaic has been taken for the bridge over the river Barada,* the "golden stream" or Chrysorrhoas of the Greeks, a bridge with shops and houses on it, like old London Bridge, or the Ponte Vecchio at Florence. What is fascinating in the mosaic is the purposeful foreshortening and distortion, a proof of centuries of experience behind the craftsmen. What we behold is a vision of classical building twelve centuries later than the Parthenon, after architecture had gone through phases which are paralleled in Vanbrugh, in Bernini, and in Borromini. We are looking at echoes of great classical Oriental towns like Ephesus or Antioch. When we read that Antioch had streets of columns with double colonnades, one of them four miles long and crossing the city from East to West; that Diocletian built a gigantic palace on an island in the Orontes; that this island later given over entirely to theatres and pleasure haunts was connected with the rest of the town by no fewer than five bridges; and that the Chinese had commercial relations with Antioch which they regarded as the capital of the Roman world, I believe we know the true derivation of the kiosques and pavilions in the mosaics of Damascus.

The Mosque, itself, still shows clear evidence of the Christian basilica of the Emperor Theodosius with its three rows of Corinthian columns that form a nave and aisles. There are rugs and carpets in profusion on which Oriental figures are sitting or lying in magnificent abandon with all their lives in front of them and nothing else to do. There can be no mosque more venerable than the Omayad at Damascus, in the knowledge that its Caliphs were rulers of half the known world as far as distant Córdoba in Spain. We are in the heart and centre of Islam, the full extent of which in the other direction towards the East is apparent when we remember that Tamerlane, taking Damascus in 1400, carried off its renowned swordsmiths and armourers and established them at Samarcand.

Midday in the Mosque is of marvellous effect because of the *muezzins* calling down from the minarets, one of which is a most beautiful specimen of the Egyptian-Saracenic style, octagonal in form

---

* Barada, meaning "cold", is the Abana of the Old Testament. The river which flows through the great panel of mosaic is more than a hundred feet long.

with three balconies or galleries. Then there are the various domed structures, raised on pillars and standing in the great court of the Mosque, being fountains for ablutions or treasure houses (with nothing in them?), but they cannot fail to remind one of the domed pulpit in St Mark's in Venice, which if one is lucky enough to have first seen it as a child forever remains a foretaste of the turban'd East. In the middle of the transept is another domed pavilion said to contain St John the Baptist's head, with prayers being said fervently at its latticed grilles, and obviously the cause of much fanatical feeling. Theodosius had built his church to contain a casket with the Baptist's head, and it is curious to think that after the Arab conquest of Damascus Christians and Moslems shared the church for over a century and came into it by the same entrance which is that Roman gate, the Moslems using half of the church for their mosque. Always, and every time one enters it, there are wonderful figures to be seen, and the flashing white cornice and architrave are never to be forgotten, suggesting, as they do, not the play but the reality of *Antony and Cleopatra* performed with fair skinned actors among the darker crowd. As we come away through the *souks* among the women in their apricot and black striped mantles we may be reminded more than ever of the painted architecture and Oriental figures of the Palazzo Labia where Tiepolo portrayed the banquet of the Egyptian Queen. But the vision fades, and there is the roof of corrugated tin, a result of General Sarrail's unnecessary and hysterical bombardment of the city in 1925. Certainly no *souks* in the world rival these of Damascus; not those of Aleppo, nor Tunis. And coming out of that dark broad tunnel into the light, an Arab who cannot be less than an Emir rides past on a fine Arab horse, surrounded by his retinue. But in a few moments all that is beautiful of Damascus is gone and we are in the modern city, which nevertheless has shop windows full of appetizing food for which Syria and Lebanon are famous, most of it in the form of hors d'oeuvres or sweets.

We may be led to think that Damascus, so old a city, has little left to show. There is a Museum, splendidly installed and full of interesting things, including an early fresco'd synagogue dating from about the third century after Christ, which was found walled up at Dura Europos on the Euphrates and has been rebuilt here. The paintings are classical in manner and naturally Jewish in subject, but curiously Russian in effect, so that it would be no surprise to be told this was a synagogue of the tenth century found near Kiev. But as a historical building, however obscure, it is of absorbing interest because of the possibility that Christ entered exactly similar buildings and saw the crude paintings. But how much more has this Museum, besides? A most curious series of fresco painting found at Dura Europos, near the Euphrates, of Mithraic subjects, perhaps, but what are remarkable are the conical white headdresses of the priests, and the sensation that this is a mysterious, an unknown iconography.* As well there is the silver mask from Emesa, or it is the face-piece of a classical helmet, but it is obviously a portrait, and oddly Red Indian in physical type, as though the mask of a Red Indian warrior. In short, this Museum of Damascus is a place of surprises; not least in the gate towers of an eighth century hunting castle of the Caliphs which have been rebuilt, stone by stone, a castle not less romantically exciting than that of *La Belle au bois dormant* for it is in unknown style, perhaps not unrelated to the castles of the Sasanids and one has to imagine for oneself the hunting parties that rode out from its gate, hawk on wrist, or tabbied cheetah on the saddle, and what nightly entertainment of dancing and dancers took place within. The ambassadors sent by Harun-er-Rashid to Charlemagne, scarcely a generation later, must have known hunting castles such as this. But there are the relics of so many gone and vanished civilizations in this Museum, including an extraordinary series of "comic strip" cartoons carried out with inlay of mother-of-pearl and coming from Mari on the Euphrates, in the far corner of that triangular piece of Syria which reaches over the desert towards Iraq, on the borders, therefore, of what of old was Mesopotamia. It is as though some one Semitic individual with a talent for caricature had brought light into darkness, and his sleight of hand had become the tradition which was rigorously kept to as if the inhabitants thought they were practising a convention as long lasting as that of ancient Egypt. Further, there are caricature statues almost of the nature of Jewish music hall jokes against themselves, depicting pastoral gods with enormous dark polyp eyes and exaggeratedly Semitic features, dressed in fleeced skirts and come straight from the sheep shearing and the bleating of the flocks, Abraham-like figures from a promised land. And even this does not end the treasures of this Museum of Damascus which must be the most interesting collection of objects and works of art in the Middle East.

In the meantime a drama of comic import was developing in the modern and comfortable hotel, its theme an expedition to Palmyra. The hotel, it should be explained, is run by Palestinian Arabs who are refugees, but it does not take long to discover that they are born and bred to all the mythical tricks and wiles of Petticoat Lane. They have, in

* "The sacrifice is being conducted by impressive-looking priests, who wear tall white, conical hats recalling those of the Persian magi or modern dervishes." (M. Rostortzeff, *Caravan Cities*, pp. 192, 193.)

fact, the legendary faults of the Jews without their virtues, and are as interested in money but lack the talent and are bad at it. The hall of the hotel has two desks; the reception at which the clerks had the manner and air, at once, of gambler and croupier, and the desk of the concierge. And here I must digress in order to say that no one who has seen it with his own eyes would believe the degree of "latinity", if that is the right word for it, achieved by the *élite* or the *jeunesse doré* of desk and counter in the two lands of Syria and Lebanon. It would be impossible for instance ever to forget the motor salesmen grouped in or outside a car mart in Beirut every time we went by, with their pressed suits, trouser creases on which you could cut your finger, the rings on their hands, their flashing and illusioned or disillusioned smiles, and curled and oiled hair; club members in some Champs Elysées of the spirit, next door to the night club and the Lido. The reception clerks in the hotels were no less polished in manner; they were, if I am correctly understood, like Oriental-Romans and, I have said, playboys and gamblers until it came to adding up your bill. I remember waiting in the hall one morning when as though to a given signal the clerks made a concerted rush to a window giving on to the street, and following them, half-expecting to see a caparisoned elephant, camel caravan, or other wonder of the East, what I saw was a young woman getting out of a motor and crossing the street into the Post Office. This is where they behave with a naïveté which is the sign of recent emancipation, and the young woman with her mascara'd face, high heels, and tottering walk was as Oriental as themselves, if rather beautiful in an alluring way. But to return to Palmyra . . . We knew the trip could be done by aeroplane, which went once a week. But at both desks, now working in concert together, they denied all knowledge of an aeroplane, and only smiled wanly when told this was exactly what we had been warned that they would say. With a shrug of the shoulders, as though implying, "We are sorry, but you can order the aeroplane for yourselves, and pay for it." And at one desk, and then the other, we were told we could hire a car for two hundred Syrian pounds (about £20). Immediately after which the chief booking clerk, following me into the dining room, whispered one hundred and ninety Syrian pounds in my ear. And there we were in the care of more Palestinian Arabs and a head waiter from the Djebel Druze.

In the late afternoon a new character entered upon the scene. The owner of "Alfredo" had given us a letter to a diplomatic colleague in Damascus, and it seemed a good plan to ask if their chauffeur knew of a car which we could hire to take us to Palmyra. By this time in a kind of infatuation I had abandoned even attempting to find out if there was an aeroplane. The chauffeur had already driven us round Damascus in the morning, and now appeared again immaculate in his white summer livery with gold epaulettes, and a cap like that of a flag captain in some Utopian navy where war was long forgotten and the only duty was courtesy and attention to the ladies. At the same time he was like an eagle dressed up as a naval officer with his aquiline nose and "Kaiser" moustache, and it was almost embarrassing to have to descend to sordid details of money with him. But his nominee was waiting outside and he called him in, unashamed, and said the price was one hundred and seventy Syrian pounds. In something near to a hypnotic trance I at once agreed and ordered the car to be at the hotel at half-past six the next morning. The eagle-chauffeur saluted debonairly, as though releasing his spell over me, and withdrew into the outer sunshine. At once the chief booking-clerk came up and enquired, pityingly, how much I was paying. Why had I not listened to him when he offered a car for a hundred and fifty, and when I reminded him that he had said a hundred and ninety he shrugged again as though to say I must have known quite well it was not his last price and he would take less.

All this time a furious intermezzo was playing at the concierge's desk where I was trying to change a traveller's cheque, and the concierge in his own words was telephoning to the moneylender to find out the exchange. This had been in progress at intervals all through the day with fluctuating results, as though according to whim, but now the moment of reckoning had come and insisting on the highest offer I began working out the sum involved on a sheet of paper, only to find the concierge looking over my shoulder and making guesses at the amount, revealing that he could neither read nor write. He, then, made a last despairing offer of a car for a hundred and thirty Syrian pounds to go to Palmyra and back, but I was now beginning to enjoy the game and told him we would decide when we came in.

For there is one other building of tranquillity and beauty, the more memorable for seeing it amid those arguments and bargainings, the Mosque of Soltan Selim, which is next to the Museum, a mosque entirely in Turkish style, the work I would say, for I do not know for certain, of Sinan, the architect who built the mosques that make so magnificent and unforgettable a spectacle against the skyline as you arrive by sea at Istanbul. One of the great architects of the world, it is certain; a mysterious personage, a Janissary and military engineer by training, no one knows of what nation, Greek, or Albanian, or Armenian, who built more than a hundred mosques all over Turkey between his fiftieth and his ninetieth year, and who in his capacity as a figure of the Renaissance had correspondence with the painter Titian. The Mosque of Soltan Selim has what I would describe as a divinity of rest and repose from worry in the Oriental mood, qualities in which Sinan, as we will see him at Istanbul, is supreme master and thaumaturge, or healer of the soul and spirit. He achieves this in the middle of noisy Damascus by simple means, an open cloister of arches, a prayer chamber like an open pavilion, a fountain for ablutions, and his usual multitude of little domes. As you walk under the cypresses, longing to stay and rest awhile, you know how and why Turkey slumbered on the Bosphorus for so many hundreds of years.

And now, delayed in the Mosque of Soltan Selim as was its purpose and object, there is little time for anything more. There are one or two old houses, one of them the Azem palace, with horrible waxwork figures wearing old costumes; there are the tomb of Saladin and the Street called Straight. But all are time wasted when one could be spending it in the *souks*. If one only had the money one would buy hundreds of yards of Damascus silks, for no particular purpose but only because they are so beautiful with their Persian or Syrian designs and gold or silver thread. This local industry, once so famous, was revived owing to a chance suggestion made by Arthur Upham Pope, and we were told that the designs are made in Switzerland. It is only a pity, as suggested elsewhere in this present book, that with all the technique at their disposal Sasanian and Byzantine silks from the Imperial work-shops are not copied and put on sale. Hand-looms, though, are no longer in use and the industry is carried on in small factories. Nevertheless, except for the silk brocades woven in Kyōto and worn by the Kabuki players, which are marvellous for their changing "shot" effects, the silk fabrics of Damascus rival the finest silks of Lyons. One dealer, in particular, has a regular warehouse of these wonders with an enormous stock of the brocades carried out in different colours. Cups of Turkish coffee are brought, and we begin to lose our heads and buy.

In the evening there is the Ghûta to drive in. It lies for some five or six miles in either direction along the river Barada, which flows in seven channels through the oasis and along conduits and watercourses beyond number. Everywhere in the Ghûta one hears the sound of running water. Looking down on the city from that terrace one sees Damascus in the middle of this watered orchard for that is the Ghûta, no more, nor less. It is this as much as anything else, and equally with the wonderful figures to be seen wandering, or sitting cross-legg'd at their counters in the *souks*, which makes Damascus into an Oriental city. For it is their conception of paradise to be among fruit trees and streams of flowing water, and after the howling deserts which take up so much of Persia, Arabia, and North Africa, the Ghûta is as beautiful to them as are green hills and snow covered mountains to a Dutchman. It does not need the sight of a minaret to know one is in the Orient, as much so as when looking down over the oasis of date palms that surrounds Marrakesh.* We had driven through the Ghûta on a previous occasion late in March when the fruit trees were just losing their blossom, and now it was early in May and full summer. It is for its apricots, in particular, that the Ghûta is famous; fruit which is, also, pressed and dried, and sold in thin cakes somewhat resembling the *membrillo* (dried quince) of the Spaniards to which it is most certainly, racially related. Whether, or not, the special varieties of apricots grown round Damascus have been examined, there are, also, water melons and several kinds of delicious grapes in the autumn. It may be that here, as at Aleppo, and at Meshed, there are varieties of fruits that have not been studied. Not a foot of land is uncultivated in the Ghûta. It is as close worked as the allotments and small holdings outside Paris. A little disappointing in itself to someone coming from the green gardens of the West, but beautiful because of the pleasure and wonder its fruitfulness afford to eyes and minds parched with the glare of rocks and sand.

Of which we were to have out fill next day, going to Palmyra. Only the night porter was awake when we left the hotel at half-past six, so we had not to run the gauntlet from the concierge and booking-clerks. For going to Palmyra, and back, in a day, by road, is not a trip. It is an expedition. The distance is a hundred and forty miles, each way, over terrible roads. At the start it was a delight to see the Ghûta so early in the morning, except for lorries driving into Damascus at furious speed having travelled all night long for coolness. They were coming from Homs and Hama and Aleppo, all of them towns in the north of Syria, and almost as soon as we were out of the Ghûta our road leads off to the east over the desert towards Baghdad. Indeed,

* No less Arabian of effect, though its elm trees were only planted at the end of the eighteenth century, is the wood of the Alhambra at Granada, kept fresh and green by the waters of the Darro, where the sound of running water is heard day and night. The singing of the nightingales is natural accompaniment to those courts of filigree and stalactite, to the fountains of the Generalife, and the view from the mirador to the Gypsy caves and blue cactus hedges of the Albaicín, whence comes the sound of guitars and handclapping and the beat of dancing. The palm grove of Elche, too, is no less Oriental than the Ghûta of Damascus, with its water channels and the pomegranates growing under and between the date palms; while the Baroque façade of the cathedral in golden stone takes its place by some alchemy as naturally in that Oriental scene as the classical cornice and architrave of white stone at the entrance to the Mosque of the Omayyads: all, or any of these, being so much evidence of how beautiful the world of human hands can be.

Palmyra is just half-way, a hundred and twenty-five miles in either
direction, from the Euphrates and the Mediterranean, and this is the
reason, precisely, for its fame and riches. There is an asphalt road
through the Ghûta to a town just out of the valley and then the stones
begin. By eight o'clock in the morning we were deep in the desert,
a vast plain with little tufts of vegetation already dried up and desic-
cated, but as important to the landscape as the myrtle bushes or low
growing trees of Piero della Francesca's *Nativity* in the National
Gallery. The far off mountains were intangible and as impersonal as
the mountains of the moon. There were no flowers, no birds, although
we searched the telegraph wires where they love to perch, and only
the black tent or two of a nomad family—how far away? An hour,
perhaps two hours' walk over the burning plain—and then there was a
figure beside the road, and it was a woman beckoning to us to stop.
A Bedouin woman who had lost her horse, and she climbed into the
car and we drove for some twenty minutes till she sighted it, no bigger
than a black speck, and got out to trail after it, and may have had a
difficult time catching it, but that we never knew for, by then, we
were some miles ahead. Most of the rest of the day she must have spent
riding it back to her tent, as though a day in her life was no more
valuable than a day in the life of a horse, or donkey, but in France
"the most civilized country in the world", as one is so often reminded,
how many old women does one not see by the side of the road whose
whole lives are spent in sitting, knitting, and looking after a solitary,
individual cow!

Presently there was, at least, a flower growing, but only rarely, and
at the rate of one or two a mile, an erect yellowish *eremurus*-like spike
of little florets, and I got out to pick one, and it pulled up straight out
of the sandy soil with a club-like base or fundament and no root, from
which I conclude that it was some kind of parasitic plant growing
in the root of another. It held in the hand like a thyrsus, rather evil
smelling, and was soon thrown out of the window. There were no
other flowers, except blood-red anemones. After a time we were going
over firm sand which was far better than the stony road, and one
could choose one's way a hundred or two hundred yards from the
track. It was possible to go quite fast over this plain of sand which
was, here, as utterly desolate as the Sahara. Indeed, crossing the Sahara
from West to East, from Casablanca in Morocco to Leptis Magna in
Libya, in the spring of 1939, we saw no stretch of it more utterly
forlorn than this. At rather more than a hundred miles, and four hours
from Damascus, we passed the ruins of that hunting castle of Quasr-el-
Heir from which the entrance towers have been taken and rebuilt in

the Museum at Damascus, a work of the Omayyad Caliphs early in the eighth century A.D., but its crenellations are those exactly of the processional stairway of Darius at Persepolis, while they closely resemble the crenellation or cresting of the Doges' Palace. What manner of life did its inmates lead? Another of the hunting castles, parts of the decorations of which are in the Museum of Jerusalem, has Salome-like paintings of nude dancers. The castles are not far from the Mediterranean, but they are Oriental, Sasanian, or Persian in feeling, achieved just in time before the blight came down and the Abbasid Caliphs forbade all representation of animals or human beings. The first century of Islam was the true and authentic era of the Arabian Nights.*

The next sensation of the glaring, featureless heat was the approach of a line of telegraph wires coming in from the direction of Homs to the north-west, our own telegraph poles having left us and gone off somewhere else at a point I never identified for I failed to miss them. It had the effect of a relief expedition coming to our rescue for the whole of this way after leaving the Ghûta we had only passed two lorries. There were cement lock-ups spaced out at long intervals, that is what they looked like, but they were clearly storehouses where tools and gear were kept. And now we had the telegraph poles to run in front of us all the way to Palmyra. Yet, where was Palmyra? For it was after half-past eleven and there was no sign of it, and we had been told it was a run of five and a half hours each way. But we were nearing the end of a valley where low hills narrowed in, and the road climbed to a little pass which was no more than a few hundred feet above the plain. Coming down over the shoulder of those hills a great mass of ruins suddenly appeared a mile or two ahead beyond the green palm trees of a considerable oasis, with the desert stretching out into infinity beyond them for more than a hundred miles towards the Euphrates. From lower down there were towers dotted here and there, which must be the tomb-towers of the Palmyrenes, there was a castle in ruins on a hill, and the pillars of an immensely long colonnade as though leading from end to end, or straight through the middle of something, with an enormous block of ruins on a square base or platform in the distance. The columns were of ripe apricot colour, while the Temple of Bel, for that must be it, was whiter in tone.

By now, we were passing the palm trees behind the mud walls of the modern village, more aware than ever of how hot it was and that there was a fierce wind blowing which raised squalls of dust. One knew, too,

---

* The façade of the hunting palace of Mshatta, another of the Saracen desert castles, is now in the Kaiser Friederich Museum in Berlin. It invokes stylistic problems of a fascinating nature.

how tired one was after nearly six hours of motoring over sharp stones. In a few moments we were near enough to the colonnade to see its Corinthian columns in detail, and coming round the corner of the village towards the great temple ended up at a hut where the custodian waited and tickets were sold.* Here we unpacked our picnic but could not eat in the room owing to the myriad flies, nor outside owing to the blazing, perpendicular heat of midday with the sun immediately over-head in the flaring, flaying wind. So we ate in gasps, standing, and waving away the flies that settled on one's wrist and sleeve, bit one's feet through the holes for the shoelaces, and landed hopefully, only to spring off again, on a sheet of paper covering a slice of bread, or on the rim of an empty tumbler.

The heat in the ruins of the Temple of Bel, only a few feet away, was as loud as some glorious noise or din. It echoed or reverberated off the paving stones of the court, which were so hot one could hardly keep one's feet on them. We are on a huge paved ramp or platform which was once fifty feet high above the plain. What a strange marriage of the Semitic and the classical for Bel was their sun-god; this pavement is like the flooring of any Roman site; the capitals of the columns are Corinthian; the fragments of frieze and architrave lying among the stones are Greco-Roman; but the carved figures on the bas-reliefs are wholly Oriental, and more so still, they are markedly Semitic! One of the great limestone beams from the cella of the temple, now lying on the ground, but once part of the pediment, shows Aglibol the moon-god, in Roman military dress, "wearing the lunar crescent on his shoulder", hand-in-hand with Malakbel the sun-god and fertility-god in company with his pine-cones and pomegranates and goat-kids, and his emblem of a cypress tree. Near to this is another part of the limestone frieze with a carving of a camel carrying a covered pavilion on its back which according to one authority† was painted red, and out of which projected an object, probably a *baetyl*, i.e. a sacred stone and a symbol of the god. The camel driver and the figures in the foreground are in native dress, a tunic over which a fringed blanket is wrapped, while the women the same authority observes are "completely hidden under long veils", proving that "the use of the veil was prior to Islam and that these were perhaps religious vestments". Later it is suggested that "the idol was sheltered in a

* Written on the day when it is announced in the newspaper that Hardwick Hall has been taken over by the National Trust, which means tickets will be sold in the front hall. Now tickets are necessary everywhere, from the Parthenon to Persepolis, and from the secularized Santa Sophia to the, formerly, remote and beautiful Hardwick Hall.

† *Palmyra*, by J. Starcky and Marrajjed, English edition, published by the Directorate-General of Antiquities, Damascus, 1948.

Bas-relief at Persepolis

Darius under his sunshade, Persepolis

A gateway at
Persepolis

pavilion of red leather, the *Qobba*, which is nothing other than a portable ritual niche". Is this not the same in principle as a portable *mehrab* which after all is a "prayer niche"? And what else is "the pyramidal wooden erection, called the Mahmal, hung with beautifully embroidered stuffs and carried by a camel", which accompanies or used to accompany, the Mecca caravan when it set out from Cairo with the Holy Carpet? The interior of the Mahmal was empty, and to the outside of it were attached two copies of the Koran? Elsewhere among the fallen stones are curious figures of *méharistes* or camel riders, who but for the absence of firearms are the equivalent of a camel corps.

Advancing into the precincts of the temple, itself, the effect is more Oriental and more Semitic still, although cast in classical idiom, but the accent is very strange indeed. It is no surprise to be told by the same authority that the pedestal of a statue from the temple bears the inscription: "This is the statue of Lishamsh, son of Taibbol, son of Shokaibol of the Bene Komara." Aramaic was the spoken and written language of the Palmyrenes (in an alphabet of their own contrivance), but the merchants and traders spoke Greek and Latin, also. It was their fashionable affectation to wear Parthian dress, the dynasty reigning in Persia (the Arsacids) being Parthian, and their costume, therefore, an adaptation of the woollen leggings worn by nomads from the Central Asian steppes. Palmyra, as so many writers have reiterated, had trading-counters or agencies all over the East, on the Danube, in Spain and in Gaul, in Rome and on the Persian Gulf, and some of its merchants were ship owners on the Indian Ocean.*

The temple of Bel, which is of course roofless, has sanctuaries to either side, a feature peculiar to Phoenician and Babylonian temples, for the Greeks and Romans put the statues of their gods on pedestals while the Semitic races hid their's in niches, and in instances of extreme holiness, as with Jehovah, preferred not to mention the deity by name. Both portals with their classical detail and curious Semitic undertones and treatment are as rich and exuberant as anything that remains at Baalbek or Leptis Magna, being in the full tide of Greco-Roman ornament of the second or third century A.D. The two sanctuaries are still sufficiently intact to be dark in their interior, which gives them a hoary air of sacrificial offerings and of burnt flesh, the more extraordinary when one considers that the temple has been a Christian church in its time and was the village mosque from the twelfth century

---

* One of the inscribed brackets in the Agora at Palmyra bore a statue of Marcus Ulpius Yarhai who owned a factory at Spasinou-Charax on the Persian Gulf, while another statue to the same individual with his curious mingling of Latin and Semitic names (no fewer than ten statues in all were erected to him) was subscribed to by merchants who had come back from India on board one of his ships.

7

down to 1929. Both of the cellars have their stone ceilings still as though they could be put back to the worship of Bel the sun-god in a few moments.

When one emerges from the temple one gets the full impression of its porticos, ranges of pillars which are still intact in several places. There were in all as many as four hundred of the columns, nearly all of which, according to the local custom, the Palmyrenes having a mania for statuary, have a bracket or a pedestal jutting out from their surface. It has to be said, as of the great colonnade which we are to see in a moment, that the rows of column would have been much more effective without their statues. It was an irritating habit of the Palmyrenes; a sort of hankering to be like the Greeks and Romans, and perhaps a craze like that which makes the modern Moroccans fill their houses with brass bedsteads and grandfather clocks. The great colonnaded street of Palmyra which we are now approaching must have been spoiled or almost ruined in effect by this swarming of statues. It runs straight through the town for a distance of some two-thirds of a mile, and a hundred and fifty, or nearly half of its columns, each fifty feet high, are still standing. But every one of the pillars has its corbel or pedestal to support a statue and the effect must have been of a chattering and noisy silence. How curious to walk home at night along this colonnaded street! I found myself thinking of the rostral columns outside the Opéra at Paris, and of the chorus of undraped females, in bronze and "all different", holding gas-lamps. It appears that such colonnaded streets were an obsession in this part of Asia Minor*; and it has to be admitted that the vision of the classical past as a golden age, if it still persists as an illusion, is given force and colour when we compare the colonnades of Palmyra with the arcades of Bologna, just as Pompeii for its wealth of works of art, even if they are copies of classical originals, gains by comparison with what could be excavated two thousand years hence at Antibes or Le Touquet. Bologna is but a town of arcades while Palmyra shows the hand, not of the house builder, but of architects. It was an architect of technical ability and much experience who designed the quadruple arch or *tetrapylon* in the middle, but not the dead centre, of the colonnaded street. For it is a

* Mr Julian Huxley "remembers Sir Leonard Woolley once saying that T. E. Lawrence had personally discovered traces of over 120 colonnaded towns within a twenty-mile radius of Aleppo". Cf. *From an Antique Land*, London, Max Parrish & Co., 1954, p. 146. Such must have been the ancient Apamaea, eighty miles north of Baalbek, which had a colonnaded main street nearly a mile long. The six hundred war elephants of the Seleucids (Seleucus I was one of Alexander's captains) were posted here, "and the slopes of the Orontes pastured the famous stud". (Fedden, *Syria*, p. 69.) It would be interesting to know more of Numenius of Apamaea, a philosopher who, Mr Fedden says, "was a capable champion of Hindu thought".

piece of tricking carried out in expert manner, consisting in a shifting or masking of the axis. Because the columns change their path and turn at an angle, but looking through the lesser or side arches of the *tetra-pylon* it is so contrived that this is scarcely noticed. The two wings of the archway are not exactly parallel with each other, and thus, turning round from one vista of columns to the other, the thinning or thickening of the perspective corrects itself. Such architectural deceit can only have been learned in a centre of experience and one suspects, and probably correctly, the schools of Antioch.

On that burning May morning the broken porticoes of Palmyra threw some fictitious semblance of shade but the heat in the theatre was something beyond ordinary experience. It was as a crushing, searing weight upon one's head and shoulders, and it had become a feat of audacity to stand out in the sun. I found myself sheltering under an archway which had been one of the stone entrances on to the stage. This theatre is not yet entirely excavated. We were told that only a few years ago there were banks of earth as high as half-way up the rows of seats. There seems to be doubt as to whether the theatre was used for plays, and it may have been intended for commemorations and the giving of honours and prizes like the Sheldonian at Oxford. Next to it was the Agora which, once, seethed with statues standing on inscribed brackets; there being as many as two hundred of them; while nearby is something more curious still, a temple built and designed as a banqueting hall with benches for the guests along the walls. Admission to these sacred meals or *symposia* was by ticket, a clay *tessera* bearing a stamped effigy of the host or donor on one side and of the food offerings on the other.

We had now to get into the car again and go off to see the tombs which are in their own way the most extraordinary relic of Palmyra. For the temple of Bel and the colonnaded streets might seem less portentous if it were not that they are out in the desert more than a hundred miles from anywhere, but the tombs are exceptional and fantastic in their elaboration and from their quantity. There are more than a hundred and fifty of the tower-tombs, some of them rising to sixty or seventy feet high and in four storeys. Then there are the subterranean tombs excavated in the ground with long passages and colonnaded halls, one of them with sixty-five "bays", by which is meant niches or recesses, and room for some four hundred bodies.

First, we went down into one of the subterranean tombs, closed, ominously, with a stone door that opened with stone hinges. And in a moment one is watching a banquet of the dead for "there they lie, each reclining in effigy in his own coffin, in festive attitude and attire, yet in silence and gloom, each with a goblet in his hand from which he seem to be pledging his fellows in the darkness of the tomb". Those are words in description of the painted tombs of the Etruscans,* and they may be applied to the sepulchres of Palmyra with this difference that they do not take into account the peculiar costume of the Palmyrenes. Even so, one conjectures what picture of our age future generations will draw from funerary monuments of our own time. At Palmyra, some of the sarcophagi are in U shape like beds around a banquet table; the fold of their garments are heavy and realistic, not in the least like the Roman toga, the ladies have high headdresses and the men are wearing tall cylindrical hats like *tarbushes*. Moreover, mummies or half-mummified bodies have been found in these tombs, wrapped in silks that had been brought from China. This, in particular, in a tower-tomb representing a ground floor with Corinthian columns and painted coffered ceiling. That will give the cosmopolitan nature of Palmyra which by the middle of the third century A.D. had become independent of Rome. Advantage was taken of the defeat and capture of the Roman Emperor Valerian by the Persian King Sapor to extract from his son and successor Gallienus the title of "Corrector of all in the East". This was on behalf of Odenath, the husband of the far famed Zenobia, Queen of Palmyra, and he went further than that, calling himself "King of Kings", the traditional title of the Kings of Babylon from the time of Nebuchadnezzar nine centuries earlier to that of the Sasanids, while their son adopted for himself and his mother Zenobia the Roman titles of Augustus and Augusta. They had taken profit from a time of dissension and defeat among the Roman legions and were defeated by Aurelian who, fresh from beating the Teutons on the Danube, captured Palmyra and brought Zenobia back with him to Rome. There, as all must know, she took part in his triumph, walking in front of her own chariot, bound in golden chains, while Aurelian followed in a chariot drawn by stags with gilded antlers.†

It is the unexpressed at Palmyra that is of even more absorbing interest than the corbelled columns or the carved and painted tombs. They lived in an oasis in the middle of nowhere, but the Palmyrenes knew Gaul and Spain, their soldiers had done garrison duty in Northumberland along Hadrian's Wall; while in the other direction, had one been able to enquire of them, individuals, and civilized ones, at that, who could read and write and had probably been to Rome,

---

* Dennis, *Cities and Cemeteries of Etruria*, first printed in 1846. One of the finest of the Palmyrene tombs, with its stone door, and tier after tier of reclining stone effigies in curious semi-classical dress, has been removed and set up in the Museum at Damascus.

† Queen Zenobia died in prison; or, according to another account, married again and lived in comfortable retirement at Tivoli with her second husband and children.

would be able to tell from their own experience of India. And not only of India for Alexander had campaigned there six centuries before— one is forgetful of the long lapse of time between the third century B.C. and the third century A.D.—but of China, with which they may have had contact not only by the caravan routes through Central Asia but, perhaps, intermediately, by sea, through their ships meeting other ships at Indian ports. There must, also, have been a few persons who had made the journey by the steppes and the Koko-Nor and through the Gobi Desert. There was, we may be certain, more information than was ever written down. Furthermore, we are to think of the Palmyrenes as living only in comparative isolation for no doubt they saw themselves as part of an entire complex of Oriental civilizations which had lasted for as long, and been as productive of arts and ideas, as to our minds have been the civilizations of the Occident which endured from, let us say, the time of Charlemagne until the old order was shaken and upset and re-cast in new shapes and forms by the French Revolution and the wars of Napoleon. If we recall no more than names, and only mention Ancient Egypt, descending to Egypt of the Ptolemies, and then Greece and Rome and Carthage, and Tyre and Sidon, and the Assyrians and Persians, it is as full a history as that of Spain and France and England, and the Venetian Republic, and the Holy Roman Emperors and the Popes. It is only surprising that the ancient world did not reach and embark upon an era of inventions and mechanizations. They must have been near to the discovery of elec- tricity and of the power of steam. But machines and engines eluded them and lay in embryo for two millenniums more. Yet it is in the light of this long tradition that one must regard the sophistication of their architecture even though it betrays a parvenu and imitative fist.

But the heat was a little too exhausting and we had to repair to the hotel. It is a long low building, cool and fly-less, with a romantic history for a former owner met with many vicissitudes, losing several husbands and reputed lovers by violent means not inappropriate to Queen Zenobia's scene. Married at one moment in her complicated trajectory to a French vicomte, and continuing to bear his name, she married at another time a Moslem in order to make the pilgrimage to Mecca. In all her actions she was dogged by ill fortune, if we give it that interpretation, her body being found at last with many stab wounds, in the sea. But this was after she left Syria and removed to Tangier. Having long been interested in her curious history, which is so well suited to be made into a film scenario with its desert setting among the ruins of Palmyra, I made every effort to enquire about her and was at last given her full history by someone I met at Beirut who had known her, and who told me, which I think makes it still more interesting and perhaps even better suited for filming, that hers was probably one of those extraordinary cases of persons who attract misfortunes, that violence played around her and she had no hand in it. All now seems forgotten in the hotel, though looking into one of the bedrooms with a dark loft at one end of it, reached by a ladder, I wondered if it was not perhaps a little sinister and alarming, not in the dark only, but when the full moon casts shadows down the pillared colonnades.

We swallowed, indifferently, iced orangeade and Pepsi-Cola while waiting at that furnace door, almost dreading the moment of first touching the leather seats of the car and knowing the windows had been drawn up so as not to let in the flies. It was indeed like opening the door of an oven when we went outside; the colonnades of Palmyra seemed to dilate and tremble with a jagged edge to their pillars; the sweat ran down one's neck and wrists. Yet one did not want to go. This was the only time. One would never be here again. But it was three o'clock, now, and when we got back to Damascus we would have been fifteen hours upon the road. So, off, looking our last on the corbelled columns and triumphal arch, and wishing we could have climbed up into the Turkish castle on its hill above the Temple of Bel and the tumbled colonnades. Once moving, with all the windows down, the air blew in with a hot edge to it and we turned the corner of the oasis, and started the climb, and could see the colonnades of Palmyra go down into the sand. In a few moments more we were over the shoulder of the hill and they were gone.

The long featureless afternoon burned itself away, meeting with nothing coming along the road in our direction, but being overtaken at that part of it where one could race on one's own upon hard sand by another car coming from Palmyra which drew level with us as though propelled forward by its own exhaust of dust, and had at last to be surrendered to and let go by. It was probably better than to be persistently followed through the wilderness. But nothing else came past going either way. We had the road entirely to ourselves for the best part of a hundred miles. Such a solitude is becoming difficult to find. And in the middle of it, at a couple of hours' journey from anywhere, though the loneliness, it is true, is made worse by a wretched village of mud huts at about half-way, I looked in the latest edition of Baedeker's *Palestine and Syria*, printed in 1912, where it says: "The route from Damascus to Palmyra is best made by carriage, reckoning five days for the journey, and four for the return journey, including a stay of twenty-four hours . . . but with a camel (now comparatively seldom used) it takes one day less. Tents, for which a guard of soldiers is indispensable, had better be pitched in the orchards. . . . The traveller should take tobacco for distribution to the escort and to Bedouins whom one may chance to meet." It was, in fact, a nine-day expedition. But the process is going on all over the world. Taxco, the silver-mining town in Mexico with the marvellous Churrigueresque church in golden stone, of which I wrote long before I went there in person in my first prose book *Southern Baroque Art*, as "being still three days' ride on mule-back over the stony mountains of the state of Guerrero", is now a two-hour drive from Mexico City on a speed road. And it is two hours more to Acapulco on the Pacific Ocean. . . .

But, at last, we reached the town with the little openwork minarets like birdcages, and the beginning of the asphalt road. A delirious, drugged drive through the Ghûta, intoxicated by its greenness, and by the excitement of the sunset and the sudden speed, and we were back in Damascus by nine o'clock at night, tired to death, but not too exhausted to be inveigled by a friend from the *souks* who was engaged in the silk business, into a night club on a terrace along the river Barada, here canalized, and opposite a Soviet-sponsored exhibition, none the less the same Abana of the Old Testament and the Chrysorrhoas or "golden stream" of the Greeks. I had never thought to find myself in a night club in Damascus. But it was pleasant enough sitting there on that summer night in the nearly empty rooms, while a pianist and violinist who looked like students from the Conservatoire in Vienna played *Ciocarla* and other Roumanian and Gypsy tunes.

Next afternoon, after returning once more to the Mosque of the Omayyads, we left Damascus, not without a last haggling at the desk over the price of a car to Beirut, to the accompaniment of pitying smiles at the way we had been cheated over our journey to Palmyra. At the last moment a new trick was played. The concierge announced a "fixed price", refused to lower it, and on acceptance stated that it was only for taking us as far as the garage in Beirut and that we would have to pay extra for going to the hotel. This Palestinian Arab, as the driver said to me later, was a man who would pocket a commission from his own mother; and an amusing argument ensued with the chauffeur as to why I should not have gone to the concierge, asked for a car to take me to Beirut, and then charged him back a commission for hiring a car from him. And we drove away from the hotel in a peculiar state of pride at having paid even more for going to Palmyra than the robbers has asked of us.

There are two villages near Damascus which we should have seen, but had not time to visit. One is Harran el Awamid, at the eastern end of the Ghûta near the mosquito-haunted Meadow Lakes, with semi-nomad inhabitants, many *seluki* dogs, and where according to Fedden "the women are astonishingly beautiful—a beauty more striking at the world's end—and go in costumes of indigo blue and faded red".* The other village is Malloula of melodious name, in its rocky gorge "in places hardly wide enough for two to walk abreast, much like the famous Siq passage in Petra", a village of Maronite Christians and the only place in the world where Aramaic, a language understood by our Lord, is still spoken. But we were on our way to Beirut, up into the hills and down again over the frontier of Lebanon into the valley of the Bk'aa, where lies the village of Chtaura with open air restaurants famous for *grenouilles* and for the red wines and *vin rosé* of Kzara and Muzar, grown largely by the Jesuits. This beautiful and fertile valley, with Baalbek in midst of it, is one end of the Great Rift Valley which according to Mr Julian Huxley begins in the gorges of Lakes Nyasa and Tanganyika in East Africa. Then, up again, and down the steep mountain road to the myriad lights of Beirut, and the Mediterranean.

* *Syria: an Historical Appreciation*, by Robin Fedden, London, Robert Hale, Ltd. 1955, p. 26.

# Chapter VII

## PETRA

ONCE more in Beirut, but in another hotel near the Grottes des
Pigeons, looking out on the sea and within full roar of its waves but,
also, of the lorries that come charging up the banked road in a series
of curves that seem directed straight into my window, and then vanish
behind the building with a hooded sound—as if gagged and blindfolded
and hurried off. The glare of their headlamps moves up and down the
walls and ceiling all night long and, as well, there is the flashing of a
lighthouse.

The bedroom furniture is built-in like that in a cabin on board ship,
giving an extra and perfunctory thrill of adventure, and indeed everything in the immediate environment points to excitement and
anticipation.

Next morning, a mechanical instrument into which coins are dropped
plays sambas and rumbas, and towards midday silent figures in grey
flannel trousers and tweed jackets are sitting about smoking their pipes,
joined later in time for a glass of orange juice by two or three pleasant
looking young women carrying tennis rackets. At luncheon they all
sit together at a long table in the dining room.

That evening, seeing me reading an English newspaper, one of them
gets into conversation with me. They are air crews and air hostesses
grounded here because of the trouble in Cyprus. But not for long. My
friend is off at five o'clock to-morrow morning for Bangkok and
Singapore, and he introduces me to a tall fair haired girl called Joan.
We talk of the Thames Valley and his home at Sonning. Later, the hotel
manager tells me they are all so quiet one would never know they were
staying in the hotel, and asks me if I have noticed that they drink
nothing. Observing them, and there was little else to do, they were fine
young people, and in view of their responsibilities it was a relief to

think they were not sitting up drinking in the night club underneath the hotel.

In the meantime a day or two was taken up with making arrangements for our journey. It is not an easy matter to go to Petra. Unless you travel under very special circumstances you must wait until there are enough passengers to fill an aeroplane. This means that the expedition only takes place at irregular intervals when advertisements in the local newspapers have been answered. There are no announcements in the normal travel agencies because accommodation at Petra and the means of getting there are in the hands of the particular firm who organize the trip.

But, also, it was extremely doubtful whether we could go at all. Petra is in a remote corner of the Kingdom of Jordan near the frontier with Israel and the Gulf of Akaba. Glubb Pasha had only been gone a few weeks. The mood of the Arab Legion was uncertain. We were warned in Tehran that visas might not be given for going to Jordan; that in any case at such times as this Petra was certain to be ruled out. A military escort would be necessary. I had, in fact, given up all hope of getting there. It was in a wild part of the country. Last year it had been closed for weeks on end. The news was not encouraging. One had better forget about going to Petra and think of something else.

Then a friend cut an announcement out of the local newspaper and sent it to me. It seemed that a trip to Petra was being organized after all and was to start from Beirut in three or four days' time. This was the most exciting prospect of the whole journey after having seen Meshed and Isfahan. It is something special and all to itself which has a particular and childish appeal, even if vitiated by an appalling line of poetry of which one is reminded at every moment. The tourist agent, of course, has it printed on his writing paper and probably it would be painted on the wings or fuselage of the aeroplane. It was almost as bad as if one was going to Petra and had written the line, oneself. A youthful excitement and an embarrassment, both at once, and I realized I had heard so much of Petra that I seldom really thought of it and had no clear picture of it in my mind. More likely than not it would be a disappointment.

"Retiring early", we were called at four in the morning, "after the ball was over", but inured, by now, to waking before dawn and able to drink coffee and eat toast while talking with nonchalance of the more serious news of the day. Thence, by tumbril, through the pinewood to the aerodrome along the *aprica littora*, the golden Mediterranean shore, while the morning sky was clearing and emptying into infinity above the stone pines, finding the benches in the waiting rooms full of our countrymen in uniform on their way, poor things, from Kenya to Cyprus, and looking forward to it because it was nearer home.

Mr Sinbad of the Sinbad Travel Agents (that is the name of the Tourist Agency, but not his own name) was already there, hatless, in shirtsleeves and sand shoes, holding a string bag. He is a big tall Maronite of the Lebanon, who arranged all the rest of our tour for us, who was honest and conscientious and to whom I took a liking. It was 5.30 a.m.; and having passed the customs we were led downstairs to the departure room where we sat waiting like the morning's victims, to be pinioned. Punctually at six o'clock, after a cup of black coffee, the moment came and we were asked to take our places, having already been told we were to travel in the first aeroplane. There were at least thirty or forty persons coming to Petra, and it was not long before one knew some part of it was a school excursion. The children, boys and girls, were from fourteen to sixteen years old, and came from the American College at Beirut. During the flight the young girls all walked along, one after another, into the "powder room" and changed into trousers. How different they were from English school children who at that age would keep in two groups and avoid the other sex. These sat holding hands, or "necking", with their hair falling over each other's faces. Coffee was handed round, with indeterminate looking rusks or wafers, unable to make up their minds whether they were cakes or biscuits.

We were over the mountains of Lebanon with snow at the level of the windowpane, soon succeeded by the green hills of part of Jordan. I had thought we might pass near the Sea of Galilee, but we had come some distance to the north of it in order to avoid flying over Israel. In about two hours after leaving Beirut we were above Amman, the capital of Jordan, low down, and able to note its unexpected character of a hill town. Some miles before we reached it the whole desert was scratched over with track marks which could have been mistaken for abstract drawings or hieroglyphs and were, it seemed, the result of tank manoeuvres. We did not touch down at Amman, and were to go there next day. So on, another three-quarters of an hour's flight to Ma'an, out in the dead desert, where the airstrip was nothing but bare sand. Here, an ambulance was standing by in case of need, and it was an Army vehicle manned by one of our mechanized cavalry regiments. How they must hate Ma'an, and what a horrible place to be stationed at! We could see their encampment not far away. At Ma'an there was a string of motors waiting for us, and after the usual unnecessary delays we climbed into one of them, and without seeing Ma'an were out in the desert, but perhaps there is no Ma'an to see.

We were three thousand five hundred feet above sea level on a sort of rolling weald or wold or down of desert with nothing whatever of interest to be seen anywhere, but having to show an interest because this was Arabia Petraea. As, often before, not a bird, not a flower was to be seen, while the character of the stony uplands made it difficult to look more than a few yards ahead. One felt sorrier than ever for the troops stationed at Ma'an. At about half-way in the two hours' motor drive we stopped in order to allow all the convoy of cars to catch up with each other, and our halt was at a water well on a bend of the road below a wretched mud built village.

Here a welcome and splendid figure made his appearance dismounting and showing himself in a scarlet cloak, chequered black and white *Keffieh* or headdress held with a gold cord, silver inlaid dagger, and long matchlock gun. He was an Arab auxiliary or frontiersman working under orders from the Arab Legion, with the aquiline features of the true desert race, and as much an object of attention from our fellow travellers with their cine-cameras as if he had been a Red Indian brave in full war paint. At last we moved on, only to halt once more at another well where women were doing their laundry and whacking it with long sticks. They were the dark crow-faced Bedouins with tribal tattoo marks. Their donkeys were tethered near them. In a few moments someone of importance came along riding an Arab pony, and he too dismounted handing the reins to an attendant with a crooked dagger in his belt. This newcomer must have been a village headman or small landowner. He wore a brown *bournouse* of fine cloth and the hilt of his dagger was inlaid with gold. A humble and pathetic small donkey came running to its mother and one knew the happy part of its life would soon be over, to be for the rest of its days and nights a beast of burden. This scene at the well is such an interlude as one remembers. It stays in the mind and is probably a memory that I share with the baby donkey.

About half-an-hour after that we came to Ain Musa or the Well of Moses (but there are many more, so called) where there is a fortress or strong point and a garrison of Arab Legionaries in a mud castle. Here we got out of the cars and were confronted with a horsefair. There must have been nearly a hundred thin, half-starved horses, some of them mares with their foals running with them, and nearly that number of thin, undersized Arabs. After another wait under a blazing sun the word was given and we all chose our mounts; mine, a wretched white mare with a rope halter and no rein. But all were the same, and an Arab took the rope in his hand and led the animal along. There was nothing to hold on to but the croup of the saddle, and the saddle had

been made for someone half my height and size. As for the Bedouin
who led me along, he was one of the smallest and thinnest and most
compact human beings I have ever seen, a pocket Bedouin in duodecimo
edition, strangely Egyptian but without a trace of the negro, and
in reminder that Egypt, or, at least, the Peninsula of Sinai was not
many miles away. With his little thin rat-face and pointed beard he
was like a walker on in a crowd scene in *Aïda* when that opera was first
performed at Cairo.

We rode down in cavalcade through the village of Ain Musa, thereby
exciting to no small degree, and no wonder, "the risible faculties" of
the natives, some few of whom, both young and old, male and female,
were made nearly hysterical by our passage, so many and so different,
and all on coursers led by hand. Perhaps the most shaming moment of
embarrassment was when we met, coming in our direction, with three
or four Arab Legionaries mounted on camels, true Méharistes, and the
picture of smartness in their uniforms. But then it dawned on me that
funny as I may have looked myself, I had, at least, some inkling of
how to ride, dating from childhood, whereas many of the American
children who came from homes in New York or in Chicago had
hardly seen a horse before. Two or three of them careered past at high
speed with their escort, dagger in belt, running in front of them while,
as with nomads on the move, the foals trotted along beside their
mothers.

Ain Musa lies on a steep hillside with a sort of glacis, immediately
below the walls of the fort, down which we slid all four hooves on the
ground. Down, down, past the windowless mud houses with all the
inhabitants standing on the street and not a sign of life within. A path
of slippery cobble stones at a tilted angle, and down past little terraced
fields of wheat under a gnarled fig tree's shade. But in a few moments
it was the stony desert, and still that perpetual descent and going
down.

Suddenly, it is no longer desert but a rocky wilderness with strange
and contorted pinnacles coming up ahead of us like those of another
and subterranean world. It could be that this is a gigantic cavern of
which the roof has been blown off in some convulsion of fire or
earthquake leaving the pillars and columns in their pristine and long
hidden colours which had lain in eternal night; or it could be some
fraction of lunar or other world struck here, and embedded, and
coming up out of the scorched sand. Whatever, these are the Dolomites
and pinnacles of another world and we are heading straight for it, not
at the speed of an aeroplane but at a walking pace. The path is no
longer strewn with boulders. It is a bed of stone; a shelf of stone down

which we slide and scramble. A pale crumbling sandstone under the darker mass above.

More suddenly still, the wall of stone opens and we have gone inside. This, almost before we realize it for it is like a hidden opening in the rock. It is the beginning of the Siq, the rocky passage leading to Petra, and in another moment we have turned a corner and are right in the deepening gorge. At first not very high, perhaps eighty or ninety feet, but almost instantly becoming sensational because it gets narrower and the walls are steeper and higher. Now so deep down that it is entirely in shadow under towering walls that have their tops lit by the sunlight. There are wild fig trees growing in crevices as they do along the escarpments of the Corinth Canal. What plants or trees, one wonders, would find foothold on the skyscrapers of Fifth Avenue for it makes one think of riding in two thousand years' time at foot of those cliff-like buildings? When we will be forgotten as if we had never lived, and what else will be remembered?

All noises in this deep gorge make a curious dead sound. Now there is scarcely room for anyone to come past riding the other way for in places it is barely ten feet wide. Oleanders grow here in quantity and are just coming into bud, but most of them are the dark red kind which is not as beautiful as the pink or white. Lovely as they are, it is a beauty conferred partly by the name, and beautiful as *oleanders* they are lovelier still as *lauriers roses*. In a few days' time the course of the Siq will be dark red with oleanders. And is it a road, or is it a riverbed? Being, in reality, both, for it was the bed of a torrent which the Nabataeans, the original inhabitants of Petra, diverted into a tunnel and then paved the passage. It is the royal road into Petra, and it is true that the walls of the gorge are of dark red sandstone. Already there have been signs of architecture. As we came into the gorge there were cuttings high up in the rock with weatherworn niches for statues, once the archway or grand portal to the city, and now although one could easily miss them for they are the same colour as the red rock they are carved in, there are altar niches and votive tablets, all defaced and crumbling. But we are now at the deepest part of the Siq with perpendicular walls of rock rising up sheer to over three hundred feet above us, while the corridor itself is never straight for more than a few yards ahead but winds about like a true torrent bed. The sides of it are almost dark, half-way up, it is so high. We have ridden for twenty minutes to half-an-hour along the Siq, and must have come nearly a mile.

All this time the colour of the sandstone deepens and gets a darker red. But it is not the red sandstone of which Gothic cathedrals are built for this has less of rust in it and is more roseate. It has at this moment long streaky marks in it but, as yet, it is not multi-coloured. Then, what colour is it? Neither mulberry, nor dark crimson, and now it darkens. It is at its darkest and narrowest—when we ride out into a gulf of sunlight, having in that moment sighted a thing quite incredible in the shade beyond and behind that sunlight, at the other side of it, so that it is like a voice from the dead out of another world. But so subtle and graceful is it that, although it is immediately in front of one, it would be possible to ride past, and look at it, and not be sure it is there. Because it might be something one was imagining for oneself as one rode along, being more appropriate to some fantasy in a dream than to anything seen in daylight.

It is the Khazné Faraóun which in Arabic means Pharaoh's Treasury, standing in a chasm that runs at right angles to the Siq, and put, of course, at that exact spot in order to be opposite this other opening, or end of it. The effect is a stroke of genius, and a moment of high drama in the world of human artifice. One will never forget the rose-petal temple beyond that chasm, that river of light. A moment, indeed, like meeting the shade of someone in the underworld. For it is so intimate and remembered, and from so long ago. But as though seen in a glass, or as though we saw the shadow of it and not the substance. Phantom, or ghost-like, as if the impersonation of someone in another generation of the same family, glimpsed or caught sight of in the moment of youth and good looks, but not of first youth, and with an extraordinary resemblance, yet not entirely the person, but the pre-cursor, or foreshadowing. Of the same parentage, but with other strains predominating because different blood has come in, since then. But it is the reticence of the Khazné that is so remarkable, as though standing straight in front of you in the shadow, holding its finger to its lips, sharing some secret of which it says no more.

This is the secret. The Khazné is not in the style of any classical temple one has seen before, but it is in the Baroque of Borromini. Of Hellenic elegance, but not in the spirit of any Grecian temple, and lacking the heavy hand of the Roman. It is a temple of Isis for it has the symbols of Isis, but it is difficult to believe it was really erected, or rather, excavated to the order of the Emperor Hadrian who visited Petra in 131 A.D. No other of Hadrian's buildings has its imprint which for delicacy is as the hand of Jacques-Ange Gabriel who built the twin palaces in the Place de la Concorde and the Petit Trianon, only for its fancifulness it is not Grecian revival, but Baroque.

The lower story of the Khazné is a portico resting upon six Corin-thian columns with a beautiful doorway, within, leading to nothing—

in fact, into a bare room or cave with cells opening from it. The upper storey of the rock temple, too, has six Corinthian columns, a cornice of rare beauty all in the rose-petal stone, and a broken pediment which is interrupted and opens of itself to show a little circular lantern or *tholos*, surrounded by columns, and with a stone urn above its conical and round roof. The colour of all is a very particular rose-petal, of that intensity when the rose is shedding and the fallen petals lie upon the ground. Impossible, too, not to allow the Khazné some connotation in one's mind with festal rose-petals, as of thrown handfuls of rose petals at the banquet, or even at the funeral feast if, indeed, it be true that the Khazné was not a temple of Isis built by the Emperor Hadrian but "the tomb-temple of one of the latest Nabataean Kings".

The *tholos* or little circular temple adorning the second storey of the Khazné is of fascinating beauty, being one of the most fanciful and delicate of all late classical inventions. It displays a degree of sophistication and experience only arrived at in six centuries of architecture since Ictinos built the Parthenon. Already in the Erectheum, which is a building of the Ionians with a more feminine refinement than the Parthenon, we can see of what the Asiatic Greeks were capable in the time of Pericles. But the Khazné shows them half a millennium later, in a mood corresponding to the experimentings of the *Seicento* and to architects of the order of Borromini or Guarino Guarini, but with a delicacy of hand that no Italian could display in that age of *bravura*, which is why I say that at the same time it looks like a work of the eighteenth century in France. What it comes to is this, that we are discussing some architect of the Hellenistic period, who almost certainly was not Greek, in the same breath as Italian, or Spanish, or other artists of the Counter-Reformation. And this is as though the Greeks had come through to the Renaissance and not been conquered by the Turks. It is the projection into the Renaissance of something that never happened.

One of the central columns of the portico has fallen and is no longer there. A beautiful feature of this strange and haunting rock-temple are the remains of figures standing on pedestals in bas-relief, mysterious shapes resembling Amazons, and a figure between two of the engaged columns of the lower storey which could be a woman mounted on a camel. The whole façade being, as it were, set back and framed in its own cutting in the mountain side, and the rock continuing for some little space above it.* Perhaps only in the case of rock-temples such as

---

* How high is the façade of the Khazné? Because opinions differ. Burckhardt, the discoverer of Petra, puts it at sixty or sixty-five feet. Baedeker (*Palestine and Syria*) says

Tomb of Cyrus at Naqsh-e-Rostam

Shapur and Valentinian at Naqsh-e-Rostam

Qashqai nomad on the move

that of Abu Simbel in Upper Egypt is a building seen emerging from a background of exactly the same colour and materials. It is this which is one of the peculiar effects of the Khazné, and that gives to the rock-temple something of a ghostly air. Out here in the stony wilderness one must not forget how near we are to Egypt.* So much for the cosmopolitan nature of the Hellenistic age. But in this remote place it is indeed extraordinary to come upon a building akin to Wren's churches in the Strand. Not only that, but, in particular, to Borromini's little church of San Carlino (San Carlo alle quattro Fontane) in Rome, "begun in 1634 in the most spirited Baroque style". For on the upper storey of its façade is "a curious little tambour-shaped pavilion.... This was doubtless suggested to Borromini by engravings of the pavilion on the upper stage of the rock-tomb of the Khazné at Petra, which likewise occupies a central position between bays flanked by Corinthian columns." We quote from *Roman Mornings*, by James Lees-Milne, pp. 124, 125. But the first modern traveller to reach Petra was Burckhardt in 1811, under the assumed name of Sheikh Ibrahim, and under the pretext of having made a vow to slaughter a goat in honour of Aaron, whose tomb is situated on the summit of Mount Hor.† And pondering on all these contradictions which make of the Khazné one of the most mysterious and intriguing buildings in the world and knowing there would be time to look at it in the afternoon, we rode on.

The way leads down the right-hand valley and soon tombs or rock-temples are to be seen in quantity, and as the valley opens it gains in colour. The rocks are now multicoloured, and in most curious veinings or striations. There is every shade of red and rose and crimson, and, as well, amethyst and violet and cornelian. Not the least curious feature of this strange circus or valley of rocks being that as though to enhance the dramatic effect it keeps back its full gamut of colours till the last. The track is now a river bed with oleanders growing in every

---

sixty-five. Julian Huxley in *From an Antique Land* (p. 121) puts it at "some ninety feet high", and I think it gives the effect of being eighty to ninety feet high.

* By a curious chance it was the same J. L. Burckhardt who was the first modern traveller to examine the rock-temple of Abu Simbel in 1812. This is the temple which has four colossi of Ramses II, hewn out of the cliff, and sitting in pairs on either side of the entrance to the temple. And the façade "is crowned by a cavetto cornice above which is a row of cynocephali (dog-faced baboons), being so arranged that at sunrise the sun's rays penetrate to the innermost sanctuary". The live experience of such a rock-temple as this of Abu Simbel is not to be disassociated from the designer of the Khazné.

† *Journey through Arabia Petraea to Mount Sinai and the excavated City of Petra, the Edom of the Prophecies*, by M. Léon de Laborde, London, John Murray, 1836, p. 19. Burckhardt was recognized by his guide as an infidel, and had to sacrifice his goat in haste half-way up Mount Hor. It is still a goal of pilgrimage, and in Julian Huxley's words "the holy man who inhabits it must lead one of the loneliest lives in the world".

8

direction and we have come out into an open amphitheatre hemmed in by coloured cliffs. A great range of them sweeps away to the right with the façades of some half-dozen tombs or temples stretching in nearly continuous line, but none of them in the style of the Khazné. Some are almost obliterated, or were only sketched out on the cliff face, but it is easy to see they are the conventional works of a drawing board in some provincial architect's office. There is no touch or fire of genius in them, which makes the isolation of the Khazné more peculiar still.

The heat was, now, of reverberant midday violence, beating and echoing off the stones, and one began to wonder where one was going, in and out of dried up watercourses among the oleanders. Then the rampart walling in the far end of the amphitheatre came in sight, and passing a stretch of what was obviously a paved Roman road, not long uncovered, we came to a military post occupied, surprisingly, by British soldiers come up from Akaba on the Red Sea, which is not much more than sixty miles away. (When I went down to talk to them next morning they had already gone.) Under the cliff at the far side, coming nearer into its shadow, we could now see an encampment of tents and some scooped out caves which were human dwellings. Dismounting, with stiff joints as though we had ridden all the way from Cairo or Jerusalem, we went in search of authority and were told we had Tent Number One. Shortly, a fly-blown luncheon of heating food was served in a marquee sewn with rays and mock suns or parhelions of coloured linen, poor relation to the tents of Tamerlane. There followed a period of rest for one was entirely exhausted, which consisted in lying on a truckle-bed in Tent Number One that like all the other tents had an earth, or, rather, a dust floor. The number of flies was prodigious and one had to cover one's head. The bed, moreover, was at an angle because nothing could stand straight owing to there being no proper floor. It was like practising to be a Chinese juggler to try and keep all four legs of a wooden chair even on the ground. A candle in a battered candlestick raised conjectures of flitting bats and huge moths, or perhaps scarab beetles singeing in the flame. If one tried to read, twenty flies settled on the book or newspaper. It was not a happy hour.

And presently, braving the heat, we decided it was better to go for a walk and look for some patch of shade beneath a rock. But our footsteps were dogged by a half-witted Bedouin who would come right up to our feet and lean on an elbow looking at us. No stratagem would drive him off. If we threatened, he retreated and came back again, and if bribed with a cigarette he lit it and came nearer still. I tried following him, but he kept perfectly still and then aped my movements like a shadow. In the end we had to accept him as he would not go away. But eventually, and we never knew how, he had gone. It must have been when advancing in the heat almost from oleander to oleander along the river bed upon the sharp stones we, at last, began the climb we had intended towards the cliff face and the line of temples. It was steep going and painful, and there were slopes of rock up which one had to scramble, taking hold of oleander or any other bush there was, and slipping backwards with a handful of leaves in one's fist. These outcrops were of white sandstone but as we climbed they became more coloured until we were standing on a ledge of dark purple, as though wine-stained stone.

This was, indeed, the platform immediately in front of one of the largest in the line of tombs. It has suffered much from erosion in two thousand years, and the surface is so blurred and rubbed away that it is like looking at something quivering in a heat-haze. The tomb is in three storeys, the top consisting of four obelisks set back against the stone of the mountain. Although of Roman date and construction (in A.D. 106 Petra and all Arabia Petraea was taken from its native Nabataean Kings and made into a Roman province) this tomb seems instinct with Egyptian feeling. Surely those who built it had seen the rock-temple of Abu Simbel, or some similar structure, coming out of the hillside.

Now we started to climb along what could have been a collapsed and delapidated terrace leading along the face of the hill, and hearing voices which were those of a family of Bedouins. They were not living in a tomb or cave, but had their miserable encampment at the edge of the platform. It was no more than a "lean-to" of poverty stricken sort, a house of hair woven of black goats' wool, propped up on a few sticks. While the Bedouin children followed us, not begging for once, there was a rush and rampage of goats and their kids; the kids leaping up on to a rock, standing there, stockstill, then prancing down playfully in front of the decrepit and age-old monument, as if all the world was young. One wondered how the Bedouins lived, what they ate, if it was only goats' milk and goat flesh, and what stories, if any, they told their children about the ruins.

More particularly, because this tomb has a façade in imitation of a palace. It has triple rows or storeys of columns, one above another, and four doors or portals with rounded or triangular pediments above them. But inside this "palace", there is nothing, as ever at Petra, and generations of Bedouins have used it for their lavatory. Here the stone platform comes to an end, and climbing to the last stretch of it to get the view it was astonishing to find a wheatfield within a few feet of

one, as though in another world from the ruins, and not a poor crop,
but loaded like the wheatfields of the promised land.* Coming back,
there is another tomb to pass, built in imitation of the Khazné, with
Corinthian columns in the lower storey, and above that a circular
lantern with urn over it between broken pediments. But it is a bad
imitation, altogether lacking in quality, by a heavy and provincial
hand.

There is yet another of the tombs along this rock face, and one of the
most imposing of all, but it was getting late and we must get to the
Khazné before the light failed. Also, the way to this tomb was a long
way round and entailed another climb. But it was imposing enough
from a distance, banked up on a substructure of open vaults, with a
square terrace in front of it and pillared porticos to either side, the
façade of the tomb itself having four tall pilasters with a triangular
pediment and architrave. One now saw the whole line of tombs
receding along the hillside, all carved, as it were, out of that matrix
of agate or cornelian, and contriving by their depth of cutting to make
full use of the different colourings. Indeed the rock-tombs of Petra,
were the bulk of them only finer in execution, could be called specimens of the art of the gem-cutter working in different layers or bands
of colour which deepen into knots like those in burr-walnut or other
cabinet woods. But confronted by this strange spectacle of rock-
façades one began to wonder what it was all about. Why are there so
many tombs and little or no signs of the living? Could it be that the
original Nabataean inhabitants of Petra lived in tents and had no
city? There are remains of the Roman Petra, a theatre and a forum, and
so forth, but no sign of earlier dwellings. This is not the least mystery
of this fantastic valley.

Now, stumbling along over the stones of the river bed, we had left
behind the multicoloured zone and were coming to the entrance to the
Siq, and to the Khazné. Why is this rose-petal rock-temple, all of one
colour, so much more beautiful than the other temples or tombs of
Petra, and by the hand of a master? And who, and what can he have
been? We were in front of it again. How humbly grateful I felt that
I had been allowed to see this, having had buildings of a similar spirit
so long in mind! Might it be possible that I could add a word of

* This is confirmed by Léon de Laborde in *Journey through Arabia Petraea*, 1836, pp.
203, 204, who says: "There is to be found here a species of bearded wheat, that justifies
the text of the Bible against the charge of exaggeration of which it has been the object;
and the vines, also, of this country, of the fruit of which we saw some specimens,
account for the enormous grapes which the spies sent out by Moses brought back from
the places which they had visited." These grapes are illustrated in a wood-engraving in
the book.

explanation to its mystery? The Khazné seemed to me equivalent to one of the buildings in Southern Italy, or in Sicily, on the edges or fringes of a culture, which a contemporary person of wisdom and experience would have looked upon exactly as the philosopher Bishop Berkeley saw the buildings of Lecce, in Apulia, when he travelled there in 1717. And his opinion, we may be certain, would have been the same had Bishop Berkeley seen Noto, in Sicily, which was rebuilt after an earthquake in 1693.* The Khazné is nearly paralleled in such places, and is surely the product of the same spiritual state of mind. Its refinement and elegance are no more surprising than that of mediaeval village churches in England miles from anywhere on the wolds or in the fens. In its own circle of culture a movement is not more remarkable which spread during a time of universal empire from a Mediterranean, with Antioch and Leptis Magna and Baalbek upon its shores, as far as remote Petra in the stony wilderness of Arabia, than that other and parallel movement which spread from Italy to half of Europe and reached over the Atlantic to build the golden churches of Mexico. The Khazné of Petra in the Hellenistic age is to be compared to some remote and beautiful monument of the Baroque age, shall we say, Wies, in Bavaria, or in Mexico, Taxco, or the Santuario de Ocotlán. It, too, is the provincial product of an universal and disseminated style.

Of what race was the architect, and what language did he speak? So much is mysterious. Is the little circular "tambour-shaped pavilion" really a *tholos*? And is it true that "only four examples of this type of façade are known, none of them from actual buildings; three are rock-cut monuments in Petra, and the fourth is a wall painting at Pompeii"?† Because the circular temples of the Greeks were one of the most beautiful inventions of the classical age. Such is the temple of the Sibyl, near the falls of Tivoli. But this is but a Roman copy of a Greek original. There were two *tholoi*, in particular. One was at Delphi, in the valley nearly below the Castalian fountain. The other, much

---

* "The most beautiful city in Italy lies in the heel. Lecce, the ancient Aletium, is the most luxurious in all ornaments of architecture of any town that I have ever seen. I have not in all Italy seen such fine convents. . . . In most cities of Italy the palaces indeed are fine, but the ordinary houses are of an indifferent gusto. 'Tis so, even in Rome, whereas in Lecce there is a general good goût, which descends down to the poorest house. . . . The square is the finest I ever saw. . . . Surely there is not a like rich architecture in the world . . . in no part of Italy indeed was there such a general gusto of architecture." And from the neighbourhood of Lecce he writes: "I have seen five cities in one day all built of white marble, whereof the names are not known to Englishmen." (*Bishop Berkeley: his Life, Writings, and Philosophy*, by J. M. Hone and M. M. Rossi, London, Faber & Faber, Ltd., 1931, pp. 103, 105, 106.) Bishop Berkeley's notes on Sicily are lost, but he visited an Italian poet and philosopher at Modica (*op. cit.*, p. 109) and so, almost certainly saw Noto.

† Julian Huxley, *From an Antique Land*, p. 122.

admired by Pausanias, was at Epidaurus. A building with exterior and interior colonnades, but of uncertain purpose; some holding that it was built over the sacred spring of the Asclepeion, and others that it served as a pyrtaneum for the celebration of sacred feasts and magic rites in the labyrinth that lay below. The younger Polycletes was architect, and was a sculptor as well, and designed the theatre of Epidaurus, the most perfect of Greek theatres. The interior of the *tholos* had frescoes of Love and Drunkenness by Pausias of Sicyon.

Such were works of the fourth and third centuries B.C., the golden age of Greece. The Khazné dates from five hundred years later. It has to be taken into consideration that such cities as Alexandria, Ephesus, and Antioch towards the end of those intervening centuries had a late classical architecture of which the Rome of Bernini is the phantom by circumstance, or if we prefer it, by historical recurrence.* How, otherwise, is it possible that the "little tambour-shaped pavilion" on the façade of the Khazné at Petra so closely parallels the façade of Borromini's church of San Carlino, at Rome? That dates from 1634, and Burckhardt only "rediscovered" Petra in 1811.

So beautiful and balanced is the façade of the Khazné that you scarcely notice the missing column on its lower storey. Perhaps its air of reticence is only because it cannot move out of its hill and speak. But now I discovered something else about it in the evening light: that it is semi-Indian. "Instead of a capital the pillars have a projecting bracket shaped like a woman . . . the frieze represents figures running with trays of offerings, athletes fighting with bulls and lions, and two lines of geese running with spread wings, each holding a flower in its beak. In the semicircular space under one of the arches is a nude female standing in a lotus bush, and holding a lotus stalk in either hand, while two elephants are throwing water over her with their trunks." This extract from notes made many years ago on Indian cave-temples could be a description of the interior of the Khazné. But the Khazné has only three little cells or chambers cut in the rock, and bare of ornament. Yet such could be its interior, which is in reality a cave-temple not far from Bhunaveshwar.

The conception of rock-temples or cave-temples is Indian, from the Buddhist caves of Ajanta with the only non-Aryan paintings that are as "beautiful" in the Western sense as paintings by Botticelli, down to the Kailasa of Ellora. This is not an interior hewn out of the rock, but the model of a complete, built temple. At Ellora there was no exposed rock or cliff face into which to dig; all the stone was under-

* Quoted from my book. *The Hunters and the Hunted*, London, MacMillan & Co., 1947, p. 14.

ground. So, first of all, an immense pit had to be dug, in places one hundred feet deep. It was a huge quarry, and as the stone was cut away they left, standing in it, a full size, double-storeyed temple. The next step was to hollow out an interior in what was already excavated. When completed, they made a pair of sculptured bridges leading to it. That is to say, both bridges are actually cut out of the rock. There would have been no span of air beneath them if it had not been cut away. The worked roofs of the Kailasa just come up to the height of the quarry walls; it is as if some landslide, some earthquake, had ripped open the bowels of the earth and revealed these temples standing inside, though, even so, the mind refuses to accept the truth about their manner of construction, and prefers to think of them as having stood within some great cavern from which the roof has fallen.* Reading further in my notes, I find mention of a Dravidian king who saw the god Shiva dancing on the seashore with his wife Parvati and built "a golden shrine" in memory of the god of dancing. And is it not an inspiration to poetry when we read of another temple built to receive the god Tivumalai for an annual visit of ten days during the hot month of May?

Such, we may think, are some of the connotations of the Khazné of Petra, could it but move out of the shadow and speak to us. There were, certainly, traders here who had been to India. And, it may be, down the coast of Africa as far as Zanzibar. But, above all, Petra, with Palmyra, was greatest of the caravan cities, if, indeed, it was a city at all and not a collection of tombs and tents until the coming of the Romans.

It was dark, already, at half-past six, when we crawled back into the camp, and found some French friends from Damascus sitting drinking at a table like a picnic party in the woods outside Paris, with the wise provision of cubes of ice in an ice-container. But after a few minutes they went off for their dinner *première service*, in the marquee, and we were left wondering, long before seven, whatever one was to do in the darkness when our dinner, *deuxième service*, would be over and finished at about a quarter to eight.

It was still too hot even to put one's head in at Tent Number One. All round, we could hear the American children talking. The young girls were to sleep in tents, and the boys in tombs or caves. Dinner in the marquee, once it started, resembled a scene interpolated into Edgar Allan Poe's *Professor Tar and Doctor Feather*, a story where, it will be remembered, the lunatics have overpowered their keepers. Murphy, a most amusing bullet-headed child with cropped hair, who came from

---

* Cf. my essay on the Kailasa of Ellora in *Touching the Orient*, London, Duckworth & Co., 1934, pp. 85–87.

Chicago, sat himself down next to me, alternately barking and roaring like a bull till dinner was half-over. Opposite was an enormous child with spectacles and a deep bass voice who turned out to be only fifteen years old. When the games-mistress came round and put her arms on his shoulder he called out to her: "Your hands are like ice, Matilda!" which, indeed, points the dissimilarity between American and English schools. Many of the children came from the "Gulf", that is to say, their parents lived at Bahrein, or Kuwait, or El Quatr, and worked at the oil wells, and all had tales to tell of the tremendous heat. Dinner was devoured at breakneck speed as though we were all being chased, and we were left, as prophesied, with nothing whatever to do except go to bed at a quarter-to-eight.

During the long night there was every opportunity for thinking of Petra, with an occasional thought for the English woman archaeologist who is carrying on excavations here, and had at the time of speaking been "in residence", we were told, for fourteen weeks. It is the first time, unlikely as it may seem, that Petra has ever been properly and systematically surveyed, and she had already uncovered a stretch of the paved Roman road. There is, obviously, a vast amount of cave exploration to be done, and much might be revealed by objects found in the dust, beads, or coins, or textile fragments. That is, from before the Roman occupation. How is it that we know there was a large city here, and there is no trace of it? There is to the rock-façades of Petra, taken in their totality, all of that disconcerting loneliness and disassociation from human activities which is the hallmark of Stonehenge.

There were hours of fierce coldness during that night amid all the incongruities of an O.T.C. or Boy Scouts' camp, and at dawn every flying insect was on the wing. I was sleepless as Napoleon Bonaparte in his tent before the battle of Alexandria, in Benjamin Haydon's hearsay account in his *Autobiography*, and for ever rising despairingly from my truckle-bed to walk in the moonlight, tripping over the tent-ropes, finding new recreation after daybreak in installing myself in the empty marquee, that was still littered with relics of last night's feasting, in order to look at the names in the visitors' book. It was a curious sensation to come upon signatures in familiar handwriting at that place and hour.

The Nabataean caravan-leaders of ancient Petra traded with Egypt in one direction and Damascus in the other, carrying incense from Arabia Felix, now called the Hadhramaut, and coming by way of Mecca on camel-back through the desert. They must surely have heard stories of China. It can have been no more unknown to them than to the camel-leaders of Palmyra. How often has one been reminded that

The Blue Mosque or Masjed-e-Shah at Isfahan

Napoleon could travel no faster from Rome to Paris than could Julius Caesar! So perhaps the ancient world was not as we see it, and Petra hardly remote at all. At no other time have the whole shores of the Mediterranean been one dominion, from end to end and round again.

It was blazing hot at seven o'clock in the morning, and we were too tired and sleepless to do anything but walk away and hide ourselves among the oleanders in one of the rocky lateral valleys. There, in a few moments we were in a lost world to ourselves, a hidden region in the lunar Dolomites, with peaks and crags rising to the height of skyscrapers, and did they feel inclined, caves for hermits and anchorites upon every floor. In this manner, passing the morning among the budding oleanders, and for once defeated, we missed seeing the other supreme sight of Petra, which is El Deir. But we were so completely exhausted that we could not face the climb, and it must be recalled in extenuation that only four days before we had made the long and difficult journey to Palmyra and back in a day, having only lately come from Persia.

El Deir—the "Monastery"—though there is no reason why it should be called that name, is an hour's climb up steps cut in the rock and along the edge of minor precipices. It is an ascent as to a Macchu Picchu, or hidden ruin, a part of its fascination being that it cannot be seen from below. It is invisible from any part of the valley of Petra. Burckhardt, apparently, had not heard of it. And travellers in 1818, a few years later, were unable to visit it and were obliged to content themselves "with having seen it at the distance of half-a-league through a telescope".* Its inaccessibility must add to the interest of El Deir.

The climb is of some fifteen hundred feet and, once reached, it is a stone façade cut out of the mountain side, more than twice the height of the Khazné; in fact, over a hundred and forty feet high, and closely resembling the Khazné except that two corner pilasters have been added to each storey, and that the beautiful ground floor pediment of

* "In midst of this chaos there rose into sight one finished work, distinguished by profuseness of ornament and richness of detail. It is the same which has been described as being visible from other elevated points, but which we were never able to arrive at. . . . No guide was to be found. With the assistance of the glass we made out the façade to be larger to all appearance than that of the Khazné, and nowise inferior to it in richness and beauty. . . . We then proceeded to visit Mount Hor, from the summit of which we distinguished with the glass another magnificent temple. But the number and intricacy of the valleys and ruins, which we supposed might have led to it, baffled all our attempts to reach this singular monument of antiquity." *Letters of Captains Irly and Mangles,* quoted in Laborde, *op. cit.,* pp. 36, 182. Miss Margaret Murray in *Petra: the Rock City of Edom,* London, Blackie & Son, Ltd., 1939, p. 56, has an ingenious solution to the problem of why the niches in the rock-hewn façades of Petra are without statues. She suggests that if there were never statues, but "merely the unhewn blocks which represented the god Dusares, a local deity, there would be no mystery".

its prototype is lacking. The *tholos* is there again; but El Deir according
to those who have seen it is altogether coarser in execution, though
extraordinary enough in all conscience when its siting is considered.
From photographs it looks to me like a typically Roman copy or
variation on a Grecian theme. Dean Stanley, who came here, says that
it reminded him "of a London church of the eighteenth century,
massive, but in poor taste, and with a somewhat debased style of ornament". And Frenchmen, who infer a compliment when something
abroad recalls a scene in France—"On dirait la Côte d'Azur", etc., etc.
—have been reminded of St Sulpice. But, in fact, it resembles that work
of Servandoni in little else but its giant scale; and a truer parallel to El
Deir would be to the Baroque churches, new built, at the heads of great
flights of steps, in that very Modica, in Sicily, where Bishop Berkeley
visited the poet and philosopher Tommaso Campailla.

Instead of climbing up to El Deir, and down again, the later morning
went by in agreeable fashion in an open bell-tent of which the canvas
walls had been taken out for coolness, talking to the pilots and co-pilots,
and air hostesses. To one of the latter I had loaned a large handkerchief
for head covering. Talk was mostly of flying conditions, of which I
know nothing but fear the worst. None of them wanted to come
again to Petra. One hour . . . two hours . . . and then a concerted rush,
like an assault party, on the luncheon marquee. The American children,
with Murphy leading, had come in already by another door. And then,
once more, the horsefair and the choosing of a likely steed, "likely",
that is to say, not to give trouble.

We set off down the valley, never again to come to Petra, and for
that reason hardly liking to look back at it. The Khazné, when we passed
in front of it, had all and more of its mystery. But, there, one turned
back. Who would not turn his head to look at it? But one could not
stop. There was the long line of guides and horses. And for a last
moment the Khazné was there still: Indian, yes! Indian, but as if the
Grecian Dionysus had conquered India, without bloodshed, and taught
to Indians "the use of the vine, the cultivation of the earth, and the
manner of making honey". The Khazné seemed in that last moment
to be one of the posts or temples of his march to India, and then was
gone and the rocky gorge closed in.

In the aeroplane flying from Ma'an to Amman a treat was in store.
The young and charming American pilot in order to please the boys
and girls took us for a joy ride down the valley of Petra. We made a
wide detour round from Ma'an, and in a few minutes covered all that
distance we had ridden and driven in cars and were approaching the
rocky mass, now looming up like the bones of a dead animal lying in

the sand. Several and lively jolts and bumpings marked our transit from the desert to the mountains. We seemed to nose about, uncertain of our bearings, or looking for something, and then, suddenly, there was the Siq below us, no more than a long crack or fissure in the painted rocks below. As one, the children rushed to the side of the aeroplane, standing and kneeling on the seats to get their faces nearer to the windows.

In front, and not more than a hundred feet away, was a moving shadow like that of a huge bird, and in front of it and flying with it was the second aeroplane. For a moment the flat nose of it was as that of some huge fish patrolling the coastal waters. But its shadow was bird-like, bat-like, a thing gliding with fixed wings. And we were round again, wheeling with our own shadow tied to us and darkening the rock, and the boys and girls rushing to the windows on the other side.

It was not to be for a few moments. We were going round and round again. The door of the cockpit opened. The pilot invited the children in to sit with him, and we saw Murphy, the boy from Chicago, whoop with joy, and go inside. Round and round Petra, and up and down we went, with the second aeroplane always in front of us and, it seemed, one or other of the children at the controls. There, below, was the encampment, and swerving over to one side with everyone at the windows, the long line of tombs which we had climbed up to only last evening. But of El Deir there was no sign at all. It must be well hidden. Not to see it was a sad disappointment, but it cannot be as beautiful as the Khazné. Yet there it is, cut back in the rock, and we never saw it. And now we flew straight out from the mountain and were over the desert on the way to Amman.

# CHAPTER VIII

# JERASH AND JERUSALEM

*Ptolemy Philadelphus — Loudspeaker on a minaret — Nightingales of Cairo — Bee-eaters on the telegraph wires — Flowering ruins — Another street of columns — Naumachia, or not? — Horseshoe-shaped forum — Down to the Dead Sea — Excavations at Jericho — Women at the Well of Elisha — Coming to Jerusalem — The Mount of Olives — Changing hotels — Church of the Holy Sepulchre — Museum at Jerusalem — Haram-es-Sherif — Dome of the Rock — Marriage of the East and West — Mosque of El Aksa — Souks of the Arab city — Easter service at the Russian convent — Monks from Mount Athos — Bethlehem — Mediaeval costumes — A Pre-Raphaelite painting.*

THE airfield at Amman, which is run with startling efficiency, is supervised by men of the Arab Legion in spiked, Crusader helmets. I thought they looked uneasily at the travellers from England. But our small pieces of luggage were soon through the customs, and a guide, but no mentor, sent to meet us from the tourist agency came forward with the sentence: "Welcome to the capital of the Hashemite Kingdom of Jordan", the only words of English in his repertoire. There followed a drive to the hotel through the crowded streets of Amman. This was the ancient Philadelphus, i.e., named after Ptolemy II of Egypt, so called by antiphrasis because he killed two of his own brothers.* There is a Roman theatre immediately in front of the hotel at Amman, which for some curious reason reminded me of the Station Hotel at Galway, not now, but as it must have been when John Leech went there with Dean Hole (they published their Irish sketch book in 1859) when "the dress of the women of the Claddagh imparted a singularly foreign aspect to the Galway streets and quays". In Roman times Amman (Philadelphus) was another of the colonnaded towns. Its street of columns ran parallel to the river and was more than half-a-mile long.†

Dinner in the hotel, which is efficient and well run, was, also, of an illusionary nature because the dining room appears to be downstairs

---

* And inaugurated a custom adhered to by later Ptolemies when he married Arsinoe, his own sister.

† In *Caravan Cities*, Oxford, Clarendon Press, 1932, p. 41. M. Rostovtzeff remarks of the theatre at Amman that "it is a lasting testimony to the ancient city's wealth and size in Roman times, and a significant reminder of the improvements which will be necessary before the modern town can even slightly resemble ancient Philadelphus".

in the basement, inducing a nightclub feeling which is not borne out by anything else in the building, or, indeed, within a long distance of Amman. True, it is a capital; but, not long ago, it was a village of Circassian refugees. The night was quiet and luxurious after the tents and caves of Petra, but only up till three a.m., or it may have been a little later, when a cannon was fired in sign that it was Ramazan, followed, almost at once, by loud and formidable roaring coming from several directions at once, as though the bull of Bashan and all his brothers had become half-human and learnt to bellow a few words.

It was, in fact, the Cairo *muezzins*; gramophone records played through amplifiers from the minarets. They are the highly paid "nightingales" of modern Islam, earning, we were told, the incomes of Italian tenors, but in this "presentation" they are a horror of the contemporary world like fluorescent strip lighting. The effect of their loud voices is most peculiar in the middle of the night. We were told of a nervous American couple arriving in Amman, being woken by the gun going off and then hearing the *muezzins*, and getting hurriedly into their clothes because they thought it was a popular uprising and that the voices were giving orders for murder and pillage. They do indeed sound as though they were inciting to a massacre of white devils. But once one is used to them, I cannot pretend I did not enjoy lying awake listening. They are voices of the minotaurs; of the mino-taur exultant, and the wounded minotaur. Sometimes the voice drops in tragedy and disaster, as of the monster with a bull's head dying, or asking for mercy in the bull-ring. Nights of Ramazan in Amman are scenes from the minotauromachia until the amplifier runs down.

In the morning we left for Jerash by road, seeing no more of Amman, and were soon in the most beautiful countryside we had known for many weeks. There were little hills covered with olives and carob trees, with wheat growing in small cultivated patches and many fig trees. Yet a wild country, all the same, for there are hyena packs in these very hills. And now on the telegraph wires were perched the only beautiful birds we had seen since arriving in the Middle East. First, an electric blue flash, such a blue as one could scarcely believe, and a spreading and a clapping of wings of brown or terracotta to show the blue beneath. They were bee-eaters, solitary individual blue birds to begin with, and then two or three or even many of them, side by side on the wires, and flying away like blue halcyons when they heard the motor. The modern village of Jerash is a white village of Circassians a little off the road. We halted at a house near the ruins, for there is neither hotel nor restaurant, and ate our picnic at a stone table in the shade of a huge old tree. Later, the Circassians came up and talked to us. They are the descendants of Moslem Tcherkesses settled here by the Turks after the Russo-Turkish war of 1877, and after only a couple of human generations still have the long heads and aquiline noses of the Caucasians.

No classical ruins can have a more lovely setting, and perhaps at Jerash it is more spectacular still because unexpected in the presumed sandy wildernesses of Transjordan. For here were flowering meadows to compare in this month, at least, with the Sicilian wild flowers of Selinunte or Segesta. There were blood-red anemones, and wild hollyhocks like thin towers or campaniles of pink bells. Jerash was the only place in our travels that we were in time to see the flowers. But it is, also, to be said that the beauty of the ancient Gerasa is enhanced because it is little known and left to itself. The city "belonged", we are told, to the Decapolis of Peraea, that being one of five districts into which Jewish territory was divided in the time of Herod, its name of "the country beyond" signifying that it was the remotest of those lands. However, its buildings of the second and third centuries A.D. date from after the capture of Jerusalem by Titus and the second Diaspora of the Jews. Moreover, it emerges as a Roman, not Semitic town. More Roman than Palmyra.

How hot and glorious it was to walk among the ruins! Weeds and flowers growing from every crevice, and in between the Roman pavements with their ruts of chariot wheels. There were squat, square lizards of a toad-shape, if one may put it so, with short tails and dark in colour, darting on the stones, lizards, we were told, of a race peculiar to Jerash, but there is not yet an opportunity of confirming this. You enter Gerasa by a triumphal arch which touches a note of originality by having acanthus leaves carved *above* the bases of its columns. Baedeker gives careful directions for the pitching of tents "near the North Gate" and remarks that "a visitation of the ruins takes a full day". Who can see himself walking round the ruins of Rugby, or Rennes, or Modena in seventeen centuries' time? In towns such as Jerash—and in how many others in Syria and Turkey and North Africa?—there is some evidence of a golden age.

We are now walking along its Colonnade or Street of Columns, half-a-mile long and leading right through the town. At a little distance down it, as at Palmyra, there is a triple gate or tetrapylon standing at the main crossing but this, with the usual niches for statues, was a domed building. And continuing, the next chapter in the flowering ruins is the Great Temple or Temple of the Sun, with porches or propylaea leading to it up flights of steps past niches shaped like cockle shells with all their flutings and ruin and wreck of fountains. It is the

heart or centre of Jerash but there is better to come. And now, by the
remains of early and not particularly interesting Christian churches
built of the old stones, we are at the far end of Gerasa, near the North
Gate where we should have pitched our tents, and looking over
orchards and more acres of wild flowers.

There is a steep climb up green banks and fallen stones and we come
to the edge of a fall or drop which is the view from above the top row
of seats of a Roman theatre. How beautiful it is to sit here for a few
moments thinking of what might have been had these lands remained
a part of Europe, or come back to it with the Crusades! For this is the
classical past, or golden age, imagined in the early Renaissance, and
here are beauties of scene and of architecture not attained in metro-
politan Rome. One cannot look at Jerash and not regret the hand of
Islam which with puritan zeal forbade sculpture and imprisoned the
arts in abstract forms. Here could have been another Italy, or a second
Spain. The country, hereabouts, is an alternative Umbria or Tuscany,
but it was to become Arabian with many vicissitudes, and then a part
of Turkey. And in spite of their hollow devotion to their ancient gods
it cannot be said that they had improved, but, rather, it has to be
admitted that the strength had run out of their civilization when they
became Christian. By the fifth and sixth century A.D. it was ripe to fall.

There are more remains of early churches at the back of the Great
Temple, and some indifferent mosaic floors. But one theatre was not
enough for the population of Jerash, and the bigger of the two with a
lately restored proscenium is built into the hillside where we complete
the circuit of the town. This theatre is of huge proportions, and looking
at it we may conjecture what will be left, one day, of the five cinemas
in Leicester Square. Further, there is a circus with a naumachia, a
theatre for the representation of naval combats, one hundred and
seventy yards long and sixty yards broad, "adjoining it".* These
sea-fights with gladiators killing one another in unusual ways gave an
extra thrill to the spectators. That is one of the darker facets of the
golden age. Vicariously, it must be compared with our ice-panto-

---

* M. Rostovtzeff in *Caravan Cities*, p. 74, comments that "it remains for him who
first gave this name to explain how a naumachia could exist, in a half-desert region,
where water was worth its weight in gold". He calls it, instead, a stadium for athletic
contests, or a cattle market with space to test and exercise the animals. But M. Rostovtzeff
seems to half-contradict himself, later, pp. 83, 84, when discussing a huge tank, or pool,
or reservoir, into which flow many springs, with a terrace and colonnade and small
theatre with seats for about a thousand behind it. An inscription proves, he says, that the
feast of Maiumas was celebrated here. "This", he adds, "was one of the most renowned
religious ceremonies of heathen Syria and was especially abhorred by Christians
because of its ritualistic submersion of naked women, in the presence of an audience
seated in a theatre-like temple of a type peculiar to Syria."

mines, *Puss in Boots on Ice*, and so forth, or with an aquaparade at
Wembley Stadium. But the golden age comes back again to Jerash
with its marvellous Ionic Forum, last item to be seen, for it is close
to the gate where we came into the town. In fact, the Street of Columns
starts from it, and the wonder and peculiarity is that it is elliptical or
horseshoe-shaped with the pillared street leading from the back of it
like the long handle of a spoon. Most of the pillars are still standing
with their entablature connecting them and much of the stone pavement is there. This Forum of Jerash seemed to me in better taste than
anything at Palmyra. Indeed, it is one of the more graceful of all
classical remains, and our parallel age from Mansart and Wren down to
Wood of Bath and Gabriel can offer nothing better, not the Peyrou of
Montpellier, nor the ovoid colonnade that leads from the Pépinière at
Nancy. The Forum at Jerash is surely one of the beauties of the ancient
world.

On the way to the Dead Sea we are still in that Arcadian landscape
for a few miles. Or Arcadian at this time of year, in the month of May,
for it may be scorched and burnt by August. But the hills become
barer. One is bracing oneself for a first sight of the Dead Sea, and gets
the impression of its huge and long basin between the hills as if, which
is the truth, it was long ago much bigger in area. The descent is not
perceptible in its early stages. At the Allenby bridge over the Jordan
we are within a few feet of the legendary place of baptism, and probably others as well as myself will have remembered El Greco's
painting, one of the pictures of his old age, and perhaps the extreme
limit of his mystical imagination. On many accounts it is the most
extraordinary painting in the world.* There are now beginnings of the
salt plain, and the landscape is a not altogether unlikely mixture of
the background of Holman Hunt's "Scapegoat" with Salvador Dali's
"pale yellow sands", only the latter have been sown with salt. Now
the cliffs lower themselves into sight, where are the caves in which the
controversial manuscripts were found, and we see the blue waters lying
into an illimitable distance for the Dead Sea is about the size of the
Lake of Geneva. Time and dimensions become irrelevant and we
appear to take an hour, at least, to cover the two or three miles down

---

* El Greco's *Baptism of Christ* is in the church of the Hospital de San Juan Bautista
or Hospital de Afuera, at Toledo. The yellow waters of Jordan have dense thickets on
their banks "which harbour wild boar" (this seems doubtful), and in biblical times were
infested by lions (Jeremiah xlix. 19). Julian Huxley (*op. cit.*, p. 168): "Here and there
in the foothill region of Northern Syria, lions survived well into the second half of the
nineteenth century." It seems extraordinary that it was only known in 1837 that the
Dead Sea lay below sea-level; it is, in fact, nearly thirteen hundred feet below the level
of the Mediterranean.

Sasanian rock
sculpture at
N a q s h - e -
Rostam

Mosque of Soltan Selim at Damascus

to the shore. Here is a gloomy bathing place, selling souvenirs, and with "export" beer from Holland or Czecho-Slovakia which is nearly as expensive as champagne. Of course it was irresistible to walk down and dip one's fingers in the waters of the Dead Sea. Not a sound comes over the lake which is its ghastly quality and attribute. The waters do not lap, they appear to be lolling in a sinister and ominous trance. Temperatures are hotter in the valley of Jordan than in any part of Palestine, and we read of the inhabitants of Jericho seeming to be "a degenerate race on whom the hot climate has had an enervating effect". As, also, being so far below sea-level; speaking personally, a sensation of a new kind, every bit as disagreeable as being too high up, and with the same feeling as though one was in a non-pressurized aeroplane. What can it be to sit here on this wooden balcony on an August or September afternoon when there is thunder coming? What sounds, then, do the small waves make? When the first murmur and rumble dies into the hills of chalk and bone, and it is the turn of the dead waters?

An apocalyptic setting of dead, dead hills lies between the Dead Sea and Jericho, too waterless even for the hermits of a Thebaid, the grey hills having no living thing upon them, so that it could become in one's imagination a prison or place of detention for those who devised the slag heaps and mounds of clinker of our coal mines down to the gehenna of open cast workings.* By road, this landscape goes on for just long enough, and not too long, until we reach the palm groves and orange glades of Jericho. But this is a transformation of the last few years since the discovery of subterranean springs of water. It must have entirely changed the character of Jericho. Now it is the place where inhabitants of the Arab town of Jerusalem have their week-end villas. But the old Jericho still exists only a little way outside its walls. Here are the astonishing pits or "digs" of excavation into mounds which even the tyro would guess to be scenes of ancient human habitation. You look down thirty or forty feet into the mound onto remains of the oldest settled site in human history. Mysterious skeletons had just lately been found there, and scraps of paper with numbers on them were nailed on the rock to mark the precise spot of recent discoveries. But strict archaeology is not my subject and is beyond my understanding.

I found the Well of Elisha, a few feet away, more interesting. This, because of the perpetual line of women coming to fill their pitchers

* This landscape much resembles the primitive painting of *The Thebaid of Egypt* in one of the first rooms of the Uffizi at Florence, a picture "sometimes given", in the words of old dictionaries, to Ambrogio Lorenzetti.

9

at the well. Hardly a moment passes without a new arrival. It is naturally warm water and the Well of Elisha is their social centre. Their dresses and the way they walk are most beautiful to watch, but we were told on no account to show a camera as they resent being photographed. They come to the well in hundreds, appearing two and three together round a corner of the road. But there are camps, near by, with no fewer than thirty thousand Palestinian refugees. Small boys came up, speaking good English which they said the nuns had taught them, and wrote down their names and addresses for us to write to them when we were back in England. The refugees are a problem one constantly hears of, but does not apprehend. There are large numbers, even tens of thousands of them, for whom no work can be found of any sort or kind. Till driven out, they were living happily in their villages. Now, without trades or land to work, and with nothing to do, they are, literally, dying of inanition. The mortality rate is appalling and tuberculosis claims many victims. They are not wanted, anywhere or by anyone, that is their tragedy. And their camps being situated in about the most lowering and devitalizing area imaginable cannot help them. If they are a problem to themselves they are no less so to the Transjordan government, a kingdom artificially composed and put to-gether, at that, and which is stifled or strangled by its weight of refugees.

Many are the human souls that would have felt themselves dying of excitement and exultation at being within a half-hour of Jerusalem. For it is no more than that. As you come nearer to it, the country becomes little and domestic in a happy and touching way. Hilly country, with castles on hilltops which you are told were built by Herod, and a background much resembling a spring landscape in a painting by Fra Angelico, only that the inhabitants are not fair-haired angels and children but the Arabs of tradition, riding donkeys, or even leading camels. As far as the Arab city of Jerusalem this is the part of Palestine occupied latterly by King Hussein of Transjordan. The frontier before that was the river Jordan. Now buildings come into sight on the tops of hills and we are told that one of them with an ugly tower is a hospital built by the Kaiserin Augusta Victoria. Next, part of a town is seen crowding a hilltop and this is the Jewish city of Jerusalem. After which, and nearer at hand, a building with familiar onion-domes is the Russian church upon the Mount of Olives.

Now appears on the left the walled city with the Dome of the Rock in midst of it. We come nearer, and below the wall, passing by the Golden Gate, still surprised at the small scale of things, the Mount of Olives being no higher than a little and inconspicuous hill among so many, and the walled city not bigger altogether than perhaps the area

of Windsor Castle. It is about seven o'clock in the evening, and we go
straight to the hotel which is newly opened and unsatisfactory, with
bedrooms like hospital cells, hospital beds, and no hot water. Moreover,
the stuff for curtains has not arrived and there are no blinds. One will
be woken at dawn, even if the street arc-lamps allow an uneasy slumber
towards morning. There is only one thing to be done. And sending for
a taxi, and having first gone there in order to be certain there is accommodation, we return, pack our bags, pay our bill, and instal ourselves
at the American Colony Hotel in time for a late dinner. This is a charming place, its tile-panels making it a little like an old house in Seville
except that the tiles are Turkish, or at any rate from Damascus, with
their cypresses and tulips, and that the night air tells one it is a hill
town. Two or three of the rooms have fine old Turkish wooden
ceilings, and in the morning the court is lively with flowers, and has
palms and climbing geraniums that are as strong growing as wistaria.

On all counts, history and religious sentiment apart, Jerusalem is
a beautiful old town. Beautiful, as are Toledo, Siena, or Avignon.
That is the scale of it. Indeed, it does not seem as big as Toledo or Siena.
But, then, one only sees a part of the town. Walls are built across the
streets to divide the Arab from the Jewish cities even within a few
yards of the hotel. There is no communication at all between the two
towns. It is a curious sensation to hear people talking during the night
and know they are in the other city. But the walled city with the
Dome of the Rock, the Church of the Holy Sepulchre, the Mount of
Olives, and nearly every site of historical or religious interest is in the
Arab part. Not a sign is to be seen of the Jewish part of the population.
The roofs of their schools and hospitals are visible, but never a human
being. It does not seem to be a situation that can possibly continue,
being as absurdly impractical as if Monaco was walled off from Monte
Carlo. I wanted to visit the grave of a great friend who was killed in
Jerusalem but the cemetery was in the Jewish city and so I could not
go. I believe I was told that it was now impossible for students to get to
the University. And another silly effect of the blockade is to make
Bethlehem more than three times its real distance from Jerusalem
(five miles) because of having to go the long way round.

Before going into the walled city by the Golden Gate we went to
the Church of the Holy Sepulchre. The ground plan of this church
must be the most complicated of any building in the world, the plan
in my guide book having no fewer than forty-eight numbers to refer
to.* In any case, the church was almost burned to the ground in 1808

* Of which the more salient are: Monastery of Abraham, Armenian Chapel of St
James, Coptic Chapel of Michael, Abyssinian Chapel, Chapel of St Mary of Egypt and

so that nothing is left of the original building but a little of the bare walls. Since that date it has become like an enormous extension to the Chamber of Horrors at Madame Tussaud's. That, too, it will be remembered, was burned a few years ago, though most of its contents were saved and carried out into the air. What is old at the Church of the Holy Sepulchre becomes, at once, suspect from its immediate surroundings. There are still remains of the circular church or rotunda with the sepulchre in midst of it, discovered, "contrary to all expectation", in the words of Bishop Eusebius of Caeserea, during the reign of Constantine. This sets the tone for nearly everything else in the building. So prolonged and intense have been the quarrels between the various Christian sects that for many years order has been kept by Moslem guardians, and the post of custodian has become hereditary in an old Jerusalem family. One of the delights of a visit to the church is to see these "Turks", of a sort now vanished and gone from Turkey, reclining in turbans and caftans on a raised platform covered with rugs at the entrance to the church, conveniently near a telephone with a direct line to the police station. There are few other pleasures, and too much strain upon credulity. This is where a Protestant past and "low church" forbears, a strain otherwise dormant or suppressed, come to the surface, for it does, in fact, make one angry to see so much ignorance and superstition. There are sticks pushed through holes and then kissed by the pilgrims (at the Column of the Scourging); a Cleft in the Rock, covered with a brass lid, less than a foot deep, but said to reach to the centre of the earth; and in the Chapel of St Helena there are columns that shed tears. A black-clad neophyte with a cracked voice and heterosexual air followed round, recounting all the miracles in an American accent to a group of tourists just behind us. Perhaps the most interesting and genuine feature of the Church of the Holy Sepulchre is the priests of the Syrian and Coptic and Abyssinian churches in their distinctive robes. They have, at least, more excuse for their superstition and it becomes them better with their darker skins and beards.

The sacred sites in the town proper are less offensive because they are in the open air. And because nearly all of them are in association with mediaeval buildings of beautiful old stone. It is as though you were pointed out the House of Dives or the Via Dolorosa in the

Chapel of the Agony of the Virgin, Greek Chapel of St James, Chapel of St Thecla, Stone of Unction, Place from which the Women witnessed the Anointing, Chapel of the Copts, Chapel of the Syrians, Passage to the Armenian Gallery, Chapel of the Apparition, Latin Sacristy, Greek Cathedral, Chapel of the Parting of the Raiment, Chapel of the Derision, Altar of the Penitent Thief, Abyssinian Monastery, Entrance to Coptic Monastery, etc., etc.

streets of mediaeval Avignon. But this without the inhabitants who in the Arab town, at least, are untouched Orientals of a Turkish tinge. Our next steps were to the Museum, which is as finely installed as that of Damascus. It possesses one of the earliest and most aboriginal of human skulls, a female with a slanting, bony shelf for forehead and a prognathous jaw. Luckily her other remains have perished; but there are other skulls and skeletons nearly as old, and descending to works of art there are the decorations of a desert hunting castle of the time of the Caliphs (eighth century) with figures of dancers half-way between a Boddhisattva and *La Sultane bleue* of Léon Bakst. There is certainly Buddhist or even Hindu influence, as though the Caliphs had heard of Indian temple dancers and after the gazelle hunt wanted entertainment by the *bayadères*. This is but a superficial account of a castle in which five centuries later, Frederick II with his hundreds of gerfalcons and his Oriental bodyguard and attendants would have felt at home.

But we will go, now, to the raised platform or terrace of the Haram-es-Sherif, which surrounds the Dome of the Rock at Jerusalem, entering the walled city by the Golden Gate. Perhaps this is the most sacred place in the world, to Moslem, Jew, and Christian, alike. The Acropolis at Athens is the only other place in the world with so much attached to it of the human spirit, but this is more sacred, and I would add, still more beautiful. To Moslems it is the holiest place in the world after Mecca. As for the Jews, the Orthodox among them never enter it for fear of committing the sin of treading on the Holy of Holies of the Temple. The Temple of Solomon stood here, and the Second Temple, and in its turn the Temple of Herod, when the whole area of the Haram-es-Sherif was enclosed by double rows of columns, with a quadruple colonnade upon one side.

Many parts of the Temple of Herod were decorated with plates of gold, and this is perhaps the ancestry of the gilded shrines of the Shiah Moslems and the golden domes of Meshed and Qom.

Setting foot on to the Haram-es-Sherif there are marvellous buildings in every direction. Wherever you look are Saracenic structures in this style which could be called the Gothic of the Orient, and long arcaded walks, and in midst of the open space a domed octagon, the Dome of the Rock, or Mosque of Omar, beyond doubt one of the wonders of the world. I have to say, in sorrow, that it is more beautiful than St Mark's in Venice, for till I had seen the Dome of the Rock I thought St Mark's was the most lovely building in the world. But the exterior is more simple and beautiful, and we will leave the discussion of the interior until we go inside.

Built for the Moslems in the eighth century, almost certainly by

Greek architects, it is a marvellous blending of Byzantine, Persian, and Arabian design. Also, it has a curious and entire timelessness, due not only to its perfection in shape and ornament, but to being, as it were, a Renaissance, where there was never a Renaissance, and so long before the Renaissance in Italy began. The Crusaders when they reached Jerusalem mistook it for the original Temple of Solomon, and its octagonal structure invested with a mystical meaning and importance which it deserves on the score of its beauty alone, inspired the Knights Templar to build their churches on this pattern in England and elsewhere.* Moreover, as a symbol of perfection and proportion and poetry it appears in a fresco by Perugino in the Sistine Chapel in the Vatican and, above all, in Raphael's famous painting of the *Sposalizio* or *Nuptials of the Virgin* in the Brera Gallery at Milan.

The Mosque of Omar stands on a little higher raised platform on the Haram-es-Sherif, and the eight shallow flights of steps leading up to it have Saracenic arcades or screens of arches of a truly marvellous grace and lightness above them. Their elegance, indeed, forms one of the chief beauties of the scene. As well, there are several *sebils* or fountains for ablution, one of them with a melon dome in Mameluke style, veined and netted like a melon, as are the tombs of the Caliphs in the desert outside Cairo.

As for the interior of the Dome of the Rock it is grand and impressive beyond words. But one could no more describe it in a few sentences than one can the interior of St Mark's. Its form, of an octagon, of course holds the attention more than do those flights and returns of the Gothic with their aisles and clerestories and their chantries and Lady chapels. It is a more rhythmical, a more planned and contained poetry, and with a deeper mystery to it. For the Dome of the Rock is, in fact, the *Sposalizio* or *Nuptials* of the East and West; and nowhere else in the world, not even in St Mark's in Venice, are Orient and Occident indissoluble and one. It is the most sacred and holy building I have ever seen, not belonging to one faith but to all religions worth the name. And in the same breath not a mosque or church at all, but a building made holy by history and poetry alone.

The interior takes the form of a columned arcade round the Rock, and we may take in evidence of this marriage or nuptials of the arts of East and West the painted and gilded wooden ceiling which is the work of Indian craftsmen of the seventeenth century, and the wrought

* The Temple Church in London, St Sepulchre in Northampton, Round Church, Cambridge, and Little Maplestead in Essex. On the continent, among others, the Cathedral or Münster of Aix-la-Chapelle, built by Charlemagne, and the monastery church of Tomar in Portugal.

iron grille of the Crusaders, between the inner row of columns, and railing off the Rock, which is the work of French ironsmiths of the end of the twelfth century dating from when the Mosque of Omar was turned into a church. We read furthermore that the mother of one of the Abbaside Caliphs presented the mosque in the tenth century with "doors made from *tannub*, a rare wood grown in Indonesia, like the wood of the pine tree". Stained glass windows, some of them of the fifteenth century, form an experience in this field all the more unfamiliar because the patterns are abstract. The capitals of many of the columns are Byzantine, as are the mosaics on the upper walls which are chiefly of flower-vases with grapes and ears of corn. How disgraceful and utterly beyond reason that this most beautiful and sacred building should have been injured by Jewish bombs during the disturbances of 1948! Coming out of the Dome of the Rock back into the world again there is the little open decagonal domed structure beside it, its columns forming a decagon on the outside and a hexagon within, a structure of sonnet-like and rhymed perfection of shape, and further away below the steps, the Mosque of El Aksa, making all in all, with the arcades and the domed fountains, a spiritual as well as architectural experience one will never know again.

Looking, once more, at the Mosque of Omar we admire the windows of open porcelain lattice, and the porcelain incrustation, for there is no other word for it, of Turkish and Persian tiles. These date from the Turkish period and were the gift, suitably enough, of Soltan Süleyman the Magnificent. The Turkish tiles came from the Isnik factory in Asia Minor, "but it is thought that the Persian ones were made in Jerusalem by Persian craftsmen brought here for the purpose". This tile revetment adds the final and ultimate beauty to the Mosque of Omar which we now walk round in order to observe from every angle.

Anywhere but on the Haram-es-Sherif, and close to that paragon, the Mosque of El Aksa would be a major architectural sensation. We go down the few steps towards it if only to get a better view of the Mosque of Omar. And now, inveigled inside by its rows of columns, it does not take long to see that this must have been in origin a Christian basilica, owing its foundation to Justinian. El Aksa is over restored, the ceiling and some of its marble columns being the gift of King Farouk, who can be mentioned here in the same intake of breath as Salah-uh-Din, or Saladin. For to Saladin is due the *minbar* or pulpit of cedarwood, of marvellous arabesque inlay with mother-of-pearl and ivory. Close to the *mehrab* was lying a man's dead body, for so holy is El Aksa that corpses are taken to lie there for a few hours before burial. Again there are beautiful stained glass windows, an

Islamic art of which one is little aware except at Cairo and Istanbul. One aisle of the mosque prolongs itself, curiously, as though not pertaining to the main building, and takes the form of a double colonnade with pointed vaulting. This is the "white" mosque, set apart for women, many of whom were praying and swaying their bodies to and fro, and it is thought that the scene of their crosslegg'd ecstasies was once a dormitory of the Knights Templar. In a world of decaying "character" the Shaikh of El Aksa must be recalled. He is so perfect an example of Oriental courtesy and good manners. With his long caftan and white turban how easily he could be a living figure out of Carpaccio's painting of the *Preaching of St Stephen,*★ the background of which is said to be the buildings of old Cairo.

The sight of the Dome of the Rock, once more, through the porch of El Aksa is an experience never to be forgotten. If only it could be said that St Peter's or Notre Dame, or Westminster Abbey were as beautiful as this! The memory of its interior eclipses all one remembers of the interior of St Mark's. Those slabs of marble which line the walls, which so much need cleaning but with a careful hand that will respect and not efface their patina, sliced marbles that on wet or bad days so much resemble *salami* or *mortadella*, or, at other times, the "ghosts" that children make with ink and folded blotting-paper, and the multitude of bad and late mosaics, but those are memories redeemed, always, by St Mark's Oriental mystery of first encounter, turbaned pulpit, and uneven floor! The mosaics of its two-angled atrium or ambulatory where one walks in wet weather, are bad, too; but there are mosaics in the baptistery with four figures of saints in the Byzantine canon in four spandrels of the dome, ecclesiastics of huge height wearing vestments patterned with black and white crosses of different sizes!† Thinking of this and that, and of the Pala d'Oro glittering with millennium gold at the high altar, St Mark's does return after all to something of its old glory. But the Dome of the Rock, the work of so many different times and races, is yet an entity and an individual and living being. As much as the Taj Mahal it could be the work of a single inspiration. I have not seen the Taj Mahal but it looks to me to be pale and feminine beside the Mosque of Omar. That, or call it the Dome of the Rock, must on all accounts be the most beautiful building of the Moslem world. Whether it is not, also, the most beautiful building of all the East and West is only uncertain in a world where all superlatives are stupid.

★ Now in the Louvre.
† Robert Byron told me he had seen the only surviving vestments of this ancient Byzantine pattern in the Sacristy of the Patriachs, in the Kremlin at Moscow.

It is difficult to drag one's eyes away from the domed octagon and to leave that holy place. But the walled city of Jerusalem is there to be enjoyed for days on end. There are cobbled lanes between stone houses and long lengths of *souks*, as unspoilt as in any Oriental town. How it compares with the other or Jewish city of Jerusalem one does not know. For there is no means whatever of finding out. One cannot look through a window, or over a wall. Only at one point is it possible to peer through a wicket and see the Wailing Wall. We may infer that the Jewish town is more modern, and that part of the charm of the Arab city is that the *souks* are fine and stone built instead of being roofed with tin as they are at Damascus.

On the day we left Jerusalem we went in the morning to the Russian convent upon the Mount of Olives in order to try and seek an interview with the Abbess, who is the mother of a friend living in London. It was the middle of May, and the delayed Russian Easter which is twelve days later than ours, and they were celebrating it with the enormously long services of the Eastern church. We stood and watched them in midst of a concourse of black-clad nuns while three bearded priests anointed all and sundry with the holy chrism. One priest, in particular, a tall young man with long black hair falling nearly to his shoulders, the high cheekbones of the Slav, and deepset eyes, was the picture of fanaticism. Many of the nuns had the round faces of peasants and were convent servitors. Some, too old to stand, were crouched on three-legg'd stools, and there were little girls two or three years old wearing miniature nuns' robes. We sent a message by one of the nuns, and were told the abbess could not leave the service to come out and see us. We stood watching for a few moments and then went away.

How pathetic these services are in onion-domed churches in so many places, in San Remo, in Florence, in Biarritz, in Copenhagen! Because it is a dwindling congregation that must die out in a few years. When we came back an hour later we were received by the abbess, a member of the former Imperial family, in a room hung with icons and portraits of the Tsars.* How simply and quickly the Russians create a Russian atmosphere! We were told that the priests, including the one who looked so fanatical, were monks from the Russian convent of Russikon on Mount Athos, and that for diet they had brought their own mushrooms with them.

---

* The custom for widows of members of the Imperial family to take the veil was long established in Russia. St Anne, daughter of King Olaf of Sweden, and consort of Yaroslav I, was the first to set an example of taking the veil, according to the custom of widowed Empresses in Byzantium. She died in 1050, and her shrine is in the cathedral of St Sophia, in Novgorod the Great. Byzantine Emperors, too, retired into monasteries, more often as a measure of prudence than a proof of sanctity.

There had been a chance, later that day, of going to Bethlehem. It is a drive through hilly country which owing to the abnormal political situation is three times further than need be. But the Church of the Nativity seems to possess all those qualities lacking in the Church of the Holy Sepulchre at Jerusalem. Yet it is neither beautiful, nor particularly interesting, although Edward IV paid for the lead upon the roof, but there is something to it that touches the emotions. And in the church and in and about the streets were to be seen the Christian women of Bethlehem wearing white wimple headdresses, rising in a peak, that are completely mediaeval in appearance. The question is, did they adopt their headdresses from the wives and daughters of the Crusaders, or did the Crusaders bring back the idea of such headdresses to Normandy and the Île de France? What is certain is that the women of Bethlehem walking along a street are like a vision of early mediaeval France.

On the way back to Jerusalem the landscape was in perpetual reminder of something. Of a painting with the conciseness of a colour slide, and I had guessed what it was. Nothing other than the picture in the Tate Gallery of *Jerusalem and the Valley of Jehoshaphat* by a forgotten Pre-Raphaelite painter Thomas Seddon, who came out here to paint with Holman Hunt, and died young in Cairo in 1856. That is an accurate and absolute rendering of this landscape in the sunlight. Half-an-hour later we were at the airport waiting for the aeroplane to Beirut.

# Chapter IX

## ALEPPO

*Tinned music — Rough flying — Armenians at Aleppo — The souks — The citadel — Mosque of Paradise — The Levant Company — Desert truffles — Irises — A brief life of St Simeon Stylite — Kalat Seman — Description of the four basilicas — 13 August 510 — Men in saffron-yellow robes — Beehive villages — Hama — Norias or water wheels — Homs — Far-off view of Krak des Chevaliers — Drive up the mountain — Stupendous scale — Crusaders' castles — Island of Ruad — Through Tripoli at high speed — Back late to Beirut — Baalbek — Compared to Leptis Magna — Country palace of Beit-ed-Din.*

ANOTHER day or two in the capital of Lebanon on this our penultimate visit, trying to avoid the wiles of the curio dealers by day, and by day and night in the new hotel hearing Rimsky-Korsakov's *Schéhérazade* relayed all over the building and through the bathroom walls. *Schéhérazade* over and over again, to ourselves but just returned from Persia! There could be no experience quite of this kind other than, let us say, going to a bull-fight in Spain and hearing the toreador's march from *Carmen*. With a needle caught in the track of the amplifier and reiterating the same phrase again and again! And in the end it is as in the beginning: however much sickened at the moment one could hear them both once more.

In the aeroplane flying to Aleppo there were raindrops on the window pane. There were, also, extremely ragged clouds on the horizon and soon we were flying through the torn fragments of a storm. Aleppo, it seems, is difficult to touch down at in fine weather, and on that windy rainy day it was a relief to land with no more than a bump and have more than the usual time wasted at the airport. The Syrians are suspicious by nature. They could not understand why one wanted to come to Aleppo. Eventually I was released, on promise to leave the country within forty-eight hours and on payment of what could almost have been an emigration fee. And on the way in to Haleb, as Aleppo is called in Arabic, it was interesting to catch sight of one of the beehive villages of Northern Syria only a mile or two away.

Before we had reached the modern town of Aleppo with its crowded streets I had already heard from the driver that he was Armenian and that there were fifty thousand of his countrymen living in the town.

A great deal of the commerce is in Armenian hands, this population being but a remnant of the race after a million had died on their way here through Turkey during, and after, the First World War. The good and comfortable hotel is Armenian-run. Yet, in spite of its many Christian inhabitants, Aleppo remains an Oriental town. Its modern streets have more of human character than those of Damascus, and there is the important difference that Aleppo has a colder climate, and though it only lies at half the height of either Damascus or Jerusalem it is a northern town. Perhaps, at first sight, it is in other ways a little chilly and depressing. The heat and enervation of the Orient are left behind though it may be fiercely hot in summer. But the solid built stone hotel is safe and sensible, soon the answers arrive to letters of introduction, and the nervous and mental climate thaws and changes.

Aleppo has one incomparable attraction. The *souks* are without an equal in the Orient. Those of Damascus and of Tunis fade beside them and lose their colour in the memory. This is, in part, because their stone vaults and passages date back to Saracenic times and it could be said almost to the day of Saladin. We were taken down some steps into a *hammam* which looked untouched during the centuries, from one room into another, hotter still, until the last had the temperature of a Victorian stove house; and into a fifteenth century house of beautifully cut stone which had been either a hospital or an early lunatic asylum, and was now a tenement for poor families. Donkeys and heavy laden horses come down the narrow passageways and at every turn there are new marvels of colour as we pass, first, the spice bazaar, then, that for slippers, or the tailors, or saddlers, or coppersmiths. And our walk through the *souks* of Aleppo was cleverly contrived so as to bring us out almost in front of the famous Citadel, that magnificent work of mediaeval military architecture, or engineering, the reply of the Saracens to the forts and castles of the Frankish paladins. It is raised on a tremendous breath-taking glacis, with a moat across which a bridged gateway leads into the heart of the Citadel, making on the way five twists and turnings for last resort in hand-to-hand fighting. The artificial hill on which the Citadel is built could be of all antiquity, and it is a pity that what is deep down inside it cannot be revealed by some scientific combination of X-ray and mine-detector. It was El Malek-ez-Zahir, son of Saladin, who built the gateway to the Citadel, and having seen his castle one would like to see his palaces.

Further walk round Aleppo revealed the Great Mosque with a square minaret of golden stone of the twelfth century, a beautiful thing comparing with any Italian campanile; and a few yards away another and smaller mosque which was once a Byzantine church with its capitals of the period so thickly daubed with whitewash that they are nearly obliterated. But another and ruined mosque in a suburb of fig trees and Moslem gravestones, built by the daughter-in-law of Saladin and known by the name of El Firdaus or the "Mosque of Paradise", is more beautiful by far. Here, the old Turkish variant of the *dolce far niente* is to be tasted while waiting for the key to be brought, and in the silence one might listen for the clacking of the stork's beak on its nest above the housetops. The court of El Firdaus is such a place of poetry in the Oriental mode as one might not believe to exist, when crossing the road at the traffic lights or travelling in the tube train. I cannot remember if it is a vine or a fig tree growing in that court, but both belong to each other and are sleeping in that shadow. On enquiring about old houses in Aleppo we were told not many existed now. But no Englishman can come here and not remember the old Levant Company.* Of another old association with Aleppo one is painfully aware, though less so than in Persia where its ravages seem more frequent. This is "Aleppo face", "a rare and painless skin-disease", we read in Baedeker, who adds with a collector's relish, "probably due to a protozoan parasite (*Leishmania tropica* Wright)". And he continues with the Arabic name for it, *habb haleb*, of obvious connotation; or another name which with prophetic insight for the phraseology of the future is translated, "boil of the year". It is now curable; but in Persia, at least, persons are to be seen with faces scarred by it.

Of this town with so many old links with England† and Europe there should be more to say. It has an identity of its own; neither Turkish, nor Damascene. We must remember its curious situation: fifty miles from the Euphrates and less than a hundred miles from the Mediterranean. On certain days the Euphrates can even be seen from

---

* This is apparently wrong. There are old houses in the Christian quarter of Aleppo with exquisite painting of arabesques and flowers . . . "more impressive than the Azem palaces at Damascus and Hama". Cf. *Syria*, by Robin Fedden, p. 36, who also illustrates the outside of an old house with stone carvings in Rococo style in imitation of the European gilded ornaments and mirrors of the time. The Levant Company, it could be added, was founded by Queen Elizabeth in 1581, numbered about fifty merchants at its apogee in 1660, and the English factory was closed down in 1791 (*op. cit.*, pp. 174, 175).

† I am, myself, descended from a Suffolk family, the Barnardistons of Brightwell, "of which the younger members had been engaged in commerce with the Levant for at least a hundred years". In my home we have old letters from Aleppo, a chestful of Turkish dresses brought back in the reign of Queen Anne, and by the will of Arthur Barnardiston (d. 1737), who made his fortune in the Levant, are in receipt of a legal anachronism of so rare a nature that few lawyers have come across it in their experience, in the form of Fee-Farm Rents. The reader will forgive this discursion which it is difficult to avoid when thinking of "Alep" as it is called in the old letters.

the top of the square minaret of Aleppo; and the Euphrates flows down from Baghdad into the Persian Gulf and the Indian Ocean as surely as the Danube flows through Roumania into the Black Sea. You can hear all of that in the music of the theatres and cafés of Vienna. It is not unreasonable, therefore, to think of Aleppo as neither Mediterranean, nor Mesopotamian, but with an individuality of its own which is not Turkish, but Syrian, and, at that, North Syrian.

Unfortunately, a visit to the museum of Aleppo in search of local colour to support this argument only reveals a hideous series of Hittite-looking statuettes from Ugarit, a town sacked and put an end to by the Philistines, of all people, who adopted and took away their fish-god Dagon. The museum is no cheerful place upon a rainy day. But in the evening we dined with a family who had had a long connection with Aleppo, and before that with the Greek islands under Venetian dominion, being indeed, as the name implies, of the family from which Marco Polo claimed descent, and under their hospitable roof in rooms furnished with objects from Venice of the *settecento* we were given a dish of *risotto* flavoured with brown truffles from the Syrian desert. There were almond sweets, too, for which Aleppo is famous.*

In the morning we were up early in order to set forth for Kalat Seman which alone is worth the journey to North Syria. And in a few moments we were passing by a beehive village. For some reason, even sillier than most, the Syrian authorities will not allow postcards of the beehive villages to be sent through the post. They will not even permit postcards of the *souks* which are the great and even sole attraction of Aleppo. We might as well forbid American tourists to buy postcards of Ann Hathaway's cottage at Stratford-on-Avon. What do they encourage instead? Postcards of the power station? We were not able to find an answer. But their xenophobia must end, logically, in their, also, forbidding postcards of anything modern and, therefore, of Western invention. Why they should be ashamed either of the *souks* or of the beehive villages one does not know.

Those latter are certainly a phenomenon and one that is peculiar to Northern Syria. But we postpone discussion of them until to-morrow's journey when we shall pass so many upon the road. For we turn off to the right, now, down a track of which those same authorities might

* As, also, for melons, cherries, apricots, and, in the words of old travellers, "good store" of other fruit. At Aleppo, as at Damascus, it is probable that there are varieties of fruit trees that have not been studied and are unknown in Europe. Typical of such possibilities is the tree, twice-grafted, so that plum, peach, and apricot were all in flower on it together, shown to Robert Byron by a landowner in a village near Yazd, in Persia, together "with his other treasure, a pip-less pomegranate for which Kew had been searching". Cf. *The Road to Oxiana*, pp. 207, 208.

understandably forbid the sale of postcards, when it is considered where it leads to! Soon it is but a bed of stones. But still there are telegraphs wires and, at last, we saw the bee-eaters in number though with difficulty, because being always on the right-hand side of the track they were in the sun and one could not catch their colour. There came a moment when the track looped, and curved right round, and we saw again the blue flame of their wings as they flew off to alight a few feet away upon the fields. At about which point there was a village, not of the beehive kind, but with more Moslem gravestones than there were houses, and the cemetery was blue with irises. They were in full flower, as though thriving from those slabs of limestone, and, perhaps, who knows, from the lime in all the skeletons buried without coffins! It was the only occasion on all our travels that we saw irises in bloom. This must have been *I. pallida* that is grown in Moslem cemeteries and was spread by that means to Bosnia and Dalmatia. What we hoped, of course, was to see the stippled irises of the *oncocyclus* family that grow in Syria and Transjordan. There are "stations" of irises near Baalbek, but, there again, too, we were unlucky. It was too early in the year when we arrived in Lebanon and too late when we came back.*

By now we are in a strange landscape that is all heaped stones. Ruined towns or villages on the tops of hills, they appear to be, with no means whatever of getting to them. We point to one or other, having the whole day before us, and the driver just shakes his head. They are ruined towns of the Byzantine period from the fourth century onwards, satellite towns of the great metropolis of Antioch from the ruins of which, though they are in Turkey, we are not much more than twenty miles away. The road becomes excruciating, or would be so to anyone coming fresh to it from Europe, and not inured by roads to Palmyra or to Isfahan. It is time to begin thinking about St Simeon Stylites, now that at any moment we may catch sight of Kalat Seman, the church built round the Stylite's column. Perhaps in all the

---

* Cf. *Oncocyclus Irises in the Levant*, by P. H. Davis, in *The Iris Year Book* for 1948, pp. 33–39. The author divides them into two groups, an Irano-Turanian and a Mediterranean "with larger and conspicuously spotted flowers". Among the former group he mentions *I. nigricans* Dinsmore, frequent in Moab, east of the Jordan, "growing in strong clumps on heavy terra-rossa soils in corn and fallow fields, where it is known by the Bedouin as 'Farouk's hat'"; *I. atropurpurea* Baker, and *I. antlibanotica* Dins: growing on a locality once occupied by bears and a forest of junipers. Among the latter group he names *I. auranitica* Dins: "known only from the Druze mountains, with fragrant flowers of old and sonorous gold"; *I. Lortetii*, one of the most lovely of all irises, "with flowers of smoky, mysteriously rosy hue"; *I. nazarena*, with pale lilac standards and brown-spotted falls; and *I. basaltica*, resembling *I. susiana*, "with heavy veiled and funerary blooms". How excellently Mr Davis writes of these flowers!

hierarchy there is no more extraordinary listing of ascetic records unless it be with "the flying saint" of Copertino.

The pillar-saint, *par excellence*, started his career in a monastery near Antioch. Here, at sixteen years old, he wore a spiked belt that drew blood, and not satisfied with that, dug a hole in the garden and buried himself up to his chin, passing in that manner what we may be correct in regarding as his summer holiday under the Syrian sun. Dug out again, at long last, after a rest he walled himself up for Lent. St Simeon was now expelled from his monastery for his excessive austerities and "took up residence" first in a cave, then in a little cell where he imprisoned himself for three years, and finally on the top of a mountain where he chained himself to a rock for several years.

Meditating on a new move, the idea of standing on a pillar out of doors in all weathers may have suddenly inspired him. But he was not the first to think of it. Lucian (d. A.D. 180) in *The Syrian Goddess*, describing the sacred city of Hierapolis, tells of two pillars a hundred and eighty feet high at the entrance of the main temple. He calls them "the *phalli* which Dionysus erected"* and, in fact, the temple was supposed to have been founded by Bacchus on his return from conquering India by "non-violent" means, and Lucian was shown garments and jewels and ivory brought back from India. But our present interest is that up one of these pillars a priest climbed, and spent a week there twice a year.

This voluptuary thereupon started his new career at Kalat Seman, at first on a plain pillar only ten feet high. Tiring of this, he went up a flight at a time, ending eventually on a column sixty feet high. But it was no ordinary column. It was formed in three drums or segments in honour of the Trinity, was three feet in diameter at the top, and had a low railing round it. Here he stood, day and night, in all weathers, and

---

* "In this entrance those phalli stand which Dionysus erected. . . . Into one of these a man mounts twice a year, and he abides on the summit of the phallus for the space of seven days. . . . The ascent is made in this way; the man throws round himself and the phallus a small chain; afterwards he climbs up by means of pieces of wood attached to the phallus large enough to admit the end of his foot. As he mounts he jerks his chain up his own length, as a driver his reins. Those who have not seen this process, but who have seen those who have to climb palm trees in Arabia, or in Egypt, or any other place, will understand what I mean. When he has climbed to the top, he lets down a different chain, a long one, and drags up anything that he wants, such as wood, clothing, and vases. He binds these together and sits upon them, as it were on a nest. . . . Between his prayers he raises a sound on a brazen instrument which, on being shaken, gives forth a loud and grating noise. . . . And I will describe another curiosity to be found in this temple, a sacred symbol of Dionysus. The Greeks erect phalli in honour of him, and on these they carry, singular to say, mannikins made of wood with enormous pudenda; they call these puppets." Quoted from *The Syrian Goddess* of Lucian, translated by Hubert A. Strong, London, Constable & Co., 1913, pp. 57, 68, 69.

A mosque at Rhodes

Archway at Palmyra

here he remained for thirty-seven years with a chain and iron collar round his neck with room to kneel but never to lie down. "Through the night and till nine a.m. he was constantly in prayer, often spreading forth his hands and bowing so low that his forehead touched his toes." A bystander once attempted to count the numbers of these successive prostrations, but at one thousand two hundred and forty-four became muddled and gave up counting. At nine a.m. "he began to address the admiring crowd sixty feet below, to send messages, write letters, etc.: towards evening he betook himself again to prayers". Twice a week a monk climbed a ladder and brought him the sacrament. "He generally ate but once a week, never slept, wore a long sheepskin robe, and cap of the same." His beard was long and his frame, as one might guess, extremely emaciated. There seem to have been no sanitary arrangements whatever connected with his long sojourn on the pillar. Once, and it is not surprising, he began to have an ulcerated foot. Theodosius I and a number of bishops sent him a personal letter begging him to come down for treatment, but instead he started a rigorous fast for forty days and cured himself.*

At last in his sixty-ninth year, in A.D. 459, "he expired, unobserved, in a praying attitude, in which no one ventured to interrupt him till after three days, when Anthony, his disciple and biographer, mounting the pillar, found that his spirit had departed, and his holy body was emitting a delightful odour". His body was taken to Antioch for burial, "and to be the safeguard of that unwalled town", and it only remains to add that St Simeon so hated women "he would allow none within the precincts of his pillar, and even his own mother was debarred this privilege till after her death, when he consented to see her corpse, and restored her to life for a short time, that she might see him and converse with him a little before she ascended to heaven".

Accounts of St Simeon must show, inevitably, a certain monotony of language for they are all derived from the same sources. He had become, and understandably, a subject of notoriety in his lifetime. Pilgrims came to see him from as far as Roman Britain and, after the manner of mirages in the desert, miracles played around his column. Evagrius, about a hundred years after his death, visiting Kalat Seman on wonders bent, "constantly saw a great and brilliant star gliding along the balustrade to the left of the Saint's pillar, while other of his contemporaries saw a resemblance of the Saint's face flitting about here and there", after the manner of a will-o-the-wisp, "with a long beard

* We should be grateful for one thing, that St Simeon lived before the human voice could be amplified on the microphone. In imagination I could hear his voice booming from the top of his pillar all over the building, and out into the countryside.

10

and wearing a tiara". The personal anecdotes of St Simeon were written by another biographer, Theodoret of Tyre, who knew him well, and incredulity should be hushed, as before the reported "air-lifts" of St Joseph of Copertino, when we remember the stories of St Thérèse of Lisieux and the showers of rose petals, all attested, and nearly in our own times.

And continuing on the track to Kalat Seman we will conclude the history of the Stylites. This order of saints, it is appropriately worded, "never found a footing in the West" if, that is to say, we do not accept the theory according to which the round towers of Ireland, some seventy in number, and two in Scotland, were anchorite towers in imitation of the pillar of St Simeon. The saint's personal disciple Daniel Stylites went up a column in the suburbs of Byzantium where he stayed for twenty years; while Simeon Stylites junior made his first ascent so young on a pillar near Antioch that in the words of Evagrius "he even cast his teeth in that situation" and remained there, man and boy, for sixty-eight years. There are stories that the "order" was abolished in the twelfth century, but a Stylite stood during some years in the middle of last century on one of the huge Corinthian columns of the Olympeion at Athens, while the practice did not die out in Georgia until early in the nineteenth century.* If we want a picturesque origin for the pillar-saints, as a whole, let us take it back into antiquity, to the pillars at the entrance of the temple of Dionysus, and conjecture that it was an India custom brought back by Bacchus from his Indian campaign. It is of the *fakirs* and *saddhus* of Ganges, ascetics who stay on one leg, or hold one arm in the air, till the limb is mortified, that the pillar-saints remind us, as of others who stand in the water, or stare into the sun and never take their gaze away. And by now we may be beginning to wonder what sort of a building the church of Kalat Seman will be.

Suddenly, we see it on a hilltop, and from down below on the stony road the first view of it is disappointing. We do not perceive the huge scale of it. The road winds round and about, and even when we have climbed level with it we do not grasp its size. It is a huge and stony hilltop, or plateau, with steep drops down of artificial con-struction when we get to the edges of it, in fact, an acropolis platform, like those at Persepolis and Palmyra and so many other classical sites. But this is a Christian building of the fifth century a thousand years after those monuments of antiquity, just about contemporary with the ending of the Roman occupation of Britain in 448. Let us recall the death of St Simeon Stylites in 459, and such contemporary events as

* Cf. *Syria*, by Robin Fedden, p. 107.

the death of Attila in 453, the sacking of Rome by Genseric the Vandal in 455, and the fall of the Western Empire in the person of the last Roman Emperor Romulus Augustulus in 476.* It was an age which had as many troubles and perils as our own.

What is of interest at Kalat Seman is that it neither resembles the Roman basilicas, nor such works of the succeeding generation as Santa Sophia in Istanbul. It is not Byzantine, but North Syrian. The surrounding country was no empty waste of boulders and fallen stones. There are more than a hundred dead cities in this region south of Antioch, with traces of vineyards and olive presses in every direction. It was, as said before, a Provence, a Tuscany, a Catalonia lost to Europe, and Antioch with its million inhabitants was the Marseilles or Barcelona of that relinquished land. In order to be convinced that Antioch in its architecture was finer than either or both of these modern cities it is not even necessary to be a believer in the golden age.

We have climbed through the stones and trodden on the wild flowers, and are now immediately in front of the basilica and about to see the extraordinary nature of its planning. Looking up at the façade we notice it is of limestone, put together without mortar, that the columns have acanthus-capitals and that they support, of course, round and not pointed arches. But perhaps the main impression is of how little, if at all, it resembles Byzantine building. They are still classical capitals with nothing of the basket-capitals of Santa Sophia, or of San Vitale in Ravenna, with their Oriental, lotus, palm, or fig-leaf connotations about them. But, more than all else, this is not an architecture adapted for the golden mosaic of the Byzantines. There are not the half-domes and wall spaces for that. It is not in this idiom which, however, has strange and most striking resemblances to Romanesque churches in France, though without their figures; to abbeys that is to say, without cloisters and carved capitals, or to churches without their sculptured portals.

Now we see that there is not one church, but four. Four basilicas forming the arms of a Greek cross, with an octagon in the middle of them. There was no high altar in the centre of that, but the octagon was built after the Saint's death in order to enclose the pillar of St Simeon, and a huge boulder of stone still lying there is the base of the Stylite's column. All four of the basilicas were not used as churches; three of them were in order to hold the pilgrims who came to see the sixty-foot pillar where the Saint once perched. Probably there were

---

* A date to be fêted by persons of left-wing tendencies, and compared to the fall of the Empires of the Habsburgs and the Tsars. Other, and similar, dates being 1453 and 1789.

stalls set along the sides for the sale of souvenirs and refreshments, equivalent to the "sandwiches and minerals" of to-day. It was the eastern of the four basilicas that was the church, and this still has more carved ornament than the others, with shell-shaped niches and delicate friezes. The central octagon is splendid in conception; but, then, what a history of architecture lay behind it! Kalat Seman is the end of a long trajectory from the Greek temples to the "Golden House" of Nero, or from Leptis Magna to Baalbek. The Syrian architects were no novices, and to them fell the honour of building this last of the great feats of architecture of the ancient world.

Was the octagon open and unroofed? It would seem probable, and that the pillar of the *fakir* rose up above it. We may picture it for ourselves as it may have looked with a dense crowd moving round the column. The church was probably completed in the generation after the Stylite's death, and it will not have been the same multitude, either in dress or language, that throng the mosques and *souks* of Damascus and Aleppo. These were Syriac or Aramaic-speaking. But no women were allowed near the pillar. They might not walk round, nor look up at it. They could only peer towards it through a wooden grille.

Half-way through our inspection of Kalat Seman we retired to eat our luncheon and it came on to rain. We were picnicking in a stone cell, roofless, of course, with a view down over the tumbling country towards Antioch. It gave time to think of this deserted and strange place, a huge church greater in area as one authority points out than many cathedrals, and with ornamental carvings of the greatest richness, but no sculptured figures. That gives to it, as a Christian building, an odd silence, or it is as though one of the senses is missing from it. At least, if it was Byzantine, it would have figures in mosaic. And what an odd contrast to the colonnades of Palmyra where there were statues standing on brackets on nearly every column! Not a sign at Kalat Seman of the Baroque, or even Rococo façades of Petra. This could be in another continent. And, as we shall see, it is as if there were no knowledge here of the temples of Baalbek. Those are some two centuries earlier in date than Kalat Seman, which one would have guessed from that might be more florid still. But not at all. Kalat Seman is in a style which might almost be called unornamented Romanesque.

The Romanesque is foreshadowed or prophesied, more particularly, if we climb over fallen stones to the back of the eastern basilica and look up at its apse. For the double row of blind arcading could come from an early church in France anywhere between Poitiers and Moissac. But, yes and no. For now, climbing further, we are outside another ruin with stone windows which have rounded tops, as though the architect did not understand the purpose of windows, and it is, recognizably, a Byzantine building; it resembles those fragments of the fronts of palaces at Ravenna and at Istanbul.* But there is nothing Romanesque about this ruined building. At Kalat Seman there are great heaps and mounds of ruins, which are parts of the monastery, or stables, or hostels for the pilgrims. And at the other end of the plateau about a quarter of a mile away is another roofless church, which has a nave in the form of an octagon and must have had a dome. It is much smaller in scale than Kalat Seman, more like a parish church in dimension, but worth walking to see, and you look out from the back of it over the ruined towns and villages in the distance.

It was tempting to proceed further and go to Antioch, but it meant getting Turkish visas and there was not time. Moreover, compared to such sites as Jerash or Palmyra, it would appear that there is but little above ground. We must catch our ship at Beirut in a few days and had, therefore, to decide against going to Antioch. That would have been the opportunity to try and visit some of the old Byzantine towns.† And had we known about it that day, we would have gone down the hill on the far side of Kalat Seman in order to see the pilgrim town of Deir Seman below the Sanctuary, its stone houses bearing such curiously precise dates as 13 August 510, and walls still standing of three-storeyed hotels. But one was becoming exhausted by so much sightseeing, and on returning to Aleppo slept for much of the late Sunday afternoon. There were two old naturalists or bird-lovers staying in the hotel. They went out every morning and spent all day in the country, coming back so tired out that they could not keep awake after dinner and fell fast asleep in their chairs. How much was their bird-count? I was told, and have forgotten. But it cannot have been

---

* Palace of Constantine Porphyrogenitus near the Old Walls at Istanbul, and the so-called Palace of the Exarchs at Ravenna, with three-arched portals in its façade, and although of the eighth century "already in the early Romanesque style".

† Fedden, in *Syria*, p. 105, mentions "the ruins of Rouheia, Serdjilla, the magnificent church of Qalbloze, the domestic architecture of El Bara, all situated within striking distance of Aleppo, but not served by any road". Of the remains of El Bara another writer has said that "in every direction there are empty houses so admirably preserved as to require nothing but a wooden roof to render them habitable, and that the vine-culture was so extensively carried on that some of the ruins are still overgrown with vines". But, after Kalat Seman, the most interesting of these North Syrian sites must be "the magnificent Christian town of Resafa", further into the desert and more to the north than Palmyra, and near the Euphrates. Fedden describes the basilica and monastery of St Sergius (Resafa changed its name to Sergiopolis); the North Gate "with its frieze of grapes and vine leaves and acanthus-capitals", a gate with but a narrow opening for there was never anything but camel traffic; the Church of the Martyry; and the water cisterns which could supply Resafa for two years. The inhabitants remained Christian for nearly a thousand years until the Mongol invasions (*op. cit.*, pp. 98–104).

higher than the number of wonders we had seen, day after day, for ten weeks on end.

Next morning there was another long journey before us, not less tiring than going to Palmyra, and back in a day. But made less monotonous, and no less wonderful, by the landscape. Starting off from Aleppo on the same road as for Kalat Seman, but keeping straight on, not branching to one side; and seeing, presently, the Roman road running beside us with unimpaired surface, mile after mile, down one rise in the land and over the crest of another, looking at moments just like a new road not yet open to traffic with its stone flags ready waiting for the chariot wheels—iron wheels, and what a noise they must have made! If ever there was a Roman road waiting for ghostly traffic to go along it, this is it leading south from Northern Syria.*

We stop to take petrol; and in all this district are men dressed magnificently in *burnouses* of saffron-yellow coming, we were told, from a town called Bab to the north-east from Aleppo. This may only mean that their saffron cloth is dyed in Bab. We had noticed them already in the *souks* and wondered who they were. And now begin the beehive villages. One of them, far away to the left, is quite a small town with what must be its mosque on a mound in the middle of it. Now there are beehive villages in every direction and there is an entire change in the landscape. It is no longer stony. We are on a huge plain, which has a character of its own from the yellow robes and conical houses, though the men in robes of saffron get rarer and soon stop altogether so that perhaps it is true that they come from Bab.

It is a redder earth than any ever seen. The red plough of Devon, or of Berwickshire, or Oxfordshire, all different from each other, is in comparison not red at all. The hide of a Hereford steer, is that red? For this is redder still. It is not red-purple like beetroot. Not a raw red: not the colour of raw meat. But a red that is as the coat of a chestnut gelding, only in terms of a red horse or steer. And as well, all that huge plain for as far as the eyes can distinguish is absolutely green with maize. There are no dykes or hedges. It is one green plain lying out of sight, with the red soil and the beehive villages. It is more open and tremendous than any landscape in Spain. Knowing the high, open tablelands of Castile in the season when they are green, around Soria in the one direction and between Salamanca and Zamora in another, there is nothing to compare with this. Redder than the deep red soil of the vineyards of Manzanares where, in the words of Richard Ford,

* Aleppo has a place of its own in the hearts of railway-lovers as terminus of the *wagon-lits* system. As such it appears on the map in the corridor, while one is waiting for the man to come along ringing his hand-bell and the door to be thrown open into the *wagon-restaurant*.

"the red blood of the vine issues from this valley of stones". For here are no stones. Redder than Valdepeñas with more vineyards and a still redder soil. For here are neither vines, nor stones. It is one huge plain of red earth, now green with maize.

And at last our wish was granted and the road led through a beehive village upon the slope of a hill. From there it was like looking out over an immense lake of which the waters as far as the eyes could see were grass-green and the banks were red. But we stopped the car in order to get out and visit the beehive houses. They are only found in this part of Northern Syria, lying south of Aleppo, are made of brown mud and are so nicely shaped and rounded that from a distance it could be that they are conical hayricks built neatly and with uncommon care. Obviously, it is one of the oldest and most primitive forms of house, and it is natural to compare it to the Apulian *trulli*, the beehive villages near Brindisi. Those are round houses with conical roofs formed by rows of stones projecting over each other, and Alberobello, a *trulli* "village" with some six thousand inhabitants has houses formed of two or three of the domed huts leading into each other, and even churches built in *trulli* shape. But the *trulli* are not really like the beehive villages of Northern Syria. These, too, are formed from conical huts put side by side. But the resemblance can only be one of accident. It could as well be said that both are like an igloo; or like the heaped earth on the sides of an old ice-house. They are just conical huts, and must resemble one another no more than one hayrick is like another.

In an instant most of the inhabitants are round the car, including two handsome boys curiously and spotlessly dressed in white, and a little equivocal. They look to be Indian with their white robes and trousers and white turbans, like neophytes of some sort or other. Women come pouring out of the beehives, all talking at once, and after a parley in sign language we are not so much invited, as dragged inside. A matriarch covered with necklaces, with the physique of a full weight Epstein figure, hustles or almost frog-marches us along. The beehives are clean and comfortable to judge from the piles of bedding and rugs upon the floor. No doubt they are as much more sensibly suited to their climate on that, alternately, burning hot and wind-tormented plain, compared to the hovels the Syrian government would build for them to live in, as are the "condemned cottages" in English villages contrasted to our universal council houses, all of the same pattern in every part of the country, in utter disregard of local climate and tradition.

But the beehive villagers were in mingled pride and fear about their houses. Pointing, one moment, to the high conical roof inside the hut, and then shrugging their shoulders, while jabbering as though it was only by some form of dumb resentment that we could neither understand nor answer them in their own language. Photography was another matter altogether, and a camera the work of witchcraft. The matriarch refused absolutely to have her picture taken, removing her hands from us and retreating to a few feet away. But moods change, and we were followed back to the car by a crowd of children who touched and fingered the clothes of the ladies of our party while uttering improper, if good-tempered comments on them.

Unfortunately this was nearly the last of the beehive villages. They must be built on old sites, but probably excavation would yield nothing. One reads of places in this ancient land where the soil is still thick with the bones and ashes of countless burnt sacrifices. Would there be nothing under the beehive houses except mud foundations and bits of broken sherds? Or are there ancient temples under the mud mosques and their phallus-minarets? Hereafter, the country is open but uninteresting, and no longer red. Often the road goes down long cuttings that are like railway embankments, and there is little to see to either side. At one point there is a steep descent into a river valley and here is the only shade for many miles.

At last on the long day we come to Hama which, because of that, we go through too quickly, missing thereby the Azem palace. But this was not so much of a loss to one who, like myself, finds little to admire in the interiors of Moslem houses. It belonged to the same family who built the Azem palace at Damascus. Another palace of the Keylani family, one of the "four families who rule the town", and more in the Turkish style, has beautiful inlaid mother-of-pearl furniture, of the sort described by Lord Henry Wootton in *The Picture of Dorian Gray* as "the work of curious bees that worked in silver", co-eval with *pouffes* of Moroccan leather and the aromatic smoke of Egyptian cigarettes. As a result of our haste, we, also, missed seeing the *souks* of Hama and its hand-printed linens. It is of more interest that the Great Mosque has in its court "a columned treasury not unlike that in the Great Mosque of Damascus", and that the fanatical Moslem character of the town is attested by Jews not being allowed to set foot in it and by an array of not fewer than twenty-four minarets. But, above all, Hama is on the Orontes and it is the Orontes valley that has the blood-red soil. The creaking of the *norias*, the great water wheels of Hama is something one becomes aware of the moment one is in the town. We stopped to look at them; they are taller than the wheels of the biggest old paddle-steamer, and far noisier. Not the even swish-swishing of the waters, for those who remember that, but a mingling of a laboured groaning with a bagpipe drone. Some despairing spirit seems imprisoned in those water-wheels, condemned to labour night and day with no intermission, and spilling almost as much as they lift of the hated element that gives life to the town.

Of Homs we saw even less than of Hama, only stopping for long enough for our driver to buy himself a sandwich, and missing, thereby, even the view of its twenty-one minarets, "square black towers of basalt", if they are still there, and "the domes of twenty bath-houses". But from all accounts we lost little by passing through so quickly. The road now deteriorated. No longer had it even that gradation in the hospital reports from, "the patient is fairly comfortable", or "is as comfortable as can be expected", to "the patient passed a sleepless and rather restless night". From now onward for some hours the road was execrable, and worse still if being mended. All the time at a snail's pace huge petrol lorries passed us, coming in the other direction and trampling the stones and mud into a worse morass. It was at a certain moment in this discomfort that looking over to the right upon the hills we saw something about ten or fifteen miles away which could, and yet surely could not be, the Krak des Chevaliers. It was so huge even at this distance and appeared to be slipping off its hill. As though it was sliding, or dropping off it, a most curious effect.

But it was the Krak des Chevaliers, and soon we turned off towards it along what was hardly a road at all. Round and about it went in no hurry to lead anywhere, and then it began to climb. For a long while it was as a "monkey-path" of sharp stones, zigzagging up the hill. After which we would come round the shoulder of it, and there was Krak on the hill opposite and still two or three miles away. No longer tumbling off the hillside, but astride on it; and now, from below and opposite, smaller and more compact than one had expected, but in a way that was equivalent to hearing some famous tune in music for the first time and finding it more simple than one had thought. And at last we are across a ravine and under the castle walls with the modern village of a few houses down below us as we go up the steep and still steeper hill, until we are afraid of the car stopping and running down backwards, and come to a halt below the damp and mossy castle walls.

There are stone steps to climb, a door to be opened with a key, and one is inside the Krak des Chevaliers. We climb up a long inclined gallery, with walls and ceiling dripping with water and only slit embrasures to let the light in, emerging into a high vaulted guard room, or dormitory, more probably the latter, and used by the men-at-arms.

The full complement of the Krak des Chevaliers being two thousand armed men.* Passing by a hole in the stone floor above a portcullis we have a first view of the moat, an astonishing thing to find filled deep with water upon this mountain top. Eventually we come out into the keep near the chapel, and near another vaulted hall built with an angle to it, which is the banqueting hall, with Gargantuan kitchens attached. Next we climb more steps in the open air on to a stone platform, and climb again, going higher and higher, inside a tower. We have now to walk along the open top of a huge curtain wall with no parapet so that one dares not go near the edge. The curtain wall sloping outward is not less than eighty feet thick. It is, next, a question of climbing to the open top of an immense tower, where the sensation is stupendous. Up there in that strong wind with the green moat far beneath one almost forgets to look over and out at the mountains and the marshy plain below. The tower at the other end of the keep is only less sensational.

Krak was held, firstly by the Crusaders, and then by the Knights Hospitaller, for a hundred and fifty years. How did it ever fall? Only by treachery, when Soltan Beibars besieged Krak, and sent in a false message purporting to come from the Count of Tripoli telling the Knights to surrender, which they did, handing it over to the Saracens, and retreating down to the coast with a safe-conduct. This was in 1271. But the empty vaulted halls and corridors still seem to be waiting for the tread of mailed feet. What an extraordinary achievement are the castles of the Crusaders, and one so nearly, if not entirely, the work of French hands! It is little wonder that the word "Frank" and its adjective "Frankish" were applied by the Moslems, indiscriminately, to every Western nation. The chief vassals of Godfrey de Bouillon, the first King of Jerusalem (d. 1100) were the Prince of Antioch, the Counts of Edessa and Tripoli, the Prince of Tiberias, the Counts of Joppa and Ascalon, and the Lord of Montroyal. Their castles were called Mirabel, Beauvoir, Belfort, Chastel Rouge, Nigraguarda and Blanchgarde, Toron and Scandalion, names taken from the Arthurian cycle and from the literature of chivalry.† The Krak des Chevaliers may be "the best preserved and most wholly admirable castle in the world", but others in the long series reaching from north of Antioch nearly

---

* Of another castle of the Crusaders, El-Merkab, built of black blocks of basalt sixteen feet in thickness "which stands out in contrast to the white chalk ridges they dominate" it is told that the double walls were guarded, night and day, by four knights and twenty-eight men-at-arms. The guard at Krak des Chevaliers must have been larger still. Cf. Fedden, *Syria*, p. 151.

† The present writer long ago indulged himself in a fantasy upon the names of these Crusaders' castles in *The Gothick North*, London, Duckworth & Co., 1929, pp. 191-197.

to Petra and the peninsula of Sinai can be little less wonderful. The castle of Beaufort, for instance; or that of Sahyun, in the Alawit mountains, where the moat was hewn a hundred and ten feet deep into the rock and an isolated column of stone of that height was left to carry the drawbridge. That there were more wonders we may be certain, for what can have been "the seven-storeyed tower in the sea", built by the Franks near Tortosa, "which they were compelled to surrender to the Moslems in 1285"?

It all seems to have been the result of a surge of energy from France almost comparable to that which took them from end to end of Europe in the Napoleonic Wars. The leaders of the First Crusade were all Frenchmen: Raymond, Count of Toulouse, Robert, Duke of Normandy, Robert, Count of Flanders, Bohemund and Tancred, Godfrey of Bouillon and his brother Baldwin. They were all, at least, French speaking. Let us recall that they took Jerusalem in 1099. The military orders of Knights Hospitaller and Knights Templar were largely French in origin, and most of the Templars when they were so cruelly suppressed had come from south-western and south-eastern France. When we add to this the Norman conquest of England which, being Englishmen, we are reluctant to admit as the work of Frenchmen, although of recent Norse ancestry (but they spoke Norman-French and not Norwegian), and the Norman conquest of Sicily and Southern Italy in almost the same years, and add further the architectural splendours of Chartres and of Vézelay, and the wonders of Cistercian building, not only in France but wherever the monks carried the Cistercian ideals, then we need no longer be surprised at their subsequent loss of energy and the many defeats in battle which the French suffered at the English hands. Krak des Chevaliers, as much as Durham Cathedral, is the work of Frenchmen in an alien land.

Another kind of cosmopolitanism altogether was in play when, coming away from the castle, we discovered that the custodian in turban and baggy-seated trousers had worked for many years as porter in the main railway station at Montreal. Did we think he could ever go back there, but one did not care to tell him "No"! He locked the door behind him and the castle was left empty on that late afternoon. The other tourists, ubiquitous French people travelling everywhere, had left before us. The castle would be alone with itself at night. There is nothing whatever to steal in it. You cannot rob cold stone, and it has no ornament except some carved corbels in the Knights' chapel and in their dining hall. No need, therefore, for a night watchman. The Krak des Chevaliers could be kept shut up, as though besieged, for months or years on end. It would be an unnerving experience to tread its long stone passages and walk its ramparts in the dark. For all is in such good condition. The garrison could move in again to-morrow. It is odder, still, to think that this huge fortress conveys no visual hint or indication whatever of the Knights Hospitaller, militant monks who held it from 1142 until 1271. That is to say, without historical knowledge gained elsewhere we would have no idea of the armour they wore, and that the stone of the building was matched by the metal of their military apparel. As a conception, the Krak des Chevaliers is not less peculiar than the three huge monasteries, one of them inhabited by militant monks, outside Lhasa in Tibet. Like them it lasted for generation after generation without women.

Coming down that track of stone from the Krak des Chevaliers was more than ever like lying on a *saddhu's* bed of nails. One dreaded regaining the main road for what it might bring of delays and punctured tyres. But we got down at last to the Mediterranean shore at a point just not within sight of the island of Ruad, a rocky islet entirely covered with houses, and with a population of sailors and sponge-fishers, in Phoenician times called Arvad when it was an important harbour, and interesting not only because its inhabitants must surely have Phoenician blood in them but because its situation on a little island near the shore is according to the prototype of Tyre and Sidon.* It was a pity not to have been able to compare the islanders of Ruad with the fishermen of Nazaré in Portugal who with their goat-profiles have certainly Phoenician blood in their veins. Twenty-five or thirty centuries ago towns no bigger than Ruad or than Nazaré could rank as great powers, and that this canon of proportion persisted until much later in history is evident when we remember Ragusa and its argosies, or that in the eleventh century Amalfi was a maritime power.

We passed through Tripoli at speed for it was getting late, not even stopping at the *tekkiyeh* of the Whirling Dervishes in order to visit their dance hall, but the sun was setting and some years before the War I had been taken to see the Dancing Dervishes at Nicosia, in Cyprus—they were refugees from Turkey—and given a letter of introduction to their Shaikh who bore a fortuitous physical resemblance to Diaghilev. We speeded along through town after town that not so long ago must have had a Turkish *Kaimmakam* to rule over it, past glades of banana palms and orange groves, in the golden

---

* The island of Ruad is a few miles beyond the frontier of Lebanon, and now in Syria. Tyre, the modern Soor, and Saida (Sidon) are south of Beirut and on the coast between that town and the frontier with Israel. It was while trying to visit Ruad last year that the Syrian police arrested my friend Wilfrid Blunt, who is an Eton master, on 4 June and kept him for the day in prison.

sunset along the shores of that marvellous blue, blue sea, with once more and again the spicy scent of the orange blossom and enough of beauty and apparent happiness in all around to make one remember the heavenly airs in *Il Seraglio* and have in one's ear tunes scarcely less lovely from Rossini's *L'Italiana in Algeri*. At last, round every curve of the coast, to Byblos which we had thought was never coming, and to the elusive lights of Beirut, approaching nearer and then retreating.

We were all so tired by now that our driver drove as though inspired, headlong through all the increasing traffic and through maddening suburbs where the trams began. Or are there no trams at Beirut? For they may have been a feverish delusion. And now, at this late hour, there was another delaying problem, that our driver, even less than the local taxi-men, knew his way into the centre of Beirut, that we did not know it, ourselves, and that it was hopeless to talk to him as he did not understand a word of any language except Arabic and Armenian. Eventually by the device of asking some pedestrian every half-minute for the St Georges Hotel, which is in a conspicuous position on the sea-front, and saying, hopefully, "O.K.", our *lingua franca* with but one word in it, we arrived at last in front of the hotel, where, in order to save time, we transferred into a taxi, and reached the hospitable Résidence des Pins long after half-past nine.

It was our last return to Beirut and for the fifth time we were in the capital of Lebanon. There was much to do in other directions as we were leaving so soon, but there remained one obligation to fulfil, which was a visit to the temples of Baalbek. It is but a two hour drive from Beirut, and we went there a couple of days later along the mountain road leading to Damascus, from which we branch off to the left at Chtaura, among the vineyards, and by the time the giant columns of the temple of Jupiter become visible through the plane trees we have climbed nearly four thousand feet above the sea. Some little dark patches high on the mountains, not long before this, were the Cedars of Lebanon, in reminder that we are still in a Semitic land. Once again, as at Persepolis and Palmyra, and so many other sites, the buildings are raised on a huge terrace. But the temples of Baalbek are so well known that I will not try to describe them in detail, but only to set down certain reflections that the sight of them gave rise to.

In the first place, having seen Leptis Magna, in Libya, it was of fascinating interest to go to Baalbek.* For it dates from the most cosmopolitan age of the whole Mediterranean basin, the only time in

---

* Cf. *Mauretania*, by Sacheverell Sitwell, London, Duckworth & Co., 1940. The ruins of Leptis Magna are described on pp. 281–294.

history when that area has been one single unit. Let us recall that Septimius Severus, who was born at Leptis, and when he was Roman Emperor called in the foremost architects of the day to beautify his birthplace, was of African origin. He spoke Latin "with an African accent", whatever that may mean. He was of equestrian or noble family, but from his busts we can see that he had a strong admixture of negro blood in his veins. His bearded face is that of a mulatto, and he must have descended from some negress concubine. Let us remember that he spent the last three years of his life in Britain, and that he died at York.

Caracalla, his son, was chief builder and benefactor of the Great Temple at Baalbek, while the grandson of Severus, the essentially silly Heliogabulus, made himself high priest of Baal. But on the subject of Heliogabulus it is irresistible to quote from Dr Lempriere : "His halls were covered with carpets of gold and silver tissue, and his mats were made with the down of hares, and with the soft feathers which were found under the wings of partridges. . . . He often invited the most common of the people to share his banquets, and made them sit down on large bellows full of wind, which, by suddenly emptying them-selves, throw the guests on the ground, and left them a prey to wild beasts." And this cautionary tale ends with the murder of Heliogabulus in the eighteenth year of his age, after a reign of three years, nine months, and four days. What emerges from all this is that the Severan family, though they were Roman Emperors, can no more be con-sidered Roman in race than the temples of Baalbek, though they are in the classical idiom, can be called Roman temples.

On the whole Baalbek is not so fine as Leptis Magna. A coarser, perhaps Semitic influence has come in. But both are monuments of the Imperial epoch upon a really gigantic scale. Given architects with the experience of six centuries of classical architecture behind them and the unlimited resources of a world empire, the Caesars could afford to be lavish in their buildings beyond anything ever possible to a prince of the Renaissance. The resources of a Louis XIV can have been but paltry in comparison. At Baalbek, as at Leptis Magna, all is on what Berlioz in his compositions for huge orchestra called the Babylonian or Ninevean scale.

Baalbek has the advantage of site, for Leptis is on a flat shore with the Mediterranean not even directly visible from the ruins. But the carved ornament of Leptis is incomparable, as in the two pairs of monolith pilasters of marble, a pair, each, for the apse at either end of the so-called Basilica. They are carved with Bacchic scenes, with clusters of grapes and vine stems, while satyrs and centaurs, and Actaeon and his stag, are revealed in the undercutting of the marble. It has been well

said that in the golden light of Africa "the columns and their capitals
are carved and jewelled as in a tryptych by Mantegna".* There is no
work quite of this quality at Baalbek.

But the excitements begin with a processional stairway leading into
a great court built in the form of a hexagon. Beyond this are the huge
colonnades of the Court of the Altar, with its four semicircular half-
halls, or chapels, with half-dome ceilings, and another stairway at the
far end leading to a yet higher platform and to the Temple of Jupiter.
It is the six standing columns of this latter temple, sixty-five feet high,
with another fifteen feet of frieze and cornice above that, that are the
wonder of Baalbek. In their day there were fifty-four of the columns,
each made of three drums or segments. Those still left are the more
impressive for standing at the steep edge of the stone platform and for
having their entablature intact. But the blocks of stone of which the
terrace is built, some of them over sixty feet long and of appropriate
width and weight, are little less extraordinary, for they fit into one
another, and by some marvel of engineering are built up into a wall.

It is, then, necessary to clamber down among the fallen stones under
the platform and approach the Temple of Bacchus. This is a Corinthian
structure of fantastic and dazzling richness with a doorway which has
jambs carved with vine branches and ivy boughs, and sheaves of corn
and poppies. It almost equals the carved portals at Leptis Magna. The
fluted Corinthian pilasters of the interior, and the architraves between
them that are like blind windows, all this is of a scale and opulence
that has no equal in the Roman world. Personally, I found the subterranean passages and long vaulted tunnels under the platform as
interesting and more impressive. And there are little rooms curiously
contrived in the substructure that could be priests' robing or waiting
rooms, or, in fact, sacristies, and that have stone ceilings richly worked
with busts and coffers and medallions.

Hereabouts it is as though one was wandering in an enlarged
Piranesi engraving. It is all, of course, very huge and wonderful. But
one wonders what would have been had this architecture continued,
as did the Egyptian temple architecture, for another twenty centuries,
indeed, down to and beyond our own time. What destroyed the
Roman Empire as much as anything else was the lack of aristocratic
tradition. Degeneration was quick and absolute, and if Septimius
Severus had some of the attributes of greatness what are we to expect
under Heliogabulus, an effeminate Caesar, half-African, half-Syrian
in descent, and the fearful Caracalla who was his uncle? Perhaps it
needed neither the early Christians, nor the barbarians, to put an end

* *A Vicarious Trip to the Barbary Coast*, by Mary Berenson, London, 1938, p. 21.

to Rome. The temples of Baalbek could be banks or palaces or baths or air-terminals. The technique and planning are superb, but not the spirit. Nevertheless, who are we to criticize, who are content with Regent Street and Piccadilly?

A little distance away from the other ruins there is the small Temple of Venus, a circular building or *cella*, not much bigger than a municipal bandstand, with a surround of Corinthian columns and a concave, not convex, external frieze and entablature, allowing for five semicircular bays; most elaborate and fanciful in ground plan, in fact, a circle indented on the outside into a decagon. This temple is described in too facile words as "a fine example of the late-Roman Baroque style", for with its cupola roof, now fallen, shell niches and swagged or garlanded pilasters, it is more suited to have been the supper room for Louis XV and Mme du Barry in the pavilion at Louveciennes. Under the late and degenerate Caesars there were as many moods of architecture as there were gods and goddesses, or dishes at the banquet.

But it was raining, and we had to run for shelter into the mouth of the subterranean passages and wait for the sun to come out, looking up, meanwhile, at the six gigantic columns on top of the stone terrace which is as an enormous breakwater or causeway. Only a few feet away was the Temple of Bacchus. Was it beautiful? Well, no! And yet... we should remember the Madeleine at Paris, the British Museum, and St George's Hall at Liverpool before we criticize the silver or Augustan age.

And we walked down the long tunnel out into the rain again, and drove away. Along a road that continued into the mountains and led to Beit-ed-Din. This was the country palace of the Emir Bechir, the Lebanese equivalent to Mohammad Ali of Egypt, or to Ali Pacha of Joannina. Lamartine, and the English traveller Warburton, went off into rhapsodies over it, but, in fact, it does not in any way resemble Isola Bella, "with all its gardens, terraces and pavilions, upheaved from the Lago Maggiore", nor, of course, do we see it, now, with the Oriental figures and the Emir reclining in midst of them, as was the luck of Lamartine. The interior has been over restored for this is where the President of Lebanon spends the summer heats. Nevertheless, from the hillside opposite Beit-ed-Din is as a far off and bucolic echo of the red Alhambra and lies, beautifully, among the cypresses. Thence, through villages full of Druzes, as we could tell from their white turbans, and down, down through the mountains till, at last, far below, we saw the lights of Beirut, arriving, late as ever, at the Résidence des Pins, where we found a letter from my kind mother-in-law that enabled us to change our plans at the last moment and go to Cairo, flying there and catching the Italian liner three days later at Alexandria.

Turkish fort and classical portico at Palmyra

Colonnade at Palmyra

Mosque of Masjed-e-Shah at Meshed (fifteenth century)

Detail of El Deir at Petra

# Chapter X

## CAIRO

*New Heliopolis — Statue of Ramses II in a square — "Bakshish, bakshish!" —
Mosque of Ibn Tulun — Mosque of Soltan Hassan — The Muski — Out to the
Pyramids — A camel called "Jack Hulbert" — The treasure of Tutankhamen —
Coptic churches in Old Cairo — The "blue mosque" — Mosque of Soltan Qalaun
— Mosque of Soltan Barquq — Mamelukes — Mosque of Qaït Bey — Tombs of the
Caliphs — Unpleasant incident — Tomb-mosque of Soltan Barquq — Qaït Bey —
Cru des Ptolémées — Rhodes — Athens — Benaki Museum — Arrival at Venice.*

ONCE more, and for the last time, we are at the airport of Beirut,
whence we had "flown out" on such interesting journeys. We take
our seats in a "Viscount" and are on the way to Cairo. It is a flight of
some three hours, but in what seems no longer than a few moments
we are over an enormous flat-roofed city, with desert all round it in
every direction and a green ribbon of vegetation in midst of it which
is the river Nile, and we come down at a dusty aerodrome. Here there
are delays of maddening nature, and we are held up for a long while
because a passenger has lost his ticket. To make it more aggravating,
several of the passport officials who have got through their work are
waiting, as we are, in the autobus, and when at last it starts off we have
to drop one or other of them at every street corner.

But, almost at once, we are in a long avenue at the end of which,
incredibly, we see the Pyramids. And, here and there, are flowering
jacaranda trees, their powdery blue blossom showing against the
tawdry buildings which look like hospitals or the offices of gas-
companies. We are in the suburb of Heliopolis, once famous for its
race-meetings. Heliopolis, we recall, was the Greek name for Baalbek,
and the spectacle of the New Heliopolis inclines one to retract, mentally,
any criticisms of the temples we were half-admiring only two days ago.
In another quarter of an hour we are at the hotel surrounded by a mob
all howling for *bakshish*, some of whom in the guise of guides or
dragomen follow one right into the building and are there, waiting,
the moment we come down in the lift. The number of hotel servants is
extraordinary. There seem to be five waiters to every table, tall negroes
from the Sudan in fezzes and long caftans, eunuch-material of the first
order, perpetually serving Turkish coffee, while the dining room has
stained glass windows of Aïda-like personages in scenes upon the
banks of Nile.

11                    161

Cairo has not changed in more than twenty years, except that it is dustier than ever and that nearly every building needs a new coat of paint. One of the only improvements is that a dark granite or porphyry statue of Ramses has been set up in one of the squares,* and is impressive enough standing up above the evil crowd. Egyptian obelisks one has seen in plenty, only to think of that in the Place de la Concorde, or the one in the middle of the Piazza of St Peter's, or Cleopatra's Needle, but never a statue of a Pharaoh in the middle of a modern town. It is of singular and particular appropriateness in Cairo, and in reminder of the first great rulers in the world. Yet it is out of place and like a whale stranded in the shallows. One cannot get it out of one's mind that a huge statue is being transported through the city and that they can carry it thus far and no further through the streets.

There was a particular reason for coming to Cairo which will make of this chapter something a little different in intention from the rest of this book. For it is an epilogue and no part of the original scheme of things, and also because Cairo may be now something of a commonplace to readers who went there during the last war. It is the best known of all Oriental towns. So this chapter must be less of a description than a comparison. For the special purpose I have mentioned was in order to have the experience of seeing Cairo so soon after visiting Meshed and Isfahan. This project had been in mind long before we started on our travels but it seemed impossible of realization. It was only made feasible at the last moment when the fact of our ship stopping for twenty-four hours at Alexandria was too good a chance to miss. I had spent a few days in Cairo during the early spring of 1931 and needed to refresh my memories of its mosques and minarets.† To be able to do so in almost a matter of days after leaving Persia was a measure of my good fortune.

Was it true, as I had written all those years ago, that "during the fourteenth and fifteenth centuries building was in progress there on a scale that belittles even Venice and Florence, and a style had been evolved which allowed of strange and fanciful developments beside which the mosques of Istanbul might be the work of one man alone"? The conclusion of my sentence, at any rate, has been curiously con-

* Ramses II, reigned 1198–1167 B.C.

† Cf. an essay on the "Mosques of Cairo" which forms the second chapter of *Touching the Orient*, London, Duckworth & Co., 1934, pp. 25–31. It is certainly true, as I said there, that "scarcely any towns of mediaeval Europe had churches of a beauty and grandeur of design to compare with the mosques of Qaït Bey, el Mu'aiyad, el Mardani, Soltan Hassan and Soltan Barquq. They give an impression of overwhelming magnificence, and from the simplicity of their appointments they gain a grandeur which the Gothic cathedrals can never possess with their crowded altars, tombs, confessionals, and choir-stalls."

firmed for it was not known at that time that the mosques of Istanbul were, in fact, mostly the work of one man, Sinan. His name was so little known that it was never mentioned. "Under Saladin", the chapter continued, "Cairo was more, not less civilized than London or Paris", leading to the conclusion that "after seeing one mosque, in particular, that of Soltan Qalaun, it is easy to realize that Cairo, and not Baghdad, was the city where all the fabulous tales of the East were set down", or indeed, the city of the Arabian Nights.

Here, and now, was the opportunity to test these theories, and an occasion the more welcome because although so much desired it was so entirely unexpected. What an excitement to find oneself without planning it once more in Cairo! Was it true that "special attention was devoted to the point of view of the street, and a long narrow street at that? The façades had to be broken, continually, into new points of interest; and therefore the exterior cornices of the mosques received a rich treatment calculated to draw up the eyes towards dome and minarets. . . . All being part of that same wonderful period, of the twelfth and thirteenth centuries, which produced so many marvels of Gothic architecture, in its purer, more primitive phases, in many countries of Europe." This present chapter is the account of an attempt to revive and correct those memories during the course of a visit to Cairo which only lasted for two days in May 1956.

That the city has much deteriorated since I saw it before is not to be disputed. There is a howling poverty and a hopelessness of dust that cries aloud. The wealthy have been robbed but it has not enriched the poor. Coming out of the hotel to a never ending chorus of *bakshish, bakshish*, we found a taxi with a Sudanese driver in a leather coat. He had obviously modelled himself upon American negro G.I.'s he had seen in the war. His home was Khartum, so he said, but it is more likely to have been some obscure village. We kept him for two days and came to much prefer him to the Egyptians. And with him at the wheel we set off for the Mosque of Ibn Tulun.

This is the second earliest of the Cairo mosques and dates from the ninth century. It has a huge dusty quadrangle and a domed fountain in the middle looking more like a mausoleum, the afternoon being so hot that it needed a determined effort to walk out to it from the shadow of the arcades. The pierced wooden lattices or *musharabiyas*, all along under the arches are marvels of pointless patience and ingenuity. But the mosque proper or *liwan* is very fine indeed; and while you walk in it the quincunx plays among its columns, there being five rows of them, and therefore, four aisles of Arabian or Saracenic arches. But that this is a Semitic architecture we are reminded on looking at the roof of the *liwan* which was originally of beams of date-palm with veneer of sycamore; and on news that the frieze of sycamore according to tradition belonged originally to Noah's Ark and was brought by Ibn Tulun from Mount Ararat! But the real interest of the Mosque of Ibn Tulun is its minaret of very ancient pattern, of spiral or corkscrew form from the outside staircase winding up it, and giving it the look of an early lighthouse. It has even been suggested that its shape was derived from the Pharos of Alexandria but its real derivation is more remote still and not less interesting. For it is copied from the minaret of the mosque at Samarra,* the second capital of the Abbaside Caliphs between Mosul and Baghdad, far away upon the Tigris, Ibn Tulun, a Turk by race, having been a native of Samarra. Thus, a tower that is really descended from the *ziggurats* of ancient Babylon serves for minaret in this mosque in Cairo. It is certainly Babylonian in appearance, of affinity to the stepped pyramids and the Tower of Babel.

Next, we went to the Mosque of Soltan Hassan which I now feel sure is the best thing in Cairo. It stands in a cleared square in front of the Citadel, but one is first aware of two buildings standing, side by side, across a street, and such is the dust of Cairo, proliferate and pullulating worse than London soot, that for a moment or two it is impossible to tell which is the Mosque of Soltan Hassan dating from the middle of the fourteenth century and which is the Mosque of Er-Rifai that was built in 1912, the latter mosque it is only fair to add being no less darkly dramatic in its steep tall shadows. But the huge portal of Soltan Hassan takes the attention and is foretaste to what lies within down dark and devious passages, carrying one's mind back to those china vaults of sapphire and turquoise and the blue courts of Isfahan. And in another moment we stand in the court of the mosque in front of a huge open cavern which is the sanctuary. It is one of the great effects in the architecture of the world, and achieved with no ornament; a court of sunlight and shadow, high walled; a cavern that is like a stage, and what is equivalent to a proscenium arch.† But the effect is enhanced by the chains of innumerable hanging lamps in the sanctuary which drop down and act as stalactites for the dark cavern. One cannot recall any more tremendous and aweful effect, in the true meaning of that adjective, in the whole of mediaeval architecture. This is a mosque built a century and a half after the reign of Saladin, Soltan Hassan being one of the Bahrite or Turkish Mamelukes, and we have still, in

* Samarra is a pilgrimage town of the Shiah Moslems, and has a mosque with a pair of gilded minarets and a golden dome, late in date, but in the pattern of the golden domes of Meshed, Qom, and other Shiah shrines, see p. 56.

† The court of Soltan Hassan has four *liwans*, four open caverns, in one of which we are standing, and it is the *liwan* opposite, the biggest of the four, which is used for prayer.

anticipation, the later more delicate works of the Circassian Mamelukes in parallel to the fan-vaulting and thin elegancies of our Perpendicular in England. After that solemn and wonderful sanctuary the tomb chamber of Soltan Hassan a little palls and oppresses, but the impression of that huge cavern and the rain of stalactites remains long in mind.

We, then, decided to drive to the Muski and walk about in the bazaars. Perhaps no steps taken, political or otherwise, will ever eradicate its Orientalism. As we entered the Khan el-Kalili two enormous young men, muscleless, but as mountainous of size as Japanese wrestlers, ran flabbily towards us, hand-in-hand. They wore identical striped *caftans*, and were in a hurry, where or whither one did not know, but we saw them a few minutes later lolloping back again. How Oriental they were, and how much a part of the unchanging East! Was Antinous as they? Antinous, to quote the rhythmical prose of Dr Lempriere's *Classical Dictionary* "a youth of Bithynia, of whom the Emperor Adrian was so extremely fond that at his death he erected a temple to him, and wished it to be believed that he had changed into a constellation". And, continuing, gaily, that Antinous was either drowned in the Nile, or offered himself at a sacrifice as a victim in honour of the Emperor, Dr Lempriere tells us in its appropriate place that: "Adrian was fifteenth Emperor of Rome and the first of the Caesars who wore a long beard, and this he did to hide the warts on his face." Bithynia being a country of Asia Minor with a Greek population, bounded by the Propontis and the Euxine. Those two young men of the Muski, it is certain, would have been as much at home in ancient Alexandria as in modern Cairo.

One may doubt whether anything worth buying will ever again be sold in the bazaars. Something which gets worse yearly is happening to the Egyptians. And with medical science to help them they are increasing in numbers and can only become worse still. We found the scent shop which had been amusing to visit years ago because of the ingratiating manner and eagerness to sell of the shop assistants, young men who should have been acting in a comedy or French farce. But the shop was shabby and unpainted. It had come down in the world. A prematurely old man with shaky voice and trembling hand stood at the counter. Could he have been one of the *jeunes premiers*, who had tried to sell us *baume de Judée*, attar-of-roses, and scented cigarettes all those years ago? And we came out of the shop and walked back to find our taxi.

It was time to drive out to the Pyramids and watch the sunset. On the way there we cross the Nile, and go down a long avenue past a former officer's club and a sad looking hotel. Once arrived in front of the

Great Pyramid which, whether one likes it or not, is an impressive moment in the life of any normal human being, all further thought is put out of mind by the roars for *bakshish* and the antics of the camel drivers. But their obsequiousness soon turns to insolence when they see you are not going to make a fool of yourself by getting on a camel, though they return to their blandishments now and again, and it emerges that for some reason I do not understand the biggest and ugliest of their camels is called "Jack Hulbert". They now talk with impertinent familiarity, and turbans and *caftans* notwithstanding, speak English, and idiomatic English at that, as well as we do ourselves. I do not think I have ever in my life experienced such a sensation of insolence and hatred as when, knowing there was no more business, they mounted their own camels and rode away. But there was something curious about their exit which is difficult to describe; and I can only put it that it was as though we found one of the conjurers who can pour any liqueur you ask for out of a tea-pot, feeeling thirsty, and availing himself of his own trick.

After the dragomen had ridden off, looking over their shoulders and uttering impertinent familiarities, we had a few moments to walk round two sides of the Great Pyramid, look at the hole in the ground from which the Sun Boat has been dug up, and at the long shed in the shadow of the Pyramid where it now lies undergoing repair and restoration. The Sphinx lay below, half in the sand, and inconspicuous for its degree of fame. And now it was time to have one last look at the Great Pyramid and drive back to Cairo, looking round once more, but it was too dark to see. And what does the Pyramid care? It has seen the loves and deaths of so many, and is unmoved. Nevertheless, who that comes to it from afar can leave it and not wonder if he will see it again, and what will be his own fate and the fate of those he loves? And to drown our cares we went for a drink to one of the best hotels, only to find that being the last day of Ramazan throughout Egypt all alcohol was forbidden, even a glass of beer. So we repaired to our own hotel to dine a little disconsolately behind those stained glass windows depicting scenes upon the banks of Nile.

In the morning we were up betimes and off early to see the treasures from the tomb of Tutankhamen in the Egyptian Museum. When in Cairo in 1931 it was not so long after the tomb had been opened * and some of the more fragile objects were still undergoing restoration and

---

* The tomb was discovered in the Valley of the Kings at Luxor and opened in November 1922. The tomb of Sethos II, which was "interpolated" into a chamber of the tomb of Ramses III, was used as a laboratory for the restoration of objects found in the tomb of Tutankhamen, and it was there we were shown those objects in 1931.

were not yet on view. However, we were shown them by Mr Howard Carter, and when at Luxor a few days later were conducted by him in person round the tomb. It will be recalled that Tutankhamen was a Pharaoh of the Eighteenth Dynasty who died at the age of eighteen after a reign of only six or seven years, in 1350 B.C. His tomb, in which the objects were found piled on top of one another in indescribable confusion, is not much larger than a fair sized bathroom (the biggest chamber is only twenty-six feet long by eight and a half feet wide). What, then, must have been the contents of the tombs of the great Pharaohs? Of Ramses II, in the next century, who reigned for sixty-seven years? Of Ramses III or of Sethos I, both of which in plan look like London Underground Stations at Piccadilly Circus or Oxford Circus with all their halls and anterooms and corridors? They must have contained treasures in gold alone of inestimable value.

Now the particular interest of seeing again the objects found in Tutankhamen's tomb was that in 1931 aesthetic opinion was so decidedly against them. I well remember that they could hardly be mentioned and, if at all, were greeted with a pitying smile. They were on a level with the monument in front of Buckingham Palace and with "official art" in France. This, from the best informed opinion, in contact with more than one of the famous aesthetes in England and one of the foremost French contemporary painters of the time. It is this that makes it interesting, for who is to be trusted ultimately but the judgment of one's own eyes? We must recall that none other a painter than Alma-Tadema was in early days the admired artist of Henry James and Roger Fry. On returning to London from Egypt in 1931 one had almost to conceal the information that one had been to Luxor and seen the objects from Tutankhamen's tomb.

But, all said and done, their effect is most wonderful and dazzling. It is not that it was a great art epoch. There were better periods during the thirty dynasties that ended with the Ptolemies.* But the official art of Egypt in the thirteenth century before Christ was of such technical assurance and so superb in execution. What a world do we inhabit, by comparison, where there is a handful of modern painters and an art of the academy which is not art at all? The mummy case, or, rather, the golden coffin of the Pharaoh is a work of marvellous solemnity and hieratic calm with all its "official" emblems and symbols of kingship; serpents and vultures upon the forehead in gold and lapis lazuli inlaid with faience, arms crossed over the breast with a flail and a crook in the hands; and figures of Isis and other gods with

* Last, and sixteenth of the Ptolemies, being Caesarion, son of Cleopatra and Julius Caesar.

outspread wings and forming, as it were, a feather covering. There is the golden mask, of burnished gold, placed inside the coffin and over the features of the mummy, and an exact portrait of the Pharaoh. And so much else; a chariot-body of gilded wood with figures of prisoners and of the Pharaoh in the guise of a sphinx trampling on his foes; a beautiful inlaid scent-chest with carvings that are of incredible delicacy of handling; a wooden casket with miniature paintings on its sides of the Pharaoh hunting lions, or in battle with negroes or with Asiatics, scenes which are conventions in the ultimate sense of the word for during his short reign he had little time for either. But most magnificent of all, not excluding the beautiful jewellery, are the two chairs of cedar wood (?) overlaid with gold, and particularly that one with "domestic" scenes of Tutankhamen and his queen. This must be in point of technique and craftsmanship equal to any work ever achieved by human hands. Nothing of the Italian Renaissance is better done. It lacks the profiled formality that is the bane of Egyptian art.

Looking closer into it one wonders what climatic changes have brought to Egypt. Cyrenaica was, then, cornland, and in the time of the Greeks was famous for its olive groves. The district of Maraeotis, near Alexandria, where the desert is in flower in early spring with anemone and narcissus, and latter with ranunculus and asphodel and yellow daisy, was once "exuberantly fertile. The lake had eight islands in it, with luxurious villas and country houses, and its white wines were celebrated by Horace and by Virgil." There have been changes in the climate of Egypt it is certain. Tutankhamen and his queen in the exquisite golden reliefs upon the chair are thinly clad but they are not natives of the desert or the tropics. They are not of the type whose energies have been impaired and enervated by the climate; neither do we find such types in any of the Egyptian sculptures. It was not an injurious climate, as it is now. Perhaps there was a return to former climatic conditions during the great epoch of the Fatimids and of Saladin? Or had it never altered since the time of the Pharaohs, and was it but dwindling under the Mamelukes to alter irrepairably when the Ottoman Turks conquered Egypt in 1517?* It is quite impossible to believe that the Pharaohs of the Nineteenth and Twentieth Dynasties, Sethos I, Ramses II and III, lived and flourished in the climate of Egypt as we know it now. Their blood was, of course, largely different for the Arab must be subtracted from it. But one of the main impressions of seeing these works of art is how African they are. They are as African as the Assyrian bas-reliefs

---

* Old residents of Cairo will tell you they remember the alteration in the climate of Egypt after the opening of the Assouan dam. The summers became hotter and the winters not so mild.

depicting Tiglath Pileser or Asshurbanipal are Semitic. African, but not essentially Negroid, for their affinity is to the Nilotic tribes, to the Dinka of the Sudan, or the giant Watussi of Ruanda-Urundi in the Belgian Congo. Who could doubt that, coming away from the Egyptian Museum in Cairo and passing the ceremonial litters of the Pharaohs, one supported by hieratic figures of cattle with wide horns like the kine of the Watussi; another by leopards simulated with their spottings; or a couch of gilded wood with sides carved in the form of fabulous animals with the heads of hippopotami, the bodies of serpents, and the paws of lions?

The rest of that morning we spent in looking at the Coptic churches in Old Cairo. They are in a quarter kept locked and barred behind a wooden door, and once within it you are in another world away from the rush and noise of the modern city.* There is the church of Abu Sarga (St Sergius) where, of course, there has to be a tradition that the Virgin and Child rested a month during their flight into Egypt. For this reason it is unnecessary to go down into the crypt, particularly when the priest on hearing it is not your first visit copies the inanities of a hostess and says he remembers you from more than twenty years before. Nevertheless, the church of Abu Sarga is humble and touching with its iconostasis and the galleries where the women used to sit. Another church attached to a college or monastery which is the residence of the Coptic Patriarch is no less charming with its early and nondescript columns and vaulted halls, but I have to admit to some confusion in my mind between the Coptic churches of Cairo and the Armenian churches in Jolfa, the suburb of Isfahan.

On the whole the Coptic churches are disappointing, particularly when we think that the Coptic textiles are among the greatest treasures of the applied arts. But, then, those belong to another tradition and are Alexandrian in origin. Are we to think of them as purposeful deformations after how many centuries of Egyptian and Ptolemaic art, as though the hand of a Matisse were at work? Or are they works of half-competence and ignorance? That seems hardly likely so near to such inveterate sophistication. And they are in undoubted connection with the Alexandrian portrait heads of Ptolemaic date, portraits of an embarrassing likeness and similitude, and of an academic competence to which there is no parallel in our own times.

But curious reversions of feeling were in progress. It was three or more centuries after the banquets of Antony and Cleopatra that hermits began to gather in the Thebaid and the Wadi Natrun. Learned opinion

* This Coptic quarter of Fostat or Old Cairo is built within the walls of the Roman citadel of Babylon, as the Greeks called what was, then, the suburb of Heliopolis.

has it that the churches in the Wadi Natrun were erected in the Meso-potamian style,* as were others much further south in Upper Egypt in the region of Assouan. The connection would be between the Copts and the Jacobites, or Assyrian Christians, all of whom are Mono-physites and hold to the doctrine of the one nature in Christ, and dating back to the time of the Abbasid Caliphs of the ninth century who ruled Cairo, but had Samarra and Baghdad as capital cities of their empire. But the Coptic textiles are much earlier still and the shreds and rags found in tombs are suggestive of nothing but a "breakdown" of the classical tradition. They cannot have been poor persons, or, without taking the Marxist view of history, their bodies would not have been found at all. They must have been persons of substance who would wear expensive materials, and what is the meaning, therefore, of the distortions and foreshortenings of pattern? Which are like a scribbling or rapid shorthand of the cupids, Venuses, gods and heroes of antiquity? It must be that the craftsman was weary and no longer believed in it. The textiles are last fragments of an age in which the hand of man could not go wrong, when the ancient world knew such a multiplicity of statues that the nomads swarming out of the desert took alarm in their puritan conscience and forbade further representation of animal and human form. Did not the same movement sweep over the Christian world with the Iconoclasts who forbade all sculpture in their churches? Outside the city there is the Thebaid of the anchorites, and the back-ground is that of that of the *Paradise* of Palladius, or Flaubert's *Tentation de St Antoine*. The hermits were even collected in sufficient number to become dangerous, and the most curious of all offensive operations in history may have been the quasi-legendary occasion when the anchorites stormed and sacked Alexandria. All this, and much more, is to be read into the Coptic textiles.

We had only the afternoon left and were determined to devote this to the other mosques, being taken immediately by our Sudanese taxi-driver, in triumph, to the so-called "Blue Mosque" which is one of the most uninteresting, but for some unknown reason the most famous of all the mosques in Cairo. It has a few blue tiles of poor quality put in by the Turks. Of the other mosques our driver knew nothing, not even their names, and we had to find our way about by map, or from memories of more than twenty years ago. Our first enquiry

* The church of Deir Suryani has "superb stuccos in the Mesopotamian style", more closely identified as "akin to the third style of Samarra", a nicety which may be lost upon most readers. Cf. "Christian Art in Egypt," by Professor Ugo Monneret de Villard, in Baedeker's *Egypt*, 1929, ed., p. cxc. The stuccos in question are probably due to the tenth century Abbot Moses of Nesibin, a town in Mesopotamia near the district inhabited by the few remaining Yezidis or devil-worshippers.

was for Soltan Qalaun, where we picked up a kind of a sacristan whom we took round with us much to the disgust of our taxi-driver, a youngish man with fair hair, probably a relic of the English garrison, and blue eyes which were sickeningly and appallingly affected, they were "oyster eyes", and indeed he was all but blind, but he knew the names, at least, and could ask the way for us.

The Mosque and Mausoleum of Soltan Qalaun date from the very end of the thirteenth century, and are to be compared to the contemporary town churches of Northern Europe. Then it has to be said that those gain by content for although mosques are a mere shell, nothing could be more intrinsically magnificent than the bare walls of Soltan Qalaun. The separate tomb-chamber where the Soltan lies in his catafalque has been a little over restored but the walls have superb incrustation of marble and of mother-of-pearl. Near by is the *madraseh* or college of Soltan Barquq, not a Bahrite Mameluke as was Qalaun, but a Circassian Mameluke, and therefore about a hundred years later in date.* It was now that, handing our sacristan-friend a paper note in order that he should get change, we saw him holding it up to the light about a millimetre away from his eyes and we realized he was nearly blind.

Hereabouts we are in a narrow street with a succession of wonderful old buildings, not only mosques but old houses, as well, and *sebils* or fountains, and the effect is of a picturesqueness to which the only equal in my memory is afforded by the two long streets in Naples that are lined down all their length with churches and Baroque palaces gone to slums. It is at about this point that one begins to admire and take note of the Mameluke style as set forth and expressed in the minarets of their mosques. It is as though they are as many in number, and show as much divergence and variety in themselves upon the same theme, as there are steeples of Wren's City churches.† Those are of the sprinkler or sugar-castor order, of near affinity to silversmiths' work of the time, what is shed forth from the openings in their tiers of diminishing

* The dynasty of the Turkish or Bahrite Mamelukes, so called because their barracks lay on the island of Roda in the Nile, reigned from 1250 to 1382, during which time there were twenty-five Soltans; and the dynasty of the Circassian Mamelukes from 1382 till the Turkish conquest in 1517. Mamelukes were originally "white" slaves trained as soldiers to form the bodyguard, who, then, usurped their master's power. Under the Turks twenty-four Mameluke Beys governed the different provinces of Egypt. The Mamelukes were eventually massacred by Mohammad Ali in 1807. It will be recollected that Napoleon had a squadron of Mamelukes throughout his campaigns attached to the Imperial Guard. For further details see my *Mauretania*, London, Duckworth & Co., 1940, pp. 263–266.
† The different forms of the City steeples are discussed and compared in my *British Architects and Craftsmen*, London, B.T. Batsford, Ltd., 1945, pp. 107–109.

octagons being the sound of the church bells. But the Mameluke minarets of Cairo are of thurible or incense-burner type and date from the Circassian Mamelukes, being contemporary to our late Perpendicular in England as displayed in King's College, Cambridge, St George's Chapel, Windsor, and the church towers of Somerset.

Immediately next door to the Barquqiya or Soltan Barquq is another mosque with a beautiful minaret, and one looks from one to other in comparison of their stalactitic balconies. Again as in the courts of the Alhambra at Granada it is the Arabian filigree, displayed, also, in the *musharabiyas*, or pierced lattices of the houses, one authority telling us that of these, since the beginning of this century, "it is scarcely an exaggeration to say that ninety per cent. have disappeared, and the streets of Cairo have thereby lost their most distinctive cachet".* The minaret-thuribles in this region of the old city are contrived, as it were, to shake forth the voice of the *muezzin* and the call to prayer. They rise up tapering with their stalactite pendentives, usually with an octagonal shaft and little domed kiosque or pavilion at the top, which is mere ornament and has no cell or chamber in it, but it just rings and echoes.

One more mosque we visited, remembered from the former time, that of Qaït Bey, another of the Circassian Mamelukes, and of such elegance that it is taken as the pattern of their style. The minaret again is excessively graceful, and almost finicky with its balconies of pierced surrounds and fastidious finish. It is the decadence or extreme efflorescence and could be carried no further in point of refinement and luxury of detail. Other mosques there was no time for; El Ghuri, El Mardani, and probably a half-dozen or a dozen more. We had seen what we wanted to see. The mosques of Cairo are the most splendid in the Mohammadan world, just as, with Istanbul, it is the other metropolis of the Moslem world. They are the two great cities of the Orient; one upon the Nile, and the other on the Bosphorus at the joining of Europe and Asia. But Cairo owes nothing to another civilization; it had no Byzantium as its predecessor and is not the heir by right of conquest to an ancient empire. Of which it took over, and adopted, not a few of the old forms. Is not Santa Sophia prototype of the Imperial Mosques of Istanbul? And within little more than a century of the taking of Constantinople in 1453 were not the Turks the chronic sufferers from Byzantinism? But Cairo is entirely the creation of the Fatimid Caliphs of a thousand years ago.

There was just time to drive out in the late afternoon to see the

* Cf. "Islamic Architecture in Egypt", by K. A. C. Creswell, in Baedeker's *Egypt*, 1929, ed., p. cci.

Tombs of the Caliphs. They are in the desert outside Cairo, but it would be more true to say they lie out in the dust of the city past the mounds of potsherds that are called the Windmill Hills. Being a feast day there was that exodus into "the country" which I have said, elsewhere, is general to all Moslem cities from Meshed to Marrakesh, and as such it is a day of animal torment. We were about to have a horribly unpleasant experience of this. There were veiled ladies about in plenty, some of them wearing the golden nose ornament, like a spoon worn on the nose, which betokens they are from the Sudan. We were already among the cemeteries and the roads were ankle deep in dust. There were the usual donkey carts taking along whole families and so heavily loaded that it was better not to look. But at one corner we came to a halt, and before we knew what was happening our taxi-driver had jumped down and was bargaining with a donkey-driver. He had offered him the equivalent of five shillings, a lot of money and probably nearly a day's pay, to put down his load of passengers. The donkey-driver had pocketed the money, but was continuing with his fares. Some ten or twelve enormously fat and ugly women, all in black, with their small children and two or three men, sat there on the cart, laughing, while the donkey-driver tried to drag the poor little animal forward, pulling at its head and kicking its matchstick legs that were so thin one expected them to snap or break. It had been too much even for our Sudanese taxi-driver who in himself can have been no tender heart. But little could be done about it. The animal was facing a steep corner and it simply could not move. There the fat women sat, not even attempting to get down, and with an appalling wrench our driver and one or two of the men somehow got the cart round that corner. It is for such experiences as this that one cannot love the modern Egyptians. We had to drive off, swallowing hard, and trying not to think of that poor donkey and its brother and sister animals on that public feast day.

By now, on an execrable road we were among low walls and lesser tombs. Domes appear, of small and private character at first. But soon we are in a maze of mausolea on every side, in the style made familiar from the domed *sebil* or fountain in the enclosure of the Dome of the Rock at Jerusalem. These are buildings of the Circassian Mamelukes, a white master race of Caucasian origin, "in general, herdsmen's sons, purchased in Georgia and the places adjacent, all extremely fair, with light blue eyes, light eyebrows, little or no beard, a very white skin and a blooming complexion".* They are not, in fact, Tombs of the

* *Narrative of a Ten Years Residence at Tripoli in Africa*, by Richard Tully, 1816. Tully was British Consul at Tripoli, and there were Mamelukes in the service of the

Caliphs at all for after the time of Saladin the Soltans of Egypt never called themselves Caliphs. The craftsmen were, of course, Egyptian but these later Soltans were Caucasian.

Twenty and more years ago, which in Egypt is but a moment in time, I had found the Tombs of the Mamelukes to be wonderfully impressive, and had written that "their crumbling disdainful grandeur made a most violent attack on the imagination": those of Qaït Bey and Soltan Barquq, in particular. And now after all these years we have arrived again at Soltan Barquq and its pair of domes which, I said, "represent the Orient in its legendary character". They are, indeed, as typical of Arabian or Saracenic art as to their own speech and kind are the blue domes of Isfahan. Said to be the earliest domes built of stone (just after 1400) they are of different pattern, though both in the shape of casques or war-helms. It is a building of large size having been formerly a convent of shaikhs or dervishes and it has long vaulted passages. On the floor of one of the passages, as we walked along with the custodian, we found a little girl lying asleep with her head and face half-hidden by an arm but covered with a crawling veil or caul of flies. Her eyes, which were shut, were completely ringed with flies crawling and swarming over one another. To what must they be accustomed, that a child of eight or nine years old can sleep with more than one fly touching or hovering upon her! This little girl was the custodian's daughter, and seeing us looking at her he gave her a little push with his hand and with no more ado put his dirty handkerchief over her face, and in a moment that was black with flies. We walked on into the Court of the Mosque and into its prayer-chamber where is a beautifully worked stone *minbar* or pulpit, and then crossing the court went on into the tomb-chamber of Soltan Barquq which is at the far corner. When we came back a few moments later the little girl was still sleeping and the handkerchief had slipped off her face, but this time her father did not even bother to drive away the flies.

The Tomb-Mosque of Qaït Bey is a little nearer to Cairo and in the middle of a huddle of mean houses where Egyptians sit out on the street all day long and for much of the night with nothing else to do but swallow noxious-looking drinks of syrupy pomegranate or lemonade. I think it is the most degraded population I have ever seen, sunk in squalor, and of entire and abject hopelessness. The mongrel curs that wander hungrily in search of garbage with their tails between their legs are at least at work looking for something, however sordid

"Bashaw" of Tripoli long after their massacre in Cairo. A certain tribe on the borders of Egypt and Cyrenaica is said to be descended from the Mamelukes. The Mamelukes may have been sold as slaves, but they were soon the masters.

it may be. But the Egyptians sitting about in their striped nightgowns are nearly universally afflicted with bad eyes, they are mostly pock-marked, and one wonders how many of them are sufferers from bil-harzia, or worse. One dreads to touch a coin or a paper-note, while the stomach revolts at the thought of drinking from a public glass or a coffee-cup in that appalling slum.

There were roars and yells for *bakshish* as we disembarked and sank our shoes into the dust and mud before gaining the dirty and stained steps into the Tomb-Mosque of Qaït Bey. It is a later building than Soltan Barquq, dating from about 1475, and is the perfection of Mameluke elegance. Perhaps it is here in midst of this moaning slum that we should think of the dress of the Mamelukes as an eyewitness saw them: "almost covered with gold and silver, adapted to constant riding, and both martial and graceful. It is in the Moorish style, but unaccompanied by long flowing coverings. Their heads are encircled with a rich embroidered shawl bound tight round their caps, leaving out a long end which hangs on the left side of the head and which appears to be solid gold from the richness of the embroidery, as does their habit. They wear their trousers extremely ample, and of the finest muslin, quite down to the ankle, with bright yellow boots and slippers." Such were the Mamelukes at the time of their extinction by massacre in Egypt, and there is no reason to think they had changed their habits or appearance in the centuries between 1475 and 1800 any more than had the Turkish Janissaries from the time of their foundation in the reign of Mohammad the Conqueror until they in their turn were massacred by Mahmud the Reformer in 1826.

The minaret of Qaït Bey is embellished with stalactite ornament of utmost richness, making an Englishman feel he would like to take the architect on a return visit to see the fan-vaulting of Henry VII's Chapel at Westminster Abbey and hear his comments upon that. The dome of Qaït Bey is melon-shaped and has a network worked over it to represent the veins in the rind of the melon. The interior of the Tomb-Mosque is sumptuously rich in marble, in carved stonework, and in its wooden ceiling, but with its perfection there is the warning that this is the end and that nothing more can happen. But, also, because that is the date at which it was most admired (and was over-restored) it is a building of 1880–1890 in some square or gardens in South Kensington. And in spite of its perfection of elegance one leaves the Tomb-Mosque of Qaït Bey with a depressed feeling.*

* Another group of tomb-mosques, known confusingly as the Tombs of the Mame-lukes, lies outside Cairo in a different direction, to the south of the Citadel. On neither visit to Cairo could I contrive to see it. The buildings are more dilapidated than the

And now we have seen everything that we had come to see in Cairo and were nearing the end of our long journey. There remained the vicarious pleasure of drinking wine again for dinner after it had been forbidden. As Mr Julian Huxley before us, we looked in the wine-list and had to choose between Aphrodite, Apollon demi-sec, Osiris dry, and Cru des Ptolémées, wines grown in the region of Alexandria, but muddling, in themselves, because of the rival Euchris and Isis and other "preparations" of the London hairdressers, not forgetting Ajax and the "celebrated Hercules". We chose Cru des Ptolémées which had a curious lingering taste not in the least suggestive of the vine. And so upstairs to bed for a sleepless night and unarmed battle with a green scarab beetle which as though offering itself for a souvenir of Lower Egypt trailed all night long to and fro on the floor of the bedroom and up the bathroom wall. At dawn, in the desolate hour of trying to sense one was in Cairo where one would never come again, a big bird like some kind of vulture began to call out at the back of the hotel looking on to low sheds and other backs, and to flap its wings. I could never see it properly, but still hear it now. Before it seemed possible the night was over coffee was brought at six o'clock by a tall crypto-eunuch from the Sudan, and an hour later we were sitting in the tumbril outside the air office waiting to drive to the aerodrome.

It is a short flight to Alexandria and the Mediterranean, but it took longer than that to drive down to the port and pass through the customs. There was a maze of different offices, currency control, immigration, certificates of vaccination, and so forth, ending in a set of last obstacles one had to jump one after another like a hurdle race. At the last desk of all, tired and exhausted, and longing to board the Italian liner before it was too late to get breakfast, we were held up by an official who having examined and stamped our passports produced in the final moment a long printed list. In order to help him and hurry things we began, desperately, to run a finger down the list looking for our names. At last, he smiled. "You are looking", he said, "for your names in my blacklist!" And with that he handed us our passports, and we went on board.

It seemed such a short while ago that we had touched at Alexandria on our way to Persia. Looking down from the deck-rail, were they the same monks and nuns waving farewell? Another, and not the same

Tombs of the Caliphs, so called, but include the early thirteenth century mausoleum of a famous religious leader, Imam-esh-Shafi, described as on a par with the best Egyptian mediaeval buildings, being two hundred years earlier in date than Soltan Barquq and Qaït Bey.

The elliptical Forum at Jerash

Mosque of Omar at Jerusalem

"galli galli" man rattled his dice-box and began his tricks. But there were familar figures, and it was now I saw the old negro gentleman in his new grey suit shaking hands all round and going ashore. There was the noise of the windlass and up came the gangway. We were leaving the Orient probably for ever. But where does it end, and where does it begin? Next morning the ship called in at Rhodes. Rhodes, where the via dei Cavalieri and its fifteenth century "auberges" of golden stone mingles the Levant with the wool-villages in the Cotswolds; where there is a Greek quarter with cubical white houses and pebble pavements in "Greek island style"; a Turkish quarter with mosques of Soltan Mustafa, of Süleyman, and of Regeb Pacha with some Persian tiles; and a Jewish quarter of Sephardic Jews, some few of whom still speak debased Castilian and still sing old Spanish songs. Flags were at half-mast and every shop was shut for two "patriots" who had been hung in Cyprus. There were armed guards outside the British Consulate. When I was a young man, and came to Rhodes before, we went to the bay of Lindos where the Rhodian plates with their designs of tulips and cypresses were painted and fired in the kiln; and another day went up into the forest of Monte Sant' Elia, where many stags were wandering and the wood was full of huge white peonies, a scene so beautiful that I made it into the setting for a long poem, *Landscape with the Giant Orion*.

Next port of call was the Piraeus, and taking the train to Athens there was an unfamiliar view of the Acropolis and the Parthenon from a train window. The Benaki Museum, for once, was open when we wanted it to be. The Brusa silks with their patterns of exploding and split pinks and carnations, the better, the simpler and bolder their design, looked Turkish but were the work of Greek craftsmen; there were showcases full of bishops' croziers and the double-handles of their staffs; there were the jewellery and embroidery of the Islands; the women's costumes and Albanian "evzone" dresses for the men, sporting the white ballet skirt or fustanella; are these all, or are they not, of Eastern origin? Late that evening, in the Gulf of Corinth, we were off Lepanto where Don John of Austria defeated a Turkish fleet of two hundred galleys and Cervantes lost an arm. The battle was fought at the narrowest point of the Gulf, and what wrecks must be down there waiting for the frog-man and his camera!

Two days later, our ship was gliding at breakfast time past low islands with the first Venetian houses. In at the Porto di Lido, and down the Canale di San Marco with Palladio's church and campanile of San Giorgio Maggiore on our left, and on the right the long line of houses and hotels and, at last, the Doges' Palace, and then St Mark's and all its

12

soap-bubble or howdah-domes, like some floating Kitaigorod or Kremlin, now obscured, vanished, and we glide past the Zattere to our berthing-place behind the shell-domes of the Salute. Coming to it from the Orient, Venice had never looked more of an Eastern or Oriental city, however classical its idiom, and we went by gondola to the station and caught the Orient Express for London.

# CHAPTER XI

## ISTANBUL

*S.S. Barletta — Naples on an August morning — The love birds — Dinner in Athens — Arriving at Istanbul — The Imperial Mosques upon the skyline — Waiters — Santa Sophia — Paul the Silentiary on the marbles of Santa Sophia — Mosque of Soltan Achmet — Mosaic pavement of the Processional Way — Secular mosaics of the Byzantines — Along the Bosphorus — Souks — "I am a magician" — Rings of the "Tulip Reign" — Sinan, the great architect of Turkey — The Süleimaniye — The Old Seraglio — The Treasure — Festivals of the "Tulip Reign" — Baghdad Kiosque — Palace of the Byzantine Emperors — Gypsy girls — The old walls — Basilica Cistern — Upstairs galleries at Santa Sophia — Church of the Pantocrator — St Mary of the Mongols — Church of the Pammacaristos — Churches of the Byzantine Emperors — Resounding titles of old Byzantium — The Hilton Hotel — Brusa — The Turbéhs — The Green Mosque and the Green Turbéh — Another visit to the Old Seraglio — Der Eunuchismus — The Kafés — Persicos domos and the Tower of the Porphyra — Tressed Halberdiers — Little St Sophia or SS. Sergius and Bacchus — Mosaics of the Cariye Cami — Mosque of Eyoub — The Night of Bairam — Circumcision ceremony in a music hall — Mosque of Yeni Cami — The "Tulip" Mosque — Mosque of Sokollu Mehmet Pasha — Mosque of Rustem Pacha — Other small mosques by Sinan — Turbéhs of Süleyman the Magnificent and of Roxelana — Sinan's mosques compared to Wren's churches — Turkish tilework — Last evening drive in Istanbul — And back to Venice.*

I

THE immediate encouragement for this book, and much if not all of the impetus towards its final realization, came in haphazard manner while I was having luncheon with my sister one day in the early summer of 1954. I found myself sitting next to an old friend, a lover and patron of poetry, who had just returned from visiting the excavations at Mohenjo-daro, and elsewhere in Pakistan. She told me of her travels, and when I said we intended to go to Venice for our summer holiday at the end of August she enquired whether I had seen the newly discovered mosaics in the Cariye Cami at Istanbul. It was twenty years since we had been to Turkey, and time we went again. Would we go as her guests and let her pay for the sea journey? This was a kindness which it was next to impossible to refuse so one day late in August in 1955 we found ourselves in the Rome Express going from Rome to Genoa, where we had luncheon in a restaurant at the top of the new *grattocielo* or skyscraper, and embarked in the evening on board the S.S. *Barletta* bound for Istanbul.

It was a small ship of much character and few passengers, and we had the purser's cabin down a long companion-way past the engines and the cooks' galleys. But the cabin was scrupulously clean, it was away from the other travellers, we could keep the portholes open and it had an electric fan. All night the marvellous air of the Mediterranean flowed in at the portholes, and the sunrises were more beautiful than words can describe. We called in at Naples where I had not been for more than twenty years, and never in August, and had an intoxicating early morning drive while the melon stalls and stalls of lilies and tuberoses were just opening for the day, up to the Vomero and the Certosa di San Martino where I enjoyed again some of those things that had thrilled and inspired me when I was a young poet more than thirty years before. Alas! that one lives but once and has no second chance. On this occasion I got as much pleasure from paintings of scenes in Naples in the late eighteenth century and down to what we would call Early Victorian times as from anything else, and there was still time for a visit to Santa Chiara and San Gregorio Armeno which were my favourite churches. Then we sat at a café in front of the Royal Palace, and I had much to think of, and we went back on board our ship which as though on purpose to please us made almost a circle round the Isle of Capri.

By this time we were for want of more serious recreation much interested in our fellow passengers. An Italian married couple who sat at our table, although anything but young, were so engrossed in themselves that they could scarcely speak to us, and this is unusual with Italians who are so generally so talkative. They never showed in the dining room twice in the same clothes, having an apparently endless repertoire of summer wear. With the husband it was a choice of immaculate white flannel, or linen, or gabardine trousers, or blue or grey ones, or shorts, and all with caps and hats to match. But the real interest was photography. They travelled with a perfect battery of cameras of all shapes and sizes, cinecameras, colour films, and so on, a complete filming unit in themselves, and their only subject was each other. At all hours from early morning onwards they were never "off the set". They even annexed a little corner of an upper deck for themselves, near the captain's cabin, and there the pair of love birds took studies of each other and slept a little on deck chairs.

At night we came through the Straits of Messina, and by morning were far out somewhere in the glorious Ionian Sea, turning by evening into the Adriatic. There was not an empty moment albeit there was nothing whatever to look at. But the Mediterranean in August is enough if one has not seen it for a long time, and one feasts one's eyes upon its colour. What a marvellous sensation to be going again towards the Orient, and passing the shores of Greece! For early in the morning we entered the Gulf of Corinth, and saw again the brown, unwooded mountains with Missolonghi to the left, and later on Patras to starboard, and somewhere away in the mountains of the mainland, not the Pelopennese, the monastery of Hosios-Loukas which I have never seen, and its Byzantine gold mosaics and floor of multicoloured marble.* And at last we were at the opening of the Canal, where once we had been tossed about at anchor in a fog for twenty-four hours on board a private yacht. We looked straight down the Canal in order to see again the curve of the earth's surface, and steamed slowly and boringly from end to end of it arriving late in Athens so that we missed keeping a rendezvous with a friend, saw nothing at all except a floodlit view of the Parthenon, and dined expensively at the Grande Bretagne Hotel when we might as well have had dinner for nothing on board ship.

The S.S. *Barletta* went at the pace of a water-beetle, of the plodding and not the darting kind, and we were a whole day in the Dardanelles and the Sea of Marmora. There had been nothing Oriental so far but one or two white minarets at Gallipoli. Also, the day was rather hazy and the sea, for once, a little rough. All the waiters and stewards on the ship came from Trieste, just as in England most ships' crews seem to come from Portsmouth. Only the barman pretended to any interest when I told him I had been to see d'Annunzio in Fiume in the winter of 1920, or responded at the mention of Sangue dei Morlacchi which was the name invented by the poet for the local cherry brandy of Zara.† Like the rest of the waiters and stewards he was unimpressed by Istanbul and only wanted to be back in Trieste. He did not mind the *tramontana*, the cold wind which blows round the corners of the streets and comes from the bare limestone plateau of the Karst. Istanbul was nothing at all, and with a gesture he showed what he thought of people who were unfortunate enough to have to live there.

The morning was unpromising with Asia out of sight and Europe too misty to be viewed. But it was a heat mist and must be very hot on land. One remembered gloomy accounts from persons who had been disappointed by Istanbul. It was universally hot and damp and grey. The low shore was objectless and uninteresting. But everybody

* *The Monastery of St Luke of Stiris*, London, Schultz & Barnsley, 1901; and Diehl, *L'Eglise et les Mosaiques du Convent de Saint-Luc-en-Phocide*, Paris, 1889.

† The Morlacchi were a mountain tribe who were famous for their cherry orchards. They were reputed to be fierce Moslems and are mentioned, if I am not mistaken, in a song in *Così fan tutte*, where there is the line: " *Wallacchi e Morlacchi*", so they must have been known to Lorenzo da Ponte, the librettist.

crowded on deck and we saw someone pointing. There were houses, and more houses, and now a continuous line of buildings, and needle-like shapes on the skyline, and a shallow dome like an inverted saucer, which was where the man was pointing. So slowly were we moving that it was fully a quarter of an hour before the shapes grew bigger and became recognizable, by which time something wonderful had happened, there was blue sky and the sun was shining, and people round us were saying "Aya Sofia", or "Soltan Achmet", as though uncertain. And now it sailed, or, rather, rose into sight, as if floating to the surface, and was indeed the Mosque of Soltan Achmet known for certain because of all mosques in the world only this and the Ka'aba of Mecca have six minarets. A domed building standing a little below it with but four minarets was Santa Sophia, and now we are suddenly approaching Asia in order to manœuvre and turn into the Golden Horn.

There can never have been such a site for a huge metropolis. The shore of Asia is crowded with buildings and mosques and minarets, and is no more than a few hundred yards away; Asia lying out to Kamschatka, or to Bangkok and its pagodas, and down the coast of Coromandel to the mines of Golconda and the lacquered seas. Asia, indeed, in any direction you prefer it, and lying so near you can almost touch it with your hand. Our ship makes a sweep towards it, and in that moment we see before and in front of us the opening of the Golden Horn, and one after another all the Imperial Mosques of Istanbul standing against and upon the skyline; the Süleimaniye, or Great Mosque of Süleyman the Magnificent, standing upon the third hill; the Mosque of Bayazit on the same hill below it; of Mohammad the Conqueror or the Fetiye upon the fourth hill; of Soltan Selim upon the fifth hill; of the Shehzade, one of the loveliest of all; and low down by the Galata bridge, so that its dome and pair of minarets come up out of the smoke of the town, the Mosque of Yeni Cami, last built of the Imperial Mosques of Istanbul. It is the most sensational revelation, one after another of these great domes, as in a panorama; they stand there on the skyline like huge kettle-drums with something menacing and martial in their air, and in that moment it is more of a capital than any other city, more than London, or than Rome or Paris; much vaster than Venice which in comparison is but a few churches and palaces upon the water at water level, or, even, it could be said, at waterlily level for the Salute apart, which like a huge shell stands upon its own steps or platform that could be self-formed of pale madrepores or coral, the Venetian buildings rise from a height no higher than the pavement.

The only city on a par with Istanbul seen from the waters of the

Golden Horn is New York City viewed from off the Battery, when the towers and skyscrapers of Manhattan appear as in some rank and order that is, really, haphazard and but anarchy and disorder; the Empire State Building, the Chrysler Tower, and Radio City being each its own master with no general scheme or plan. But at Istanbul many of the mosques look to be, and are, the work of one man. Perhaps if one could sail to London up the Thames, diverting on purpose and at length through the East India and other docks, and then see the City steeples of white Portland stone with St Paul's in midst of them as in Canaletto's painting, it would be like the entrance into a great city. But London is not a capital of Europe and of Asia, and the second Rome; and the Thames is not the Bosphorus. In this moment Istanbul is alone and tremendous. No water city can compare to it; no other city of the Orient climbs upon its seven hills above a trident or triple lane of calmed and inland waters. It must be the most wonderful site for a great capital there has ever been.

As we come in to dock illusions pale a little at sight of decaying paint and peeling plaster, and we berth near a small mosque which could have been built sixty years ago as an advertisement for a cigarette factory. It looks to be still in use. Can anyone go to worship there, or believe in it? But there is no time to think of it, or of anything else, when the assault party of Turkish dock porters swarms aboard, one of whom mysteriously makes straight for me waving a piece of paper in his hand. He then drags me to the rail and points down to a *kvass* standing below, and with no more ado ties a length of thin rope round all our luggage, amounting to some seven or eight suitcases, hoists the whole lot of it on to his back and leads the way ashore, this apparent Sandow or Hercules being no more than the typical Anatolian peasant.

After moderate delays we are through the customs and driving along the narrow streets of Galata, past an old house which I remembered from before bore an inscription saying it was the residence of the Consul-General of the Republic of Ragusa, and so up the steeper streets of Pera to our hotel. Here we were given a room with a delightful balcony, but the heat of Istanbul at the end of August was so huge and tremendous that we were only able to go out on it if one woke up in the middle of the night, or at early morning. The view from it was superb, over the Bosphorus to Asia and up a little corner of the Golden Horn with the dome of one of the Imperial Mosques riding like some aircraft carrier trimmed for action on the skyline, and down below, far down the hill, some cypress trees and at the water's edge a little mosque with one minaret from which round about dawn we could hear the voice of the *muezzin*.

We now came down to luncheon, and were at once aware of the
waiters who were most of them old gentlemen with bald heads,
Phanariots, that is to say, persons born in the Phanar or Greek quarter
of Istanbul, but, curiously, to my mind they were much less Greek
than Turkish, as were the youths in long aprons who carried trays up
from the kitchens. What was remarkable in these old waiters was that
they had evolved their own way of walking which was conditioned by
the slippery marble floor. They shuffled and never raised their feet,
and one must suppose, found the floor "drew their feet" and was
painful. The maître d'hôtel was White Russian, and the food Russo-
Turkish with Greek or even Armenian accents. The old waiters were
friendly, and in manner like down-at-heel decrepit ambassadors of
some forgotten Oriental state which had existed when one was young,
and since disappeared. But the floor waiters were more enterprising;
one of them lent us guide books, collected signed editions of modern
authors, and asked every morning if he could change money for us on
the black market as he brought our breakfast.

Walking to the door of the hotel we fell, automatically, into the
hands of a retired Turkish naval officer, a "captain" as he told us, but
with his Tartar features he looked much more as though he had served
in the Chinese navy, now, owing to the smallness of his pension
become one of the hotel guides. With him we set off at great expense
down the Grande Rue de Pera in a taxi. It is the distances that are the
drawback of this city, and going twice a day from Pera to Istanbul,
for sightseeing is costly both in time and money. But conditions had
improved in one direction. When last in Istanbul in 1930 the taxi-
drivers had no homes of their own and lived and slept in their cars with
a companion who they took round with them for protection. In
consequence, it was something of an ordeal to set foot inside a taxi.

On this first afternoon we went immediately to Santa Sophia. At
the time of our previous visit it had only just been secularized and turned
from a mosque into a museum. It had even been proposed to set up
gambling-tables and turn it into a casino. We were taken upstairs into
the galleries where, before we could stop him, the guide threw up a
piece of stone against the ceiling and offered us a handful of mosaics,
the same experience that Lady Mary Wortley Montagu describes as
happening to her two hundred years ago.* Now there are all the
mosaics uncovered by Professor Whittemore but their beauty and
importance have been exaggerated. There are some delicate mosaic
patterns on a vaulted passage and a number of indifferent and coarsely
executed Imperial portraits. These discoveries which were so eagerly

* We saw the same thing happening in the court of the Great Mosque of Damascus.

Dome of Madraseh Chahar Bagh at Isfahan

anticipated, and hailed as though the excitement was as that of discovering the treasure of the Incas, amount to very little. But neither is
Santa Sophia in itself ever anything but disappointing, for you expect
something which is more beautiful than St Mark's and find yourself
in an Albert Hall—only it is fifteen hundred years old. It is the immense
age of Santa Sophia which begins to grow upon one. Then the lightness of the huge dome dawns upon one's mind; and perhaps more
than all else the marvellous columns of porphyry* and of green Molos-
sian marble and their carved capitals, and the beauty of the half-domes
which rest, as the Byzantine author Procopius says, "on columns
standing upon the floor, which are not placed in a straight line, but
arranged with an inward curve of semicircular shape, one beyond
another like the dancers in a chorus". The ghost-marbles are older
and dirtier and more faded than those of St Mark's, marble veneer
resembling in effect the child's trick of scrawling its name on blotting-
paper and then folding the paper so that it smudges and makes a
double "ghost".

But for this wondrous array of marbles fifteen hundred years ago,
when fresh and new, one can but quote Paul the Silentiary for his
account written in the lifetime of Justinian: "Yet who even in the
measures of Homer, shall sing the marble pastures gathered on the lofty
walls and spreading pavement of the mighty church. These the iron
with its metal tooth has gnawed—the fresh green from Carystus,
and many-coloured marble from the Phrygian range, in which a rosy
blush mingles with white, or it shines bright with flowers of deep red
and silver. There is a wealth of porphyry, too, powdered with bright
stars, that has once laden the river boat on the broad Nile. You would
see an emerald green from Sparta, and the glittering marble with wavy
veins, which the tool has worked in the deep bosom of the Iassian hills,
showing slanting streaks blood-red and livid white. From the Lydian
creek came the bright stone mingled with streaks of red. Stone too
there is that the Lydian sun, warming with his golden light, has
nurtured in the deep-bosomed clefts of the hills of the Moors, of
crocus colour glittering like gold; and the product of the Celtic crags,
a wealth of crystals like milk poured here and there on a flesh of
glittering black. There is the precious onyx, as if gold were shining
through it; and the marble that the land of Atrax yields, not from some
upland glen, but from the level plains; in parts fresh green as the sea

* Paul the Silentiary says that these columns of porphyry "were brought from the
cliffs of Thebes, which stand like greaved warriors by the banks of Nile". For this, and
other passages by the same sixth century writer, one of the last poets of the Greek
Anthology, see *The Church of Sancta Sophia*, by W. R. Lethaby and Harold Swainson,
London, 1894.

or emerald stone, or again like blue cornflowers in grass, with here and there a drift of fallen snow—a sweet, mingled contrast to the dark shining surface." This celebrated description of the marbles of Santa Sophia, often quoted before, it is irresistible to quote again, perhaps with a particular indulgence in the case of the present writer who was familiar with it when he was a schoolboy at Eton, and copied it into his notebook from the school library, at about that wonderful time in his life when he discovered Flaubert's *Salammbô*, in the Lotus edition, in the village post office at his home, and was in correspondence with the Italian Futurist poet, F. T. Marinetti. Probably nothing more than that, and certainly nothing better, is to be said of Santa Sophia, though, coming away, I looked and looked in vain for the beautiful little yellow tiled library dating from the Turkish golden age.

After this we went as a matter of course to the Mosque of Soltan Achmet which stands near by, beside the Hippodrome. It seems that there has ever to be a "blue mosque", and this is the "blue mosque" of Istanbul. Beautiful, indeed, are its courtyard and its half-dozen minarets with their stalactitic balconies, though they are not so much stalactites as icicles. The interior of Soltan Achmet has blue tiles from Nicaea around its waistline, and above that is stencilled or arabesqued in blue. There is a tribune or gallery for the Soltan, raised on pillars, with a gilt screen, very different from the golden grilles in churches, which were made to hide the nuns; and there one may think of the Grand Turk sitting crosslegg'd, probably with an enormous emerald in his turban which gives a taste of India that we shall find again and again, and for a reason, in Istanbul. And now having seen enough for one day we returned to our hotel, where we found the love birds from the ship, who had incredibly not booked rooms anywhere, although it was the height of the holiday season, now being refused with ignominy at our hotel desk and repairing with all their luggage and cameras to a Turkish "hotel" in Istanbul. That evening we went to a restaurant famous for its Turkish food where we ate grilled swordfish from the deep waters of the Black Sea.

Next day, or the day after, we lost touch with the ex-naval officer who was too deeply in collusion with the taxi-drivers, and made contact, instead, with first one and then another Armenian taxi-man both of whom are now indistinguishable from each other in my memory. Both were "natural", "born" comics, perhaps the second of them, whichever he was, being the more intelligent, but they were indeed, both of them, extremely funny. They would tell with wealth of gesture how the Ghazi had forbidden the dock porters, all of them peasants from Anatolia, to make public exhibitions of themselves by carrying such things as grand pianos or motor-cars on their backs up the steep streets, and the manner in which one of them would say "absolument défendu" with a sweep of his hand was a proof that national character never changes and that heads would fall. Both of them, as indeed everyone else, seemed devoted to the Ghazi's memory and they would begin talking about him as soon as we passed his monument on Taxim Square. They would tell us how he made no money for himself and only left an insignificant sum to his sister. And one or other of them would ask if we realized that the Ghazi was a Macedonian like Alexander the Great, and had eyes of different colour, a blue and a brown, as had that hero of antiquity. In the meantime we would be crossing the Galata bridge, and swirling up the one-way street past the shop of Haci-Bekir ("confiserie turque, produits d'Orient les plus renommés"), with jars of *loucoums* and sugared almonds in the window, on our way to put on *babouches* and go into a mosque.

But probably our next objective was the newly uncovered stretch of mosaic pavement of the Processional Way. Or, according to other accounts, it is the floor of one of the colonnades of the Imperial Palace, but, whichever it is, this is Roman mosaic at its most splendid, still in classical style untouched by the Byzantine, with hunting scenes, vine-trellis borders, muscular athletes, and a scene of children playing with push-carts. There is the possibility of still more to uncover; and it was curious in one corner where a particularly delicate pavement had been roofed over to find two barefoot and personable young women making a copy of it, and hear them talking in the accents of South Kensington or Ladbroke Grove.

What is most to be desired is that work should be found of later date, but that is unlikely upon this present site, and in any case the prospects are unfavourable for Byzantine mosaics were upon walls and ceilings, and not upon the floors. But, in its day, the quantity was immense. Theophilus the Iconoclast in the ninth century, having forbidden all portrayal of religious themes, ordered mosaics of trees and flowers and animals (somewhat in the manner of those in the court of the Great Mosque at Damascus?), weapons and war-like arms, lion-hunting and scenes of fruit-gathering; while a part of the palace called the Triconchos, comprised the Heros or arsenal with still lives of weapons and armour, and also the Camilas with a roof flecked with gold and scenes of harvesting and reaping upon the walls.

What other news is there of mosaics in this Imperial Palace which stood upon the present site of the Old Seraglio, upon the Golden Horn, "forming the highest achievement of the arts of decoration in the Western world, and probably in all human history"? We read of mosaics of Justinian and Theodora, with the conquered towns of Italy, Libya, and Spain, and their general Belisarius bringing the loot and the prisoners to the feet of the Basileus. Also, of a banquet and festival in celebration of triumphs over the Goths and Vandals, all in mosaic. And later additions made to the Imperial Palace by Basil the Macedonian in the ninth century included a summer garden, open to the Bosphorus, with its walls adorned with hunting scenes. Wall surfaces of mosaic, it is evident, were as large in area, and made as much use of, as were coloured tiles in Persia. It was another architecture in colour but with scenes and figures, and not composed only of abstract geometrical patterns and inscriptions in calligraphy.

The golden background was most appropriate to those blazing August days when we would go perhaps for an excursion along the Bosphorus, its winding banks no further apart than those of a fair river, with a white palace across the water in Asia built by a Soltan for the Empress Eugénie, and through Arnautkeui, the "village of Arnauts", which is to say, Albanians, and other little towns with tilted roofs and kiosques, to a further village where the Spanish Embassy had owned a villa for upwards of a hundred years. A few of the old Turkish wooden Rococo houses are still standing, and there is the bay of Büyükdere, a theme on which the old guide books become ecstatic: "On fine moonlight nights, when the dark-blue sky mingles with the deep blue of the Bosphorus, and the twinkling of the stars with the phosphoric illumination of the sea; when kaiks full of Greek singers and guitar-players glide with their tunes along the banks, and the balmy air of the night wafts the softest melodies over the waters; when the silence of the listeners is interrupted by soft whispers", etc., etc.,* ending a little uncertainly as to what *does happen* when all this is going on. Other villages are famous for their chestnuts, or their cherry orchards. Decidedly a beautiful and favoured part of the world, of langorous intent, and affording to anyone of poetical instinct a terrestrial pendant or parallel to the Grand Canal of Venice.

Then there are the *souks*, and although a great part of them was burnt down a few years ago they are still wonderful, particularly the jewellery *souk*. But I knew the *souks* of Istanbul before the fire, and had that curious adventure referred to by my brother,† when we were examining together some of the enamelled watches made for the

---

* Murray's, *Turkey in Asia*, 1878, p. 11, which, also, carries the information that the Bay of Beykoz, opposite on the Asian shore, "is celebrated for its swordfish which are caught in great numbers in August and September and supply a good article of food". See my p. 186.

† *The Four Continents*, Osbert Sitwell, London, Macmillan & Co., 1954, pp. 99, 100.

Oriental market rather more than a hundred years ago. The supply
must be exhausted for you never see them now. We were looking at
one of the watches, and making an offer for it to the shopman until,
in my brother's words, "a figure sitting behind and above the stall, at
the level of the proprietor's head, on one of the stone tiers of seats, rose
to his feet . . . a most impressive apparition, a very tall man, with a
handsome aquiline face, and with dark eyes, melancholy, but yet
burning with a fire of their own. . . . He wore a flowing black cloak
and a wide-brimmed black hat. . . . And he said, in a voice without
accent, pointing to the stall-keeper: 'It is of no use trying to bargain
with him. He is the one man here who never varies his prices.'"
Startled by this interposition my brother enquired, "Who are you?"
And to his question, received the proud and unusual answer, "I am a
magician." But he would, as my brother says, divulge no more about
himself. Yet it was a reply in some fashion appropriate to the background, and to the city in which it had been given.

This was not the end of our adventures. For we had noticed a little
dwarf, like a six or eight year old boy, in the hall of the old Tokatlian
Hotel, and also in a Russian restaurant and night club where we saw
him dancing with a very young girl, a child dancer who was part of the
cabaret, and whom afterwards he invited to sit at his table. A day or
two later we saw him in the carpet bazaar bargaining for rugs, and
when he left the shop and we enquired who he was they seemed
surprised that we did not know, and told us he was a German count
who knew more about carpets than almost anyone else and drove the
hardest bargains.*

In the jewellery *souk* the nicest objects now are the rings, looking
rather like turbans, which date from the "Tulip Reign" (Achmet III,
1703–1730). A tray with a dozen or more of these "tulip rings" was
a beautiful sight. Not far away, in the middle of the main alley of the
bazaar, stands the wooden *yoghourt* kiosque, a fascinating top-heavy
two-floored structure dating from the eighteenth century, and as
"Turkish" as anything in Istanbul. And a little further away still,
round another corner of the bazaar, in the textile section is a tall old
creature with a bowed back, bald head and imberb features, who is one
of the last surviving eunuchs of the old regime, and it was very
evident that he did not like being looked at.

We had by now made friends with Lesley Blanch who was staying

---

* Later on, I wrote a short story on this theme which appeared in *Far from my Home*,
London, Duckworth & Co., 1931. Many years after, to be exact in about 1949 or 1950,
I read in the papers of the death of one of the smallest men in the world, a German count
who had been in the U.S.A. in the war and had just returned to Germany. No doubt
this was he.

at our hotel, and is a great lover of Istanbul. With her we went sight-seeing to the mosques, and for exquisite sunset drives with our Armenian taxi-driver at the wheel. What a marvellous city, in spite of so many grumbles at it! But I have seen Istanbul in the snow, and also in the rain, and it rains and snows in London and in Paris. It is impossible after the first days not to begin wondering who was the architect of the great mosques which, in fact, follow the plan of Santa Sophia but improve upon it. This great man was Mirmar Sinan, born in 1489, who lived to be ninety years old. He was not Turkish, but Greek, or Albanian, or, possibly, from his name, Armenian by origin, except that it is unlikely an Armenian would be a Janissary and it was in the corps of Janissaries that Sinan started his career as a military engineer. He campaigned in Egypt and Persia and built his first big mosque when he was more than fifty years old. The Mosque of Soltan Achmet is not by him; and in order to appreciate this architect of genius one has to see the Süleimaniye, the Mosque of Süleyman the Magnificent,* the effect of which is as though Sinan had tidied up and put to rights the exterior of Santa Sophia reducing its domes and buttresses to symmetry and order. He was nothing less than a master of the leaded dome. Yet, in spite of its external resemblance to Santa Sophia which there is no mistaking, and its "sharpened pencil" minarets which are so wholly Turkish, there is something Indian, or, rather, Moghul, about the court of the Süleimaniye and about its domelets which are like the segments of a peeled orange and could persuade one to the epigram that Sinan cut an orange in the Indian way. The interior of the mosque is a huge open hall freed from the upper arcades and galleries, and therefore with more sense and space. All in all, it is surely the best and finest of the mosques of Istanbul.

There is a certain and inevitable sameness about all mosques and it is better to take them little by little and not see too many of them in one day. Instead, let us embark on one of many visits to the Old Seraglio. Different parts of this are open, irritatingly, on different days, and in any case there is no general indication of what there is to see. In the result we never saw the silk brocades of the fifteenth and sixteenth centuries found recently in the storerooms of the Seraglio in unopened bales.† There are the extremes of disappointment and fascination in

* Soltan Achmet was by an architect called Daoud (David), presumably of Jewish origin. The Mosque of Fetiye, or of Mohammad II the Conqueror, largely rebuilt, but still imposing from its position on the fourth hill of Istanbul was, confusingly, by a Greek called Christodoulos, or Atik Sinan, *not* Mirmar Sinan, but another Christian turned Moslem.

† Described and illustrated in *Anciens Tissus Turcs*, by Tahsin Oz, Istanbul, 1950? Another, similar publication on the decorative arts of Turkey illustrates some splendid

the Old Seraglio. But, more than everything else, gone are the old pantomime costumes now that the corps of Janissaries no longer guards the gate. The fountain of Achmet III, the "Tulip Soltan", that "chef d'œuvre de l'art turc" is just opposite, more Indian looking than Turkish and as though it should be a kiosque by the side of a lotus-tank, now dirty and uncared for, but striking just the right note, for what we shall see is no palace but a collection of pavilions, as though the Soltans were in the habit of sleeping in tents and could not get used to permanent buildings. And immediately inside the gate there is an open loggia or verandah with a wall painted as though with bad pantomime scenery. This is in prelude to the Hall of the Divan where the Grand Vizir gave audience, which is like a built scene from a pantomime.* Now that the figures in their extraordinary dresses are gone there is nothing to hold the attention. One is in the hall of the Divan, and out again in a moment.

Another day we saw the Treasure, and another day the Soltans' carriages. There are attractive berlins and coupés for the ladies of the harem with space for eunuchs on the hammer cloth. But, of course, it is the Treasure that is the attraction of the Old Seraglio. You walk to it down a silly asphalt path whence, again, the ghosts and the gazelles are fled. But, at least, it is housed in the kitchens under two rows of little domes by Sinan, where his hand is immediately apparent, and it is a pity there is no more building by him in the Seraglio. The enormous collection of *celadon* and blue and white is more tiring than beautiful, but there are astonishing gewgaws and all that a thieving magpie would admire most in the Treasury, jewelled holders for cups, aigrettes, and a full size snuff box carved from one emerald. Perhaps the kitchens were more admirable when they ministered to the sweet tooth of the Soltans and their ladies, not forgetting the eunuchs, both white and black. In the eighteenth century, and during the "Tulip Reign", prodigious quantities of sweetmeats, and even scented soaps were made here.

As to Laleh Devri or the "Tulip Reign", we may read of its festivals in an account left by Flachat, who had it from the Kislar Agha or Chief Black Eunuch.† Shaikh Mohammad Lalezari was Master of the

brocaded robes, and not the least beautiful of its plates are those of marbled papers, an art at which the Turks were past masters.

* J. B. Vanmour of Valenciennes (1671–1737) spent his life in the Levant and painted many pictures of Turkish scenes. Three of them in the Rijksmuseum of Amsterdam have for subject the reception of the Dutch Ambassador by Soltan Achmet III, and one of them shows the banquet in this Hall of the Divan. It is reproduced in *The Netherlands*, London, B. T. Batsford & Co., 1948, p. 109. See also, *Les Peintres du Bosphore*, 1909, by le Baron Bopp, a Belgian diplomat, a book unimportant as it is delightful.

† For further details of the Tulip Festivals, which were held on such a scale that

Flowers. Above all it was the tulip that was beloved by the Turkish fanciers who saw in it a resemblance to a turban. Tulips were cultivated with very long pointed and recurved petals, and brilliant colouring. Wild tulips, we are told, were brought from Anatolia, and the florists came in the spring to Magnesia to dig the bulbs. In addition, the cultivated sorts were imported from Persia and from Holland.

"Tulips sent by the Court Grandees were exhibited in the Soltan's pavilion where they were banked up in an amphitheatre, arranged in glass vases upon staging, with little lamps and glass bowls filled with coloured waters in between. Songbirds hung from the ceiling in gilt cages. In the distance, here and there, were towers and pyramids built down the gardens, and there were *ombres chinoises* or Chinese shadow plays. Eunuch confectioners in high caps handed round sweetmeats. There were sherbets made of violets and sugar, and of the yellow nenuphar that grows in ports and rivers . . ." sweets which we may think would cloy upon a modern palate. When all was ready the Grand Signior caused the state of Kalvet or absolute privacy to be proclaimed, and the women, so the communicative Kislar Agha informed Flachat, "rush forth like a swarm of bees settling on the flowers".

A pavilion, which looks no more important than any of the others, except that it is isolated and stands in the middle of the court, contains the Mantle of the Prophet, his Staff and Seal, and according to some accounts, his Sword. This pavilion is still inviolate, and no one knows what is inside it, but the contents are surely not works of art. And keeping the women's part of the harem for another day we look into the Baghdad Kiosque which, as certainly, does not live up to its reputation as "perhaps one of the most beautiful rooms in the world". On the contrary, it is pre-eminent for that terrible ennui and boredom of all Oriental interiors, though it may be that the more perfect the workmanship the more abject the listlessness and lack of interest. Murad IV built this pavilion when he had taken Baghdad, but it would seem doubtful if it can be, as alleged, a copy of a kiosque in that city for it is most typically in Turkish style. Coming away, I wondered in which pavilion it was on my previous visit that a little wizened dwarf in a blue suit and peaked cap had asked to see my ticket, for he was the last of the White Eunuchs, come down in the world, we are to presume, from being as important as Mr Baldwin or Mr Neville Chamberlain.

"they actually began to interfere with State business, and to prove a drain on the national resources by the reckless extravagance of the fêtes which seemed to be regarded as even more important than the national festivals themselves", see *The Hunters and the Hunted*, London, Macmillan & Co., 1947, pp. 119–121.

Krak des Chevaliers

Baalbek

## II

How much more wonderful by far must have been the Imperial Palace of the Byzantine Emperors that stood upon this site! With instead of the Janissaries, Doryphores, and Hoplites, two of the seven detachments of the Imperial Guard on duty at the gates of the Chalce with drawn swords. Excubitors and Candidates were two more detachments, so called from the white uniforms they wore. And there were others with golden bucklers, a gilt battle-axe, and golden helmets with red plumes. And as well the "axe-bearing Barbarians" or Varangian Guard, in part recruited from Saxon English who fled here after the Norman Conquest, and in part from Danes or Norsemen. Another corps was the Immortals founded by Michael VII Ducas in 1078, and copied from the horsemen who were the household cavalry of the old Persian Kings. There were also the Noumera, and the rowers of the dromons or State barges. When Constantine VII received the Saracen ambassadors the watermen stood by the throne.

The great halls of the palace were the Octagon, where the Imperial robes and crowns were kept; and the Triclinos of the Nineteen Couches with beds or sofas, *accubita*, where the guests feasted, reclining in the ancient pagan manner, at eighteen tables twelve to each, while the Basileus had twelve guests at his table, making in all two hundred and twenty-eight. The three golden vases of dessert were so heavy that they had to make a circus entrance in three chariots, harnessed and upholstered in scarlet. The next hall was the Magnavra, in the form of a basilica with three naves, and containing the throne of Solomon on which the Emperor was raised by some hidden mechanism until he nearly reached the ceiling, what time the ambassadors prostrated themselves and closed their eyes. Then, the Triconchos, by way of the Sigma, a hall the shape of an apse or hemicycle, the Lausiacos and Justinianos, and so into the Chrysotriclinos built by Tiberius II in the sixth century, an octagon about twice the size of San Vitale at Ravenna, with eight arches leading to as many apses, and mosaics of flowers and trees with gold and silver for ornament. Here were posted the corps of the Immortals with golden apples for handles to their spears.* Later, in the second half of the ninth century, there were the additions of Basil the Macedonian, who built the Kenourgion, in the form of a basilica with sixteen columns, eight of green Thessalian marble and eight of onyx. Compared to such wonders the Old Seraglio is little more than an encampment of permanent tents and lean-to's.

* Constantine Porphyrogenitus had a dining table of silver made for this hall; but its chief feature was the Pentapyrgion, a display cupboard with five towers, made by Theophilus (829–842), where the golden treasure was on view.

13

The August heats brought gaiety, and as I came out on to my balcony in the mornings, but only for a moment because it was too hot to stay there, I repeatedly heard singing. After a morning or two I determined to find out whence it came. The terrace outside the dining room was a good vantage point for it had a covered balcony. Sure enough there came sounds of song and laughter, and looking down I saw two Gypsy girls carrying heavy hods of stones upon their backs. They were carrying them for the roadmenders. One would put her load down, look up at the balcony and sing and click her fingers to be thrown a cigarette. It was the only sign of this sort of gaiety one had seen in Istanbul where there are no *fandangos*, *siguiriyas gitanas*, or *sevillanas*, no *boleras*, *polos*, or *peteneras*, nothing, in short, of Antonio and his company of clacking and grinding castanets. You had only to open your cigarette case, and empty out a little tobacco dust, to be greeted with imitation Gypsy song. Then one girl would help the other on with her heavy hod in order to show how hard they had to work, and they would come nearer still, just beneath the balcony, and put out a hand for a cigarette. One would be lit from the other, and pretending to dance and sing they would slowly go away.

There are a lot of Gypsies living under the old Byzantine walls. Typically enough their dwellings, for they could never be called houses, have been torn down and demolished on one side of the wall. But they are in full strength on the other, and have somehow contrived their whitewashed vine-shaded hovels, where even a four-legg'd chair seems incongruous, but an empty petrol tin looks like a piece of furniture. The walls in many places are on a steep slope, but still have their battlements and shivered towers, though almost falling to ruin, and here the same race are living who have made their homes in the hollow cement blocks of the unfinished breakwater at Almería; in the caves of the Albaicín between blue hedges of cactus looking over to the Alhambra; and in Triana the Gypsy suburb of Seville, where are born the *bailerinas* and *toreros*. In spite of their dirt and squalour it is, always and everywhere, wonderful to see Gypsies. We used to drive down past the old walls at sunset when it was getting dark and they were moving like figures by Callot across the lit doors of their houses. A sinister neighbourhood all the same and one where it would be better not to walk alone at night.

But perhaps it was always so, because not far from here one of the towers was called the prison of Anemas, from the person of that name who was imprisoned here for conspiring against the Emperor Alexius I Comnenus. Anna Comnena, the Emperor's daughter, describes how by chance she saw Anemas and his fellow conspirators taken from this tower on their way to be blinded; they were dressed in sacking, their beards were torn out, their heads were shaved, and they were crowned with the intestines of sheep and oxen. They were mounted on oxen which they were made to ride sitting sideways as a further mark of shame. Anna Comnena fetched her mother, and together they interceded with Alexius and persuaded him to spare their eyes.* But the messenger only reached them just in time. There was a point on the wall marked with a carving of two hands transfixed by a spear, and the Imperial mandate only carried thus far and no further. No sentence could be commuted once the prisoners had passed that spot.

One afternoon we were taken on a tour of the old Byzantine churches, going first to see the famous Basilica Cistern, or Underground Palace as the Turks call it, built by Constantine the Great and repaired by Justinian. With its brick vaulting carried on twenty-seven aisles of columns, the parabola playing in and among them, and each column lengthened by its reflection in the water, it is as impressive and as much of a phenomenon as the Mosque of Córdoba, not a water cistern but a scene of mystery and of magic. No other Byzantine building in Istanbul is upon this scale except Santa Sophia to which we went immediately afterwards to climb the ramp into the women's galleries. From one of them a wonderful winged female figure, pied wings, and late classical physiognomy with arched eyebrows and a fillet round the forehead, is to be seen, and it is the great triumph of Professor Whittemore's in Santa Sophia, for we were told that not only was it too expensive but impossible, as well, from a practical point of view ever to put up a scaffolding from which to clean the mosaics in the dome. Yet this was done successfully more than a hundred years ago when an Italian engineer made drawings of the mosaics; and if a scaffolding is impossible to erect in the middle of the twentieth century how was it that the Byzantines built the dome of Santa Sophia fifteen hundred years ago?

The other churches we were to see that day were all small and unimpressive, with one exception. The Pantocrator is a jumble of three churches all built next to one another according to a custom of the so-called "dark ages". Mosaics of Christ and his apostles could still be seen here as late as the beginning of the eighteenth century, and this cheerless place which suggests a set of cisterns with the water run out is more interesting because of the huge green sarcophagus in the square outside, which is said to have been the tomb of an Empress, and because

* Cf. *The Alexiad of the Princess Anna Comnena*, translated by Elizabeth A. S. Dawes, London, Kegan Paul, 1928; and, also, *Anna Comnena, a Study*, by Georgina Buckler, Oxford University Press, 1929.

of the old and inflammable Turkish houses with their wooden balconies. The next church we saw, now called the Gül Cami or "Rose
Mosque", is little better and it comes as a shock of disillusionment
when one is told that the last of the Byzantine Emperors Constantine XI
Palaeologus together with the Patriarch and Senate spent some hours
of 28 May 1453, the day before the fall of Constantinople, praying in
this church. Many men and women remained to pray all night, and the
next day were taken off into slavery by the Turks. It was the feast of
St Theodosia to whom the church was dedicated, but was this small
and insignificant church, then, one of the chief buildings of Byzantium?

St Mary of the Mongols or the Mouchliotissa is more warming, at
any rate in sentiment, for it is the one church which has come down
untouched by Turkish hands. It is, or was, a clutter of icons and carved
woodwork,* but has nothing interesting except the legend of its
founding, if it be true that its patron was the illegitimate daughter of a
Palaeologus who went to Samarcand in order to marry Hulagu, the
Mongol Khan. He died before she reached his town of tents, and
instead she was married to his son, and on return home built this
monastery. St Mary of the Mongols stands in the Phanar, near the
church of the Patriarcate which is even less interesting, and in a quarter
of steep cobbled streets with Greek priests walking about in their tall
hats with the brim at the top, all overshadowed by a red brick
seminary of such ugliness that it effaces most other memories of the
afternoon. But not that of a most curious little old church down the
hill, belonging to Copts from Egypt who had affiliated themselves to
the Eastern Church and were, therefore, in relation with Catherine
the Great of Russia who gave them a silver altar for their church. We
went into the Priest's house and spoke to his family, newly arrived from
Alexandria, and not overfond of their Greek neighbours in the Phanar.

But the one exception I mentioned to this tale of disappointments
is the Fetiye Cami or church of the Pammacaristos where we waited
and admired the view for, maddeningly, we never got inside. It was
built by the grandfather of Anna Comnena, the Curopalates and Grand
Domestic John Comnenus and his wife Anna Dalassena.† It is a beautiful little brick church of the human generation of William the Con-

---

* St Mary of the Mongols was burnt down during the anti-Greek riots in September
1955.
† Robert Liddell in his *Byzantium and Istanbul*, London, Jonathan Cape, 1956, p. 82,
tells that further restoration was made in the fourteenth century by Michael Ducas
Glabas, the Protostrator, and Maria Ducaena Comnena Palaeologina Blachena, his wife.
Clearly, and understandably, he is unable to resist their names. Alexius and his daughter
Anna Comnena were buried in the church of the Pammacaristos.

queror and of Lady Murasaki, if we like to think of it in world history; a brick elevation of three storeys with round-headed windows and an agglomeration of five cupolas or domes. So compact is it in shape that it could be a reliquary in the form of a church, or a model of a church held in the donor's hand in an early painting. That it must have been important in its time is proved because before their tombs were desecrated by the Turkish conquerors it was the burial place of the Comneni and Palaeologi. Therefore it was probably the most important of the later churches of Constantinople. That St Mark's in Venice shows the influence of such a building is evident from the first look at it, but little brick churches with delicate exterior arcading and a multiplicity of domes and turrets were typical of the last phase of the Byzantine Empire from the eleventh century onward, as can be seen in the churches of S. Caterina and of the SS. Apostoli at Salonica; in the church of Chilandari, actually a foundation of the old Serbian Kingdom, on Mount Athos; and in the "red" church of the monastery of Vatopedi upon the same "one-way" island.* But the aggravation of not seeing the interior of the Pammacaristos was made worse in the knowledge that one of its domes has a beautiful mosaic of Christ and the prophets and that the restoration of this, and probably other discoveries, as well, is to be the next work of the Byzantine Institute of Boston, U.S.A.

Is it possible that the great church of Santa Sophia was the only building in Constantinople upon this scale, and that the other churches were no bigger than the Pammacaristos? It seems probable, and that the halls of the Imperial Palace were far from being enormous though built of very rich materials. What were the other churches? There was the church of the Saviour, built by Constantine the Great, with a special body of clergy attached, and a Skevophylax or guardian of the sacred treasures, which were chiefly relics, then, of course, more precious than any works of art. Constantine caused a statue of himself, which was really a converted statue of Apollo set with a new head in a halo of golden rays, to be set up near this church. It was raised on a column of eight drums of porphyry, and in the plinth Constantine enclosed for good measure the twelve baskets from the miracle of the loaves and fishes, the alabaster box of spikenard ointment, the adze with which old Noah shaped the ark, and the crosses of the two thieves. It is little wonder the Crusaders sacked Constantinople and brought its relics home.

The Macedonian Emperors of the ninth century were cathedral

* *Le Mont Athos*, by F. Perilla, Salonica, 1927. The same author has published a work on the monasteries of Meteora.

builders. They built a new cathedral, not less magnificent in its decorations than the Coronation church of the Virgin of the Pharos (Lighthouse) which had been finished twenty years before by the previous dynasty. That had five cupolas roofed with copper, and had doves of white gold, studded with emeralds, and carrying cruciform sprigs of pearls in their beaks, that hung from the ceiling. The new church, for one better, had six domes of bronze, and an altar formed of a composition "more precious than gold itself". Neither of these churches sound as if they were big buildings. Basil the Macedonian also built the church of St. Elias which was octagonal with seven altars, and the Oratory of the Saviour where the floor was entirely covered "with a thick silver leaf, enriched with inlay and niello. The treasures of the Indies were lavished on its sacred fittings. Another oratory, that of St Paul, had a floor formed of circular plaques of precious marbles with surrounds of silver."* Leo VI, the son of Basil (886–912) rivalled with his father in the Church of St Demetrius, next to those of Elias and of the Virgin of the Pharos, in fact built touching on one another, like the cathedrals of the Kremlin. The church of SS. Sergius and Bacchus (Little St Sophia), which we have not seen yet, had next door to it the church of SS. Peter and Paul, now destroyed, with which it shared in common the atrium, the porches, and the marble columns of the entrance.

But let us finish the day with a recital of the curious sounding titles of Byzantium, a subject upon which Anna Comnena is the authority to be consulted. She tells how her father Alexius invented a new name by compounding together Sebastos and Autocrator and making his brother the Sebastocrator, "exalting him a step above the Caesar who was now counted third in the acclamations". And then and there Taronites, who had married the sister of Alexius, was created Protosebastos and Protovestiaros and, finally gazetted Panhypersebastos. "Now my father was inventor of all these new honorary titles. Some he made by compounding names, of which I gave an instance above, and the others by applying them to new uses."

There were the Great Domestics of the East and West, exercizing authority in their different spheres; and the Great Primicerios who was chief of the household and held high appointment in the army. Other titles carrying office in the army or navy were the Phalangarch, or Protostrator, Thalassocrator, or more simply Dux of the fleet. There is mention, too, of the Great Hetaeriarch of the Foreign Palace Guards,

---

* I am quoting from my own book, *The Hunters and the Hunted*, London, Macmillan & Co., 1947, where a reconstruction of the Imperial Palace of Byzantium is attempted, pp. 17–31.

and of a very special official the Exousiocrator of Alans, a race of barbarians who have disappeared from history. And the list can end with the Decurion, the Toparch, or Topoteretes, and the Tagmatarch. With last of all, not least, the Great Drungary of the fleet. And Anna Comnena concludes, unctuously, "And if anyone were to reckon the art of ruling as a science of all sciences, then he would certainly admire my father for having invented those new titles and functions in the Empire." And the amazing fact remains that Alexius I Comnenus died in 1118, and that the Byzantine Empire lasted with vicissitudes until 1453.

### III

A DIVERSION in the form of a lazy morning we spent looking over the new Hilton Hotel. It must be the most salutary thing that has happened to Istanbul for very many years. For it is as modern as the Lever Building, or any of the new skyscrapers on Fifth Avenue. The whole of the ground floor is in effect one large glass room round an open court with shops down one side of it. There are dining rooms downstairs, and again most of the top floor or penthouse is treated as one unit centring round a bar and night club, the only discordance being the water-tank which breaks up the space, and spoils the modern symmetry of the building when seen from any distance away. Each floor is decorated in a different colour scheme, and a subtle and clever Oriental note has been imparted by getting advice from a Turkish woman designer who certainly deserves well of her country.\* "Sweet music", as that is understood in America, is relayed all over the building but not loud enough to distract, or interrupt a conversation. There is the sense of living in the middle of the twentieth century, even if one's own financial resources cannot support the strain for more than a few minutes, and this is enjoyable indeed after the tortuousness of the Old Seraglio.

As we walked away there was the sound of pipes and tabors in the distance. Catching up with it, we found it was the folk dancers from all over Turkey who were to give a performance in an open air arena in the evening. They were marching through Pera in their costumes, including a group from Trebizond on the Black Sea who were to perform sword dances, and others who looked like Circassians. The procession must have been some half-mile long with several bands, and

---

\* Eren Eyüboglu. Her husband, Bedri Rami Eyüboglu has painted decorative panels in the hotel. They are the two best painters now working in Turkey (*The Times*, 3 December 1956).

we stood to watch it in the door of a travel agent who was standing there, and with whom we had already made friends. He was a young man from the Lebanon with beautiful manners, who liked talking of Cannes, and the whole proceedings pained him exceedingly. It was just the sort of thing he detested. This Orientalism made him feel sick, and he could not bear it. This was no longer 1955; it was going back to the unpleasant memories of his youth. And in order to console him we had to talk of Monte Carlo and tell him we had just come from the new Hilton Hotel. But he hated that, too, and only wanted to talk about the Côte d'Azur.

There now arose the question of going to Brusa (Bursa). A friend had offered us a single air ticket which was not needed, and it was just a matter of buying another. But I still had memories of going there before, when we started early in the morning by boat, a sea-journey that lasted about five hours. During the course of it I had the curious experience of being addressed by two young men in what even to me seemed an antiquated sort of Spanish. They were a Sephardic family settled for some four centuries in Turkey. The boat to Mudanya was followed by about another couple of hours in a motor and we reached Brusa fairly late in the evening. That was a tiring day, and I have to admit that it had never dawned on my intelligence that Brusa is so short a distance from Istanbul direct by air. So we did not go, having only become "air-minded" a year later when it was necessary to make so many flights in order to travel in Persia. I believe my calculation was that it must take about two hours to fly to Brusa, and in fact the "flying time" is sixteen minutes. Had one known we were to make a journey in the next year to nearly every place in the Middle East where there are works of art we would, of course, have gone. But the glorious heat kept us in Istanbul and we did not set foot in Asia.

But Brusa does not fade in the memory and it must be the prettiest town in Turkey. There are, or were, painted wooden houses in quantity with latticed balconies, and streams of running water. Also a *souk* with embroideries for sale such as we have at my home, brought back from Smyrna or Aleppo two hundred years ago, and Turkish towelling. And the silk industry, partly in French hands with Lyon connections, as a result of which the hotel was owned by Mme (Veuve) Brotte. The mulberry trees to feed the silkworms are on the slopes of Mt Olympus, and the inhabitants of Brusa could be seen in their houses "weaving the silk into a gauzy material with stripes at intervals, which is employed throughout the Levant for the vestments of females of the richer classes". This is all that is left of the velvets and silks of Brusa which in their day were the most potent and tremendous of all textile patterns, and even though the work of Greek craftsmen, the true art of Turkey. Designs of formalized tulips and carnations, of splayed petal and exploding calyx. Then there are the Turkish baths, famous all over the East, and of old foundation; one of them with a floor of rose marble, lapis lazuli, and verde antique, and a wonderful tiled panel of white calligraphy on a blue ground, enlaced with the same tulips and carnations, not as in the Brusa velvets about to explode or burst, but in foretaste of tiles in other Turkish mosques to come.

For Brusa was taken by the Ottoman Turks a hundred years before they took Constantinople, and was their first capital. The arts of Turkey are in Brusa except for the Mosques of Sinan. The Ulu Cami is, or was, so whitewashed that little is left, and it appears to have been treated summarily for some epidemic. Low, elephant-height, with howdah domes; that is how I remember the Ulu Cami. But at the far end of the town there is a whole group of *turbéhs* or royal tombs into which at that time one was allowed to enter. It would seem that now, as at Istanbul, most if not all of the *turbéhs* are closed, probably because of a nervous hesitancy about so many strangled princes. It is a pity because the *turbéhs* are more beautiful than any of the pavilions of the Old Seraglio, and are one of the typical things of Turkey. Those of the Muradiye at Brusa are of the early fifteenth century and of the golden age. I do not remember them in detail, but recall one *turbéh*, probably that of Prince Musa, which was octagonal and lined inside with marvellous green tiles, and another with a fantastic wooden porch carved into stalactites.

But the Yeşil Cami or Green Mosque is the wonder of Brusa and among the most lovely of all Moslem buildings. Not, I would think, now I have seen them, so breathtaking as the mosques of Isfahan but, in fact, two hundred years earlier in date, more perfect in detail, and pertaining to a more vernal and a more flowering age. It is, of course, a much smaller building. Probably because there is a so-called Green Mosque at Tabriz it has been said that the architect was a Persian, but it is, indeed, wholly and entirely Turkish in inspiration. Before the earthquake it had a pair of minarets which were tiled an emerald green, but these have gone, and I must admit to having no very distinct memory of the marble exterior which may have been a little of a disappointment. However, the inside of the Green Mosque is a revelation. The prayer-hall is tiled in blue, which is more of a sapphire-blue than green. But the pair of transepts opening on either side have hexagonal tiles with an emerald green predominating, and marvellously patterned with arabesques and flowers. The *mehrab* and its stalactite canopy are tiled. There are little china balconies like opera-boxes—though where was there ever such a theatre!—one of them for the Soltan at his prayers, with little tiled rooms below them. Here again, as I remember it, the colouring was more of a sapphire-blue.

This same Soltan Mehmet I el Chelebi is buried in the Yeşil Turbéh or Green Turbéh nearby. It is a china pavilion in octagonal form with an interior which is entirely flowering or blossoming in tiles. My memory is that there is more of green in the Green Turbéh than in the Green Mosque. But, in default of having seen them both again, there exists an old book in which one can study them in detail.* I think it emerges from this that the finer tiles are in the Turbéh. Persian potters were brought from Tabriz who established kilns here, but probably they only taught the art and did not practise it for the flower-panels and arabesques are Turkish and not Persian. Nowhere in Persia is there work resembling this. As to where the Green Mosque and Turbéh of Brusa stand in rank beside other Moslem buildings it can be said that their china revetments are more beautiful than those of Shaikh Lot-follah at Isfahan, that acknowledged masterpiece of the reign of Shah Abbas. The Turkish work is livelier and fresher. Mohammad I el Chelebi died in 1422 so that the Green Mosque and Turbéh are two hundred years earlier in date. There is the breath of the early Renaissance about them, and to see them is to have confirmed the Oriental figures in paintings by Carpaccio and the Bellinis.

After which ghost excursion we repair again to the Old Seraglio for a visit to the harem. Little apartments are now open that we had not seen before, but some of the eunuchs' quarters which I remembered are not on view. They, too, it seems are being expunged as much as possible from Turkish history. But I summoned up courage to ask our guide about the White Eunuch whom I remembered, and sure enough what I said was true. The guide had known him. He had retired in about 1940, had gone back to live in his native village in Anatolia, and was dead now. His condition was due to an accident in childhood, and not to an operation. But eunuchs, of course, go back in the history of Constantinople much further than the Turkish Soltans, and there are eunuchs attending on the Empress Theodora in the mosaics of San

---

* *Architecture et decoration turque au XV siècle*, by Léon Parvillé, Paris, 1874, with preface by Viollet-le-Duc. Parvillé was a ceramic expert who was charged with the restoration of the Mosque and Turbéh in 1863. The earthquake which destroyed the minarets was later. This book has splendid coloured plates of individual tile-panels which it is interesting to compare with the flower-panels of Fatehpur Sikri, Moghul work two hundred years later in date, due to Akbar (d. 1605). A late Victorian publication in four volumes by W. E. Smith, produced by the Archaeological Survey of the Government of India, is devoted to these. They are certainly nearer in spirit to Turkish than to Persian Art.

Vitale at Ravenna.* They had played a part in Byzantine history for ten centuries before the Turks. Their quarters, it must be owned, are suitably mingy and depressing.†

One of the curious features of the harem is that it has more than a spiritual resemblance to the *petits-appartements* of Versailles. The little rooms look out on to the same squalid courts. And there was one place, which one could probably never find again in this rabbit warren, where one looked from a dirty window down over some sheds and outhouses to the railway embankment, for the railway runs at foot of the hill of the Seraglio along the shores of the Golden Horn, and one could not help comparing it to those "backs" of London houses which give upon a railway viaduct. A few of the larger rooms are in faded pantomime-Rococo, but always with the inference that in spite of their extraordinary history they are no more than ordinary *mauvais lieux*. How were the little rooms and salons in the Parc aux Cerfs?

Other parts of the harem no longer open, or on this visit we were not shown them, are the *Kafes* or Cages, where the princes were kept once the custom of strangling them was abandoned. Before this, on accession to the throne the new Soltan had all his brothers murdered. It is for this, one must presume that entrance is forbidden to the *turbéhs*.

* The traveller Bertrandon de la Broquière, courtier to Duke Philip the Good of Burgundy, has left a description of a later Empress. She was the Palaeologina, Maria Comnena, sister of the Grand Comnenus Alexius IV of Trebizond, a family famous for their good looks, and wife of John VIII Palaeologus. He had seen the Basilissa during a service in Santa Sophia, and waited all day without food or drink in order that he should see her again. He saw her mounting her saddle-mule from a bench, behind a cloak which was outstretched for screen. She wore a long cloak and a pointed hat, with three golden plumes, and long golden earrings set with jewels. Her face was painted, "of which she had no need for she was young and fair". She was attended by two ladies-in-waiting, some courtiers, and a corps of eunuchs. This was in about 1430, nearly a thousand years after the time of Justinian and Theodora.

† On this subject *Der Eunuchismus*, by the scarcely credible Dr Pelikan, is to be consulted. It is in the Library of the British Museum. The learned doctor was with the German army in Roumania in 1915 and had opportunities of studying the Skoptsi cabmen of Bucharest and Galatz, members, like Origen, of a voluntary sect, in this instance, of Russian religious dissenters. For an account of the Skoptsi, see my *Roumanian Journey*, London, B. T. Batsford, Ltd., 1938, pp. 51–53, 73, 79–81. There was a meeting of the eunuch's society or association in October 1955, just after we left Istanbul, and about fifteen members attended. One hundred and twenty-seven eunuchs were in the employ of Abdul "the Damned" when he left Yildiz to go into exile at Salonica in 1908. At the same time two hundred and thirteen "females of the harem" were returned to the Circassian villages in Anatolia whence they came. Cf. Francis McCullagh, *The Fall of Abdul Hamid*, London, 1910. The late Lord Berners as a young man was an attaché to the British Embassy at Constantinople, and was given audience on at least one occasion by Abdul Hamid. The Sultan told him he knew of his own reputation for being cruel, but that he was kindness itself. "Look", he said, "I have brought up my family on birds' milk" (or words to that effect), pointing to the trademark of two birds on a nest upon a piece of Nestlé's milk chocolate.

But here are instances. The tomb (*turbéh*) of Selim II (d. 1574), which is in the precincts of Santa Sophia, has the bodies of seventeen of his sons strangled by their brother Murad III at his accession. When Murad III died in his turn in 1595, his son Mohammad III held a veritable holocaust and all nineteen of his own brothers were murdered, while, as well, he caused to be drowned seven of his late father's concubines, who were pregnant, in case they should have male children. Or so the story goes, for it is possible a new Soltan had his hand forced by the eunuchs, or other palace attendants, there being another account that Murad II pleaded for his brothers' lives. However that may be, they all lie buried round their father's tomb with turbans to mark their headstones. It was the age of mass decisions, and Ibrahim (d. 1649) made a clean sweep and drowned all his harem. They were put in sacks, weighted with stones, and dumped into the Golden Horn.* The murdering of brothers seems to have stopped at the accession of Achmet I in 1603.

But now began the imprisonment in the *Kafes* or Cages of the Seraglio, and this continued until recent times. Süleyman II had been imprisoned for thirty-nine years when he succeeded in 1689; Osman II had been in the *Kafes* for fifty years when he came to the throne in 1754; and Abdul Hamid I when he became Soltan twenty years later had been imprisoned for as long, or longer. It has been rightly said that the *Kafes* "has been the scene of more wanton cruelty, misery, and bloodshed than any palace room in the whole of Europe. . . . These unhappy men were kept without knowledge of the outside world. . . . Their education was entirely neglected, except for what they could learn from their companions, who consisted of deaf mutes and a handful of sterile women", or odalisques. Although one of the most "romantic" places in the world the Old Seraglio has too many unhappy memories and is overfull of mouldering relics of its stultifying past.

So, too, must the palaces of the Byzantine Emperors have had their unpleasant associations. But they must have been more beautiful, by far, as works of art. What can have been that part of the palace known as the Mouchroutas, dating from the end of the eleventh century, and deriving from the Arabic word which means a "cone", also called

---

* The indispensable authority on the Old Seraglio, N. M. Penzer, *The Harem*, 1936, tells a story of a diver sent down to a wreck off the Seraglio Point: "Almost immediately he signalled to be drawn up again, and explained in a voice quaking with terror that at the bottom of the sea was a great number of bowing sacks, each containing the dead body of a woman standing upright on the weighted end and swaying slowly to and fro with the current." One wonders whether this was before, or after the building of the railway. Further quotations from N. M. Penzer, pp. 197, 198.

*persicos domos*, or the "Persian house"; with a staircase leading to it of blue, white, and green, with purple from the mussel shell and cupolas wrought into honeycomb vaults and stalactites, the craftsmen being Greeks who had worked for the Seljuq Soltans at Koniah (Konya) in Asia Minor? Or the apartments built by Basil the Macedonian at the end of the ninth century which from their great elevation were called the "Eagle"? But most of all one would like to have seen the famous tower of the Porphyra, upon a square base ending in a pyramid, and made of red porphyry flecked with white. This was the tower of the Porphyrogeniti, princes and princesses "born in the purple", for it was in this tower built in the shape of a pyramid that the Empresses gave birth to their children. Anna Comnena has this to say of the Porphyra in the sixth book of her *Alexiad*: "This purple room was a certain building in the palace shaped as a complete square from its base to the spring of the roof, which ended in a pyramid; it looked out upon the sea and the harbour where the stone oxen and lions stand. The floor of this room was paved with marble and the walls were panelled with it but not with ordinary sorts nor even with the more expensive sorts which are fairly easy to procure, but with the marble which the earlier Emperors had carried away from Rome. And this marble is, roughly speaking, purple all over except for spots like white sand sprinkled over it. It is from this marble, I imagine, that our ancestors called the room 'purple'."* Which account makes one conjecture if the Porphyra was not like the Seljuq buildings at Koniah, *tekkiyes* which are square at the base with roofs in the form of pyramids faced with green tiles. And in the monastery of the Chelebi dervishes the tombs of their founders are in the same shape. Perhaps this is the secret of the Porphyra; and that, as has been suggested in respect of their other buildings on analogy with the Byzantine churches, none of them was of great size. The curious shape, it is thought, may be due to Basil the Macedonian who as an iconoclast Emperor was anxious to be an innovator, and to introduce architectural forms hitherto unknown. Such a thing, it could be added, has not happened again at Istanbul until the building of the Hilton Hotel.

What more there may be in the Seraglio one does not know, and cannot tell. But it is only four or five years ago that discovery was made of the unopened bales of Brusa silks. When in Istanbul on the previous visit, the church of St Irene just within the Seraglio was on view as a kind of military museum filled with a collection of figures of Janissaries and other extraordinary figures in their pantomime dresses,

* *The Alexiad*, translated by Elizabeth A. S. Dawes, London, Kegan Paul, Ltd., 1928, p. 170. Anna Comnena was, herself, born in the Porphyra in 1083.

but this has been discontinued. Perhaps they are in course of being rearranged. And there was a story that in a shed or boathouse there was the gilded barge of Süleyman the Magnificent, but one met no eye-witnesses. One leaves the Seraglio regretting more than ever that the actors are no longer upon the stage; wanting to see the *peiks*, a branch of the halberdiers whose costume was taken over *in toto* from the Byzantine Court; so far fetched a body as the *Zülüfli Baltajilers*, or Tressed Halberdiers, so called because two false curls hung down from their tall hats to prevent them seeing the women when they took the monthly supply of wood into the harem; or the *kapicis* in their huge headdresses of white ostrich feathers, who walked beside the Sultans in their processions so that they seemed to move "surrounded by a white feathery mass".*

And now the day came when we were to see the Cariye Cami which had been the prime object in our coming to Istanbul. Permission had to be asked because work was still going on and it was a matter of climbing up into the scaffolding. On the way we were to see Little St Sophia, or Kuçuk Ayasofya, triple-named for it was, of old, SS. Sergius and Bacchus. After Santa Sophia, itself, they are by far the most imposing relics of Byzantium, if we except the Cistern Basilica, for in tokens of its own greatness the capital of the Byzantine Empire takes second place to several other cities.† But the absorbing interest of seeing "Little St Sophia" and the Cariye Cami in one afternoon is that they are recognizably in the same style of architecture and yet eight hundred years apart in time. For "Little St Sophia" was built by Justinian and is in the Justinian canon of proportion, all Byzantine buildings known to us for nearly the next thousand years erring on the side of smallness. But "Little St Sophia" is as large as San Vitale at Ravenna, also built by Justinian, and has points of resemblance to that. Like San Vitale it is an octagon, but not framed like San Vitale within another octagon. Also the upper galleries of "Little St Sophia" are more emphasized and the accent is more upon architectural form than decoration. The capitals are splendid (though not so boldly beautiful as at San Vitale) and the paired columns on both storeys are of verd antique and a red-streaked marble. The state of disorder of this church is remarkable even for the

* N. M. Penzer, *The Harem*, 1936, pp. 95, 96, 110. On recent occasions the old Janissary uniforms have been worn in processions at Istanbul, and we were told, brought admiring comments from the crowd, who seem otherwise impervious to the tremendous history of the city. Perhaps the best illustrations of the Sultan's processions are the two folding plates in colour in *Voyage à Smyrne*, 1811–1814, by J. M. Tancoigne. They are by I. A. Melling, a German painter (1763–1831), who has so contrived his pair of panoramas that they include specimens of all the old dresses except those of the Tressed Halberdiers.

† To Ravenna, Salonica, Palermo, Torcello, and Cefalù.

near Orient, and the floor was ankle-deep in a very special and inexplicable mud, aftermath of an inundation. Twenty, and more years ago it was conjectured that "Little St Sophia" was the most promising field for the discovery and cleaning of more mosaics, but now these hopes are transferred to the Pammacaristos. None the less, it is as a mosaic-less San Vitale that it is to be admired. How odd to think that in the manner of the Kremlin so many hundreds of years later, Justinian built another church of SS. Peter and Paul in prolongation of this with entrance from the same atrium.

The Cariye Cami is at the other end of Istanbul, close to the Byzantine walls and near where the road leads off to Adrianople. Its ancient name was St Saviour in Chora ("Christ in the Fields"), and it was rebuilt and redecorated in about 1320 by Theodore Metochites, Grand Logothete, or Lawgiver or Treasurer, to Andronicos II Palaeologus. That is its interest, that it is so late in date, half-way between the Frankish Emperors and the fall of Constantinople. So much has been found here, and so careful and splendid are the restorations by the Byzantine Institute of Boston, that almost every memory of a previous visit is obliterated except that of the mosaic of the kneeling figure of the donor wearing an immense striped turban of peculiar form, in proof that such headdresses were not the prerogative of Moslems, and in his instance it is almost certainly a badge of rank. Another headdress of fantastic shape appears in a mosaic of the *Enrollment for Taxation*—it could be thought an unrewarding theme—in a lunette in the outer narthex. But this is a kingly headdress, and resembles the special hat worn by the Emperors of Trebizond.* There are two sets of Gospel scenes in continuous narrative, as it were, on the two floors of the outer narthex, and scenes from the life of the Virgin on the inner porches. The scaffolding gave opportunity there may never be again for seeing the mosaics from a few feet, even a few inches away. On the inner narthex there are a pair of domes, not flat, concave surfaces, but ribbed, and lending themselves, therefore, to elongated figures of prophets or disciples. It is a fascination of its own to see this art of the fourteenth century, and recognizably that, without the pointed arch. There is no sign of Gothic tracery. Where a city is shown, for instance

---

* The headdress of the Palaeologi, of conspicuous form, appears over and over again; in Piero della Francesca's frescoes of *The Battle of Constantine* at Arezzo; in frescoes by Benozzo Gozzoli in the Palazzo Medici at Florence; and in medals of Constantine XI Palaeologus by Pisanello. It was made familiar by the unavailing journeys of John VIII (d. 1448) all over Europe, including England, in search of help against the Turks. There are magnificent colour plates of some of the mosaics of the Cariye Cami in *Byzantine Painting*, Skira Edition, Geneva, 1953, but much additional cleaning and restoring has been done in the last three years.

Nazareth, all the doors and windows are square or oblong openings. In the dress, for it is the daily dress, that is most interesting, there are still signs of classical, i.e. Roman tradition. The soldiers in the taxation scene are in "Roman" armour, and the ordinary individuals wear leggings, and some garment that is not too far in descent from the Roman toga.

But it is the freshness and originality of the colour schemes and the power of lively invention that delights and astonishes in the Cariye Cami. At last it was possible to see mosaics from the distance of one's hand. Just the borders in themselves are a pure delight for they display such a wealth of motif and invention. This art of mosaic which was by then nearly a thousand years old shows no signs of tiring. It is impossible on seeing the Cariye Cami not to wonder what would have happened had the Turks been driven back by a strong and combined effort on the part of Europe. Then, Byzantium might have come down to us as another land like Italy or Spain, though I think it is enough to have seen the mosques of Sinan on the skyline of Istanbul to know this could not have been. Their personality is too strong and militant and portrays the military ardour of the Turks. No alliance of Pope and Doge and Holy Roman Emperor, had the inconceivable happened, could overcome them. The Turks were the strongest power in Europe, and tottering and aged Byzantium the weakest.

Nowhere in Europe is there such a display of mosaic as in the Cariye Cami and it gives rise to all sorts of problems. The drawing is so much more easy and fluid than in Italian early fourteenth century painting. The iconography is practised and assured as though the artist had no difficulty in presenting any subject asked of him. One writer has noticed a deficiency in the physiognomy: "The profiles are never good . . . nor are full faces always much better." But it could be that this comes from seeing them so near to, under strong electric light and only a few inches from one's eyes. For the art of mosaic is ever more of a "mystery" in the mediaeval sense than any other of the visual arts, and the closed or secret sense of mosaics could not be better expressed than in this sentence in criticism of a great musical composer: "It will never be decided how much of his originality represents the heaven-sent windfalls of genius and how much the technical incompetence of an insufficiently and sporadically trained craftsman."* This is true in front of such acknowledged masterpieces as the mosaics of Justinian and Theodora in San Vitale at Ravenna. There are little touches, for instance a red spot on the ear of one of the clergy attendant on Justinian,

* From a leading article on Mussorgsky, in the *Times Literary Supplement* for 9 November 1956.

Giant columns of the Temple of Jupiter at Baalbek

The Khazné at Petra

Church in "Greek Island style" at Rhodes

when the mosaic is examined in detail, some of the modelling of Justinian's face, or touches in the marvellous likeness of Theodora, that must have been the hazard of a moment. They cannot have been long premeditated. So it is, too, with the mosaics of the Cariye Cami. But perhaps in order to understand the art of mosaic it is only necessary to watch any woman at her embroidery. She will worry and fuss end-lessly about what to do next when a difficult point is reached, and almost anything she decides upon will have an equally good effect. All who have ever possessed competence in any of the arts would agree to this if they were truthful, just as anyone who has written poetry knows that it is, in part, reason, and the other part, unreasoning inspiration.

Another truth which emerges is that even so large a scheme as this of the Cariye Cami was the work of the proverbial "two men and a boy". The task was both quicker and less laborious than one would suppose, and probably in all was only the work of a few years.* The subjects from the early life of the Virgin are fresh and touching in their naïveté. Perhaps they are the most beautiful of the whole series, par-ticularly the scenes of her innocence and motherhood. There is life and colour in all the details. No one who has seen it could forget a glorious peacock in a pendentive of the inner narthex, and another opposite. This cerulean vision, with something of red and purple in its wings, and a fan-tail tied in, as it were, and not spreading—but it is the moment when the peacock lifts its tail and carries it—stands in front of the door of a house on a blue-green ground, turning with its head and crest to peck a low bough which is in echo of the shape of its own head and tiara of feathers, forms which are repeated again in weeds or flowers growing in the blue grass.

Again in this little pendentive there are small and inexplicable touches, as though the craftsman made a new move, and then left the traces of it knowing that it would not matter. One carried the vision of this Indian peacock, and of the rounded and not Gothic doorways of this Orient scene, into the body of the church, where there is a frescoed chapel which may be by the same painter who made the designs for the mosaics. This chapel, when the process of cleaning is finished, will mean the rewriting of a whole chapter in the histories of art for it is by a more experienced hand than many then at work in Florence or Siena. From the unfolding of the narrative in the outer and inner narthexes there must have been more mosaics on the walls of the church depicting the later Gospel story, but those have perished. But for its

* One of the more important revelations in the text of the monumental *Survey of Persian Art* is that carpets supposed to be the labour of many years, or even decades, were completed in a much shorter time.

14

outer and inner porches alone the Cariye Cami is worth the journey
to Istanbul, and when the process of restoration is finished it will be
one of the most beautiful things of the world.

After the Cariye Cami one felt in no mood for such sprawling trifles
as the Dolmabahce Palace of which there were lingering memories
of ennui and irritation even after twenty years. We used to pass its
marble portals every day. Neither were we tempted by Yildiz, nor
other soltans' palaces. It was more pleasant to spend the day upon the
water, picnicking near the islands where there are little and delightful
wooded harbours and one can watch the curious spectacle of whole
Oriental families taking their siesta, and then coming down to paddle
in the landlocked waves. On the way back, there would be the marvellous spectacle of this Eastern city from the sea with the domes of
the Imperial Mosques rising on the skyline,* and near at hand in
another continent the cypresses and white minarets of Scutari even if
marred by an enormous Crimean barracks and a huge railway station.

One of those places on earth of which the character never alters, and
that is as typical of Turkey as in its own way Covent Garden market
is of London, is the approach to the Mosque of Eyoub, which is inland
along the Golden Horn. The day we went there it was the feast of
Bairam, and the crowd made it nearly impossible to move along. This
meant, also, that one could not enter the mosque, remembered from
long ago with its fountain of ablutions and its plane trees. It is a long
street of shops, selling every kind of toy and sweet and holy amulet,
and with incongruous and lurid film-posters for which the Turks must
breed a special race of artists—or are they, more probably Armenians?
—and with *turbéhs* and little tombs, or just cemeteries with turbans and
fezzes on the headstones, in every direction. There were mosque-
pigeons galore, but, being late August, only the storks' nests without
the storks. The scene, *d'une turquerie délicieuse*, is haunted by P. Loti as
much as the ghost of Hogarth haunts ever the coffee-stalls of Covent
Garden. It is, and stays, more "Turkish" than anything else in Turkey.
Going on beyond Eyoub there is a road that threatens at any moment
to become "ideologically impossible" and that leads up and up, and
round and round, past more cinema and circus posters pasted on the
walls of houses, and more cemeteries, to a place where one walks a few

---

* And every now and again a flight of those sea-birds that fly low over the water,
never uttering a sound. They are supposed to be the ghosts of women drowned in the
Bosphorus. Mr Julian Huxley, *From an Antique Land*, p. 101, pronounces them to be
shearwaters, of the same species (though not the same subspecies) as our Manx Shear-
water. But in their silent flitting by they made me think of the cycling clubs who rush
past, never speaking, but pedalling in grim earnest, with bunches of bluebells tied behind
their bicycle seats.

yards over the top of a hill, and the view down over the Golden Horn and the Sweet Waters of Europe to Istanbul is beyond words beautiful and wonderful. Here, indeed, is the café to which Pierre Loti used to come. Having seen the view in the morning and the afternoon one does not know when to prefer it, but it is marvellous to come down out of the evening into the darkened street of Eyoub.

For the night of Bairam our Armenian taxi-driver made a promise that much would be going on, instancing fireworks, though we saw no sign of them. But he came to fetch us at nine o'clock, and we drove over the Galata Bridge into Istanbul, stopping by one mosque which stood on a terrace in order to look out over the city. It was lovely but unsensational, and we drove on. First of all to a café where nothing at all was happening. And then, tiring of that, to a larger café which was, as well, a music hall. It was in the open air, with bright lights, and here and there were trees. We sat down at a table, but our chauffeur wanting us to enjoy ourselves moved us to another table nearer to the stage. A middle-aged woman in a "gown" of mauve sequins was singing an interminable song, "all about love", our chauffeur told us, who stood close by. After a good deal of this we became aware of what seemed to be a linen stall a few feet away at the end of our row of seats, and another one just behind it. Moreover, it was finely embroidered linen like a set of hangings, and feeling intrigued by this and moving nearer in order to have a closer look, this was what we saw.

The whole centre of the auditorium under the trees and all the back of the music hall was filled with beds so close to each other that there was hardly room to walk between them, and in every bed there lay one or two small boys. Little boys of from six or seven years old up to twelve or thirteen. By, or on the beds, sat their mothers, their grand-mothers, and every sort of female relation, with quite a few males as well. They were delighted with the foreigners, and invited us to sit down on the beds and talk. It was a social occasion. The small boys all looked pale; some looked rather tearful, others were sleeping. I held the hand of one child for some moments, I felt so sorry for him, not knowing what it was all about and hoping, I have to admit, that one was by now more or less proof against the epidemics that used to mow down everyone at my first school, usually during the Easter term.

But we were not left long in ignorance. Doctors or surgeons in dirty white coats were coming round from bed to bed, whipping off the top sheet, doing something quick and drastic, and replacing it again. Then we knew. The small boys were being circumcised, then and there. It was the matter of a moment, and they went on to the next. The children, we were told, would be up and about again in three or four days' time. So it was a circumcision party. A rich man pays for it all and entertains all the children and their families in his parish, as it were; or two or three persons will join together to give it. Last year, a rich man had hired the huge open air Stadium and given his party in it. The music hall entertainment was in order to make things merrier and help to pass the time, and it would go on for most of the night. Essentially a feast for the poorer classes, at the same time, in significance it was not unlike the ceremony in London each summer when the debutantes drag in the wedding cake at the Queen Charlotte's Ball. The greatest good humour prevailed and it was a time for congratulation, though no one we met in the English colony had ever been present at a circumcision party. It was, I have to say, among the more curious evenings in my own experience. When they come out again after the operation, in token of their suffering and of their new condition, the small boys go about for a week or two wearing charming little round caps of all colours which are sewn with spangles. We had noticed stalls of these caps on sale at Eyoub, and were told that the previous year a liner had arrived at Istanbul on a luxury cruise, and the young American girls on landing had immediately bought these caps and sported them all over the town. This appealed to the Turks' sense of humour and much amused them.

Another night we dined in a Turkish restaurant on a sort of wooden pier, near where the Byzantine walls come down to the water, and drank arrack, with a friend from the Bazaar who could not stay late because he lived in Asia, which was as if his home was on the other side of the Grand Canal and it was difficult to get across when the *traghetto* had stopped working. And on another night we went again to a music hall and were taken to see the idol of the Turkish *jeunesse doré*, a youth wearing a white satin tail coat, and singing songs which had so many verses that it made one's brain reel to think of them. He was of the school of Liberace and had improved upon his master, of whom he had surely never heard, by some contrivance that made his eyes glitter. Perhaps it was simply that he wore contact lenses. He had, too, his own peculiar technique with the microphone, alternately caressing it and singing woodenly, with his hands straight down his sides. For fear of an encore we had to leave after about one hour.

But, even now, on our last days there was much to see and do. There was the mosque to go into which one was always passing on the way to the Bazaar. Within it has a plenitude of Turkey rugs and no less than a galaxy of chandeliers.* And there was the Yeni Cami, the last

---

* The Nuruosmaniye Mosque built in 1748-1755, begun by Mahmud I and completed by his brother Osman III.

of the Imperial Mosques, and the one which is near the Galata Bridge
and built low down, so that its dome emerges out of the smoke of the
town and not upon the skyline. It is difficult to get into because it is
in the middle of a whirl of one-way traffic. The builder was a remarkable lady, wife of Achmet I, and mother of Murad IV and the fearful
Ibrahim, he who drowned his harem, but surviving her dreadful
progeny she became too powerful in the reign of her grandson, and the
eunuchs killed her. There is no sign of these tragedies in the beautiful
and calm court of this mosque, which has good tiled columns support-
ing the dome, of enormous width and size. Upon the same morning
we continued to the Laleli or "Tulip" Mosque, attracted by its name,
although that has nothing to do with the "Tulip Soltan", Achmet III.
Decidedly, it is one of the more beautiful of those later mosques which
show traces of the Rococo, and at the time of our visit it was full of
women. They were sitting on the floor, crosslegg'd, in their dozens,
listening to an address from an extremely handsome, bearded *molla*, in
a turban and coffee-coloured caftan, who spoke with great emphasis
and rapidity. It must have been some kind of ladies' service; and every
now and again with a rapid movement he would stroke and smooth
his beard. None of the ladies looked in our direction or paid attention to us. They were too engrossed in what the *molla* had to say.
Nothing could have been more appropriate to the "Tulip" Mosque
than this Liotard-like scene.

In the middle of nearly every night one would waken and hear the
*muezzin* calling from the minaret of a little and Rococo mosque down
by the water. And in the morning, coming out onto the balcony, the
outline of the martial and splendid Süleimaniye would come up out
of the mist. Seeing that, one had no longer to ask oneself how
it was that the Turks took Constantinople. The race who built the
Cariye Cami or the Pammacaristos could be no match for them. And
it is doubtful how Henry VIII of England, or François I of France, or
the Doge of Venice would have fared against them. Admiration for the
Imperial Mosques of Istanbul, two of the six of which, in all, are by
Sinan, the Shehzade and the Süleimaniye, makes one wonder what this
architect who was so huge in scale could accomplish in little. Of these
there are two examples which are among the most lovely things in
Istanbul, of the sort one would return to again and again. They are the
Sokollu Mehmet Pacha and the Rustem Pacha, names to remember
because nothing could be more beautiful.

Sokollu Mehmet Pacha is in a quiet corner behind the Hippodrome,
though our Armenian in order to quicken our interest told us that the
loud chanting coming from a building on the slope of the hill was the

work of Moslems from Bokhara, who were fanatical, did not like being looked at, and refused categorically to be photographed. But when standing in the court of this mosque all is quiet and peaceful. It soothes and calms as does no other architecture. What a delight that it should have been built by a Grand Vizir and his wife who was a Soltan's daughter! And that Sinan, himself, was eighty years old then! On the steps of the mosque sat an old doorkeeper or mosque attendant who tied on our *babouches*, and showed us round with exquisite and touching manners, and he was, we were told, nearly, if not quite a hundred years old. How beautiful it is, looking from the arcaded court with its fountain in the middle, to the facetted or chiselled minaret of many sides, polygonal, with stalactites under its balcony as though it has known, not the heats only, but the frosts and dews! The lovely interior of Sokollu Pacha is a hexagon, and like all Sinan's mosques one great prayer-hall, unimpeded, with superb tiling. The columns have dripping stalactites as capitals. One wall of the mosque is nothing but china flower-panels in full blossom, and even the pulpit or *minbar* is spired with tiles, a thing quite unique, and a *turquerie* not of the decadence, but the grand century.* What a poetical conception, this china hexagon, for the interior is nearly all china behind its splendid proportion, the arcaded cloister outside and the pierced, openwork balcony to its pencil minaret!

Rustem Pacha is of another kind, in midst of all the noise of the Oriental city. Indeed, it is in the middle of the most marvellous and unspoilt part of Istanbul down a steep cobbled street, if you come to it that way, with horses loaded with sacks, and perhaps a porter carrying a wardrobe on his back, jostling you at every step, and shopkeepers standing in front of their stalls, down a row where they sell wooden trunks painted with roses in canal-barge style, somewhere near the Golden Horn and the Galata bridge for it is nearly impossible to find it or say where. Then, down a narrower, and still steeper and narrower alley, and up a dark and winding staircase in a stone wall and so into the courtyard of the mosque. Rustem Pasha was married to a daughter of Süleyman the Magnificent, and the architect Sinan displays all his artifice and technical skill in this town mosque where there is no large space to play with. This time it is an octagon, with but a small court or cloister, where can never have been peace and quiet, and so attention is taken by the glorious tile-panels, perhaps the most gorgeous display of them in all Istanbul. The *mihrab* of Rustem Pacha

---

* Mr Robert Liddell says there is another *minbar* "with a pointed spire of faience" in the Mosque of Çinili Cami at Scutari, across the Bosphorus (*Byzantium and Istanbul*, by Robert Liddell, London, Jonathan Cape, 1956, p. 175).

is patterned with blossoming trees, all in faience, wreathed with lilies, tulips, and carnations, a display in kind only second to that of the Green Mosque and Turbéh in Brusa, and an art that is wholly and entirely Turkish in inspiration. If only in the shape of the long petalled tulips it is nothing Persian. Rustem Pacha, and not Soltan Achmet, is the "blue" mosque of Istanbul.

After enjoying these two mosques by Sinan we were always hearing of another of his mosques, Piyale Pacha, built for an admiral, but had not time to get to it. It is out of the town, on the Pera side of the Golden Horn, and it seems, has beautiful tile panels. The minaret is in an unusual position in front of the door of the mosque, in order to signify, so it is said, the mainmast of the admiral's ship. But there were other mosques we should have seen, also by Sinan; that of Kiliç Ali Pacha, another admiral, at Tophane, that is to say, below our hotel windows down on the Bosphorus, and I do not know why we never managed to see it. Neither did we see the Mosque of Mihrimah, wife of the aforesaid Rustem Pacha, and daughter of Süleyman the Magnificent and Roxelana (what a parentage!) which is on the summit of the sixth hill and at the highest point of Istanbul. Nor the mosque built for the same princess by Sinan, close to the wharf at Scutari, but, then, as described, we never crossed to Asia.

In all this mention of beautiful tilework, which is one of the arts of Turkey, there is little said about the *turbéhs* for the reason that it is next to impossible to get into them. On the previous visit we were admitted into the Turbéh of Süleyman the Magnificent, which is beside his mosque the Süleimaniye, and I have to presume the Turbéh of Roxelana, as well, which is near to it, but I must confess to little memory of either. The dome of Süleyman's Turbéh is carried on an arcade resting on eight columns of porphyry with stalactite capitals, and the dome has a decoration of "roses of rock crystal", "cabochons, cut diamond-wise", "with emerald centres". The railing round the tomb is of ivory and precious woods inlaid with mother-of-pearl, while chandeliers and ostrich eggs hang from the ceiling. Another *turbéh*, that of the Sheyzade or Shah-Zadeh, the two sons of Süleyman by another wife who were murdered owing to the jealousy of Roxelana, has superb yellow faience tiling and the most beautiful stained glass windows in Istanbul. So it is said. I have not seen it.*

* Before we part from the Turkish tilework let us quote what Mr Robert Liddell reports on it in succinct phrases: "five floral panels in the Mosque of Atik Valide at Scutari, where tomato-red vases hold sprays of blue fruit blossom; the lovely red-current panels in the little Tekiedj Ibrahim Agha; and panels with marvellous tomato-red borders" (a tomato red, he tells us, made with liquefied coral) "in the Mosque of Ramazan Effendi". (*Byzantium and Istanbul*, by Robert Liddell, London, Jonathan

A mosque can never be so interesting as a church because there is so little inside it. Even the Great Mosque of Damascus must yield on this score to the Cathedral of Toledo. But it is certain that for structure alone there is nothing in the Christian world that quite compares with the mosques of Istanbul. What city in Europe has twelve or more churches of the golden century that are the work of the same hand? It is of no avail to cite Wren's City churches because those are so trivially small in scale. But this great architect of Turkey does, at least, compare with Wren in one respect, and that is in his endless experimenting to bring variety into the same forms; in his choice of the octagon or the hexagon, of the square domed chamber, in the different methods of varying the arcaded cloister, and of floating or securing the dome. In his *madrasehs* with their rows of cupolas, in the domed kitchens of the Old Seraglio, he shows of what he was capable in other ways. Considered as a feat of engineering in aesthetics Sinan's Süleimaniye is not less magnificent than St Paul's Cathedral. There are mosques built by Sinan, or under his direction, in Ankara and Damascus and Sarajevo, and throughout the ancient Turkish Empire. Akbar's mosques and palaces in Delhi and Lahore and Agra were built by Sinan's pupils. But his masterpiece, built by him when he was well over eighty years old, is said to be the Selimiye, the Mosque of Selim II, son of Süleyman, in Adrianople which the Turks call, mistakenly, Edirne.* With a huge dome resting upon eight piers, and a great arcaded fountain court, it is according to all accounts the most simple and perfect of all Sinan's creations although upon a huge scale, and the one in which he finally resolved the problems on which he had been working all his life. I remember seeing the dome of the Selimiye and its four minarets from the train when returning from Istanbul by the Orient Express some twenty-five years ago, but that is all.

And now there is time for nothing more but a last evening drive for to-morrow we go home to England. Already we are across the Galata Bridge, climbing the hill, and before we know it are by the Mosque of Bayazit, where are all the pigeons, and near the Turkish café underneath the trees. It is getting darker, and after a while we come to the Shah Zadeh (preferring it in that spelling). For good fortune it was a new moon, and one could walk in the court of the mosque and get the

Cape, 1956, p. 175.) Mr Liddell's fine book, and *The Harem*, by N. M. Penzer, are the two indispensable works on Istanbul. I have to express my indebtedness, also, to the learned and valuable article on "Sinan: Architect in Chief to Süleyman the Magnificent", by Spencer Corbett, in *The Architectural Review* for May 1953.

\* This town was the capital of Turkey in Europe, as was Brusa their capital in Asia, from 1360 for a hundred years before they took by sword the dwindling Empire of Constantinople.

crescent, first against a cypress tree, and then shining on the balcony of the minaret. The Shah Zadeh is perhaps the most beautiful of all, and now in the half-dark its architecture looked almost Indian. Yet, was it the Shah Zadeh? It delights me, who am precise in most things, not to know which mosque it was. The next day we left Istanbul by ship and watched the domes and minarets of the Imperial Mosques, one after another, sink below the skyline. We saw the Parthenon, once more, in a thunderstorm; and a day or two later reached Venice, not having seen it for seventeen years, and found the most beautiful city in the world more beautiful even than before.

# INDEX